Excel® 2013

ABSOLUTE BEGINNER'S GUIDE

Tracy Syrstad

800 East 96th Street,
Indianapolis, Indiana 46240

Excel® 2013 Absolute Beginner's Guide

ISBN-13: 978-0-7897-5057-0
ISBN-10: 0-7897-5057-0

First Printing March 2013

Trademarks

All terms mentioned in this book that are known to be trademarks or service marks have been appropriately capitalized. Que Publishing cannot attest to the accuracy of this information. Use of a term in this book should not be regarded as affecting the validity of any trademark or service mark.

Warning and Disclaimer

Every effort has been made to make this book as complete and as accurate as possible, but no warranty or fitness is implied. The information provided is on an "as is" basis. The author and the publisher shall have neither liability nor responsibility to any person or entity with respect to any loss or damages arising from the information contained in this book.

Bulk Sales

Que Publishing offers excellent discounts on this book when ordered in quantity for bulk purchases or special sales. For more information, please contact

U.S. Corporate and Government Sales
1-800-382-3419
corpsales@pearsontechgroup.com

For sales outside of the U.S., please contact

International Sales
international@pearsoned.com

Editor-in-Chief
Greg Wiegand

Executive Editor
Loretta Yates

Development Editor
Bill Abner

Managing Editor
Kristy Hart

Project Editor
Andy Beaster

Copy Editor
Karen Annett

Indexer
Lisa Stumpf

Proofreader
Dan Knott

Technical Editor
Bob Umlas

Publishing Coordinator
Cindy Teeters

Cover Designer
Anne Jones

Compositor
Nonie Ratcliff

Contents

About the Author

Tracy Syrstad is the project manager for the MrExcel consulting team and also handles many of the tech support calls. She's been helping people with Microsoft Office issues since 1997 when she discovered free online forums where anyone could ask and answer questions. She discovered she enjoyed teaching others new skills, and when Tracy began working with the MrExcel team, she was able to integrate the fun of teaching with one-on-one online desktop sharing sessions.

Dedication

To Bill Jelen and Loretta Yates who believed it was time for my training wheels to come off.

Acknowledgments

Years ago while I answered Microsoft Office questions at online forums, I met Anne Troy, aka Dreamboat. She introduced me to Bill Jelen, aka MrExcel, and my life took a major turn. Bill opened several doors for me, including the one that has led to this book. Thank you both.

Juan Pablo González Ruiz and James Crawford helped me maintain a positive attitude through the long days it took to get this and another book done so quickly. Thank you to my SP friends, Brados, Safaribabe, Daisy443, and Mslzzy—your positive encouragement has helped in so many aspects of my life. And thank you to all the MrExcel clients who have asked how to do something in Excel. Those questions helped guide me in choosing the subjects to cover in this book.

We Want to Hear from You!

As the reader of this book, *you* are our most important critic and commentator. We value your opinion and want to know what we're doing right, what we could do better, what areas you'd like to see us publish in, and any other words of wisdom you're willing to pass our way.

We welcome your comments. You can email or write us directly to let us know what you did or didn't like about this book—as well as what we can do to make our books better.

Please note that we cannot help you with technical problems related to the topic of this book.

When you write, please be sure to include this book's title and author as well as your name, email address, and phone number. We will carefully review your comments and share them with the author and editors who worked on the book.

Email: feedback@quepublishing.com

Mail: Que Publishing
         ATTN: Reader Feedback
         800 East 96th Street
         Indianapolis, IN 46240 USA

Reader Services

Visit our website and register this book at www.informit.com/title/9780789750570 for convenient access to any updates, downloads, or errata that might be available for this book.

INTRODUCTION

INTRODUCTION

Familiarity with Microsoft Excel is a requirement for many jobs today. Workers in numerous offices use Excel to track and report information. Sales reps track leads, prospects, commissions, and travel expenses in Excel. Workers on the factory floor log schedules and quality data in Excel.

Excel is an amazingly flexible program. A new Excel worksheet offers a seemingly endless blank canvas of rows and columns where you can enter, summarize, and report data of any type. Charts and other data visualization tools can convert a page full of numbers to a visual snapshot. Pivot tables can summarize thousands of detailed records to a one-page summary in a few mouse clicks.

If you've never opened Excel, or if you've used Excel only to neatly arrange lists in columns, this book will get you up to speed with the real-life skills needed to survive in a job that requires familiarity with Excel.

When a potential employer asks if you know Excel, you need to ask which *version* of Excel. There are a lot of products available that have Excel in the name but offer a different subset of commands.

- Excel 2013 is the most recent version of the full-featured Excel program. The full version of Excel is what you will find in use in most job environments.

- Excel Web App is browser-based version of Excel. Whereas the browser is great for displaying existing Excel worksheets, the Web App allows users to enter new data and formulas in an Excel workbook while online. Those users do not need to have Excel installed on their computers. Mobile workers today might use Excel Web App to access their Excel data while they are out of the office. You also might expect college students to use Excel Web App to collaborate on group projects using this free version of Excel.

- Excel 2007 and Excel 2010 are similar to Excel 2013. If you learned how to use Excel 2013 and begin work where the company uses Excel 2007, you will be able to transfer most of your skills. Some features, such as sparklines, are missing. The Excel 2007 File menu offers far fewer choices than the Excel 2010 and Excel 2013 File menus. (In Excel 2007, the word *File* was replaced with an Office logo inside a round circle in the upper-left corner of the program. This was a bad idea and Microsoft went back to the word *File* in Excel 2010.) For the most part, you should find yourself comfortable working in Excel 2007 or Excel 2010 using the knowledge that you learn about Excel 2013 using this book.

- Excel 2003, Excel 2002, Excel 2000, and Excel 97 are collectively known as the legacy versions of Excel. Although the concepts of entering data and formulas in the worksheet are the same, the entire command structure is different in these versions of Excel. Instead of the intuitive ribbon interface, you will find long text lists of commands organized on menus, such as File, Edit, View, Insert, and so on. Although the menu system is harder to learn, hundreds of millions of people originally learned about Excel using these menus. Nearly half the companies with Excel installed are still hanging on to their legacy installations of Excel. Be prepared to have a steep learning curve as you try to find where the Excel 2013 commands are located in the old Excel menus.

NOTE   If this is your first experience with Excel, going to work in an office that is still using Excel 2003 is going to present some frustrations for you and the employer as you try to adjust to the older version of Excel. If the company is still using Excel 2003, it either means that the company didn't have the money to upgrade or that the people at the company are firmly entrenched with the old version of Excel. Be up front with your manager. Explain that you learned Excel using Excel 2013. That manager resisted upgrading to Excel 2013 because he or she didn't want to take the time to learn the new ribbon interface. As someone who learned on Excel 2013, it will be just as intimidating to learn where familiar commands are in the old Excel environment.

Who Should Read This Book

Excel 2013 Absolute Beginner's Guide is recommended for anyone who wants to use Excel. Whether this is your first time entering data in Excel or you've used Excel before but need to get caught up on the new functionality, this book walks you through the steps and gets you comfortable using Excel.

How This Book Is Organized

This book teaches you the important functions and uses for Microsoft Excel. As each chapter progresses, it builds on skills learned in previous chapters. The concepts in this book allow you to get started by entering data and formulas in Excel. However, the later chapters on pivot tables and charting provide you with enough advanced techniques to allow you to thrive in any job requiring Excel.

Downloading the Example Files

You can download the sample files for this book from quepublishing.com.

Conventions Used In This Book

The following conventions are used in this book:

- At the beginning of each chapter, you'll find a quick overview of the major topics that will be explained as you read through the material that follows.
- The end of each chapter reviews key points you just learned about.

Most steps in this book require the use of the mouse. All mouse instructions are based on a right-handed mouse. *Click* refers to a single click using the left mouse button. *Double-click* refers to a double-click using the left mouse button. *Right-click* refers to a single click using the right mouse button.

If a *keyboard shortcut* is provided, you have to press two or more keys on the keyboard at the same time. The two keys are shown with the key names joined with a plus (+) sign. For example, Ctrl+V requires you to hold down the Ctrl key, press the V key once, then let go of both keys.

Special Elements

This book also includes a few special elements that provide additional information not included in the basic text. These elements are designed to supplement the text to make your learning faster, easier, and more efficient.

 TIP A *tip* is a piece of advice—a little trick, actually—that helps you use your computer more effectively or maneuver around problems or limitations.

 NOTE A *note* is designed to provide information that is generally useful but not specifically necessary for what you're doing at the moment. Some are like extended tips—interesting, but not essential.

 CAUTION A *caution* tells you to beware of a potentially dangerous act or situation. In some cases, ignoring a caution could cause you significant problems—so pay attention to them!

IN THIS CHAPTER

- Recognize and manipulate the Excel interface.
- Learn to move around a worksheet.
- Install additional applications.

1

UNDERSTANDING THE MICROSOFT EXCEL INTERFACE

If you already know how to add a custom tab to the ribbon, select cell D28, or install an add-in, then you've probably spent some time using Microsoft Excel. However, if what you've just read makes little sense to you, then this chapter is especially for you. This chapter explains the basic parts of the Excel window, how to use them, and the terminology used to refer to them. It also shows you how to navigate around a sheet and how to install add-ins and apps to expand on Excel's amazing functionality.

Taking a Closer Look at the Excel Window

When you open Excel 2013 for the first time, you should see a window similar to Figure 1.1. It's a list of templates that you can start off with. Chapter 2, "Working with Workbooks, Sheets, Rows, Columns, and Cells," covers the details about templates. For now, click once on the Blank Workbook item in the upper-left corner to open a blank spreadsheet, as shown in Figure 1.2.

 NOTE If you see Figure 1.2 when opening Excel, that's OK. That just means a previous user turned off the Start screen. See the "Troubleshooting the Excel Options" section later in this chapter for instructions to turn it back on.

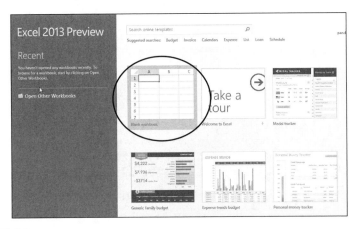

FIGURE 1.1

Select the Blank Workbook item (circled) to open a blank spreadsheet.

That big grid taking up most of the Excel window is the spreadsheet, also known as a worksheet or, simply, a sheet. Each little box is a cell. Multiple cells selected together are commonly known as a range.

Right above the grid are letters known as column headers. Down the left side of the grid are numbers, also known as row headers. The intersection of a single column and a single row is a cell. Each cell has an address made up of the column letter then the row number. Figure 1.3 shows cell C8 selected. Note the C in the column header is highlighted as is the 8 in the row header.

Quick Access Toolbar (QAT)

Name Box   Formula Bar   Ribbon   Column Header

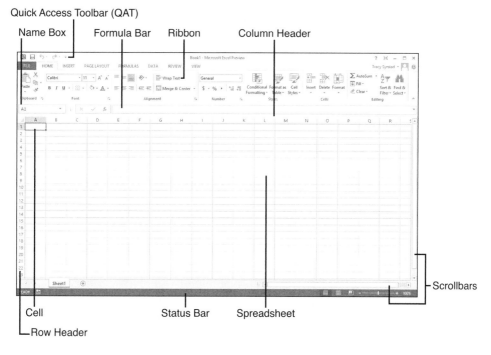

Scrollbars

Cell   Status Bar   Spreadsheet

Row Header

FIGURE 1.2

The Excel window is made up of many components that you'll use when working on a spreadsheet.

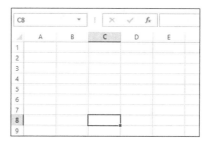

FIGURE 1.3

The intersection of a column and a row is a cell. The cell gets its name from the column and row headers, in this case C8.

Above the headers and to the left is the Name box. This box shows you what you have selected on the sheet. This can be a cell address, a named range, a table, a chart, or some other object on the sheet. When you first opened Excel, the

Name box was likely showing A1. If you've selected another cell on the sheet, the address has changed to show that cell's address, such as C8. Later in this chapter, you learn how you can use the Name box to quickly move to another area of the sheet.

To the right of the Name box is the formula bar, which is a slight misnomer. Although that is probably the most common use of this field, the formula bar actually reflects anything that's been typed into a cell, not just formulas.

At the top of the Excel window is the ribbon, where you choose what you want to do on your sheet, such as formatting text or inserting a chart. See the section "Making Selections from the Ribbon" for information on the different types of buttons on the ribbon. As you use Excel, you'll notice new tabs in the ribbon appearing depending on what you're doing in the sheet area. These tabs are context sensitive—they only appear when they are useful. Other times, they stay out of your way.

The Quick Access Toolbar, also known as the QAT, is located in the upper-left corner of the Excel window. It is always visible, even when the ribbon is minimized and, unlike the ribbon, the commands aren't dependent on what you are doing in Excel, such as working with a chart.

Below and to the right of the grid are scrollbars, which can be used to move around the sheet. You can either click and drag a bar or use the arrows at either end of the scroll area.

The status bar is along the bottom of the Excel window. Not only does it show the status of Excel, such as Ready or Calculating, on the left side, but it also includes buttons for changing the page view or zoom. In the right corner of the status bar is the Zoom slider. You can use the slider or the - and + buttons to change the zoom of the active sheet.

To the left of the Zoom slider are three buttons for changing how you view the active sheet: Normal, Page Break Preview, and Page Layout. The default view is the **Normal** view, showing just the sheet.

With **Page Break Preview**, you can see where columns and rows will break to print onto other pages. Dashed lines signify automatic breaks that Excel places based on settings, such as margins. Solid lines are manually set breaks. See Chapter 9, "Distributing and Printing a Workbook," for more information on setting and moving page breaks.

The **Page Layout** view is like an editable Print Preview—you can see what your page will look like when it prints out, but you can still enter data and make other changes. Columns and rows will move between pages as you adjust their widths or the margins of the page. You can also enter information directly into the header and footer of a page. See Chapter 9 for information on adding headers and footers.

Making Selections from the Ribbon

Along the top of the ribbon are tabs (File, Home, Insert, Page Layout, Formulas, Data, Review, View), which you can select to show new options in the ribbon area below the tabs. Each tab consists of multiple groups containing buttons and drop-downs of similar functionality. For example, on the Home tab, you have an Alignment group, which consists of buttons and drop-downs for aligning, wrapping, and merging data.

 TIP If you point your cursor at an option in the ribbon, a tip box appears, providing a brief explanation of what the option does.

Some groups have a small arrow in the lower-right corner, as shown in Figure 1.4. Clicking this arrow, the dialog box launcher, opens up a single dialog box with all the options of the group and more. If you can't find the option you want on the group or you want to use multiple commands (for example, changing the font type and alignment of a cell's contents), you might want to use the dialog box.

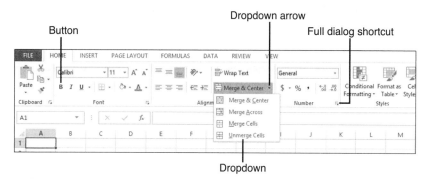

FIGURE 1.4

The ribbon consists of multiple types of controls.

Arranging Windows So You Can See Multiple Sheets at the Same Time

Sometimes you might want to compare data in two or more workbooks. If you have multiple monitors, you can simply drag an Excel window to another monitor. But if you need to show data side by side on the same monitor, Excel offers two methods. Clicking View, Window, Arrange All opens the Arrange Windows dialog box, which allows you to arrange all the current windows in a Tiled, Horizontal, Vertical, or Cascade view. Clicking View, Window, View Side By Side provides a quick way to view two windows horizontally. You can then select Synchronous Scrolling to lock the scrollbars together and move the data on both sheets at the same time.

Zooming In and Out to Better See Your Data

The ability to zoom in and out on a sheet is an often-forgotten functionality in Excel. Instead, large fonts are used when designing a sheet, then the designer later wonders why there are problems, such as the validation text being too small to see. Instead of relying on font size to make text on the sheet larger, zoom in on the sheet.

There are three ways to change the zoom on a sheet:

- **View, Zoom**—On the View tab, the Zoom group contains three options for zooming on a sheet:
  - **Zoom**—Brings up the Magnification dialog box
  - **100%**—Sets the zoom to 100%
  - **Zoom to Selection**—Zooms in on the selected range
- **Wheel mouse**—While holding down the Ctrl key, use the scroll on your mouse to zoom in and out.
- **Zoom slider**—In the lower-right corner of the Excel window is the Zoom slider. You can use the slider or the - and + buttons to change the zoom of the active sheet.

Getting to the Built-in Help

There are two ways to bring up the Help interface in Excel. You can press F1 on your keyboard or click the ? icon in the upper-right corner of the Excel window. If an Internet connection is found, you'll be able to search Microsoft's online database. Otherwise, your search results will be limited to the Help files on your system.

Once you have the Help dialog box open, you can change your source for help. If you have an Internet connection but would rather use the Help files on your computer, click the arrow to the right of Excel Help and select Excel Help from

Your Computer, as shown in Figure 1.5. From then on, search results will be from your computer. You can always switch it back to getting online Help if you don't find what you need locally by selecting Excel Help from Office.com from the drop-down.

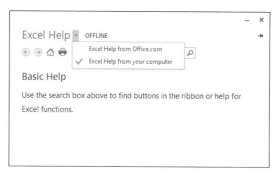

FIGURE 1.5

You can choose whether to search the online Help or the local Help files.

Troubleshooting the Excel Options

There's nothing more frustrating than opening Excel and finding out something strange has happened to the way Excel works. Table 1.1 reviews possible scenarios and the settings under File, Options that could be the source of the problem.

TABLE 1.1 Possible Situations and Solutions

Situation	Check This Setting
The Mini toolbar[1] is gone; make the Mini toolbar go away	General, User Interface Options, Show Mini Toolbar on Selection
Column headings A, B, C have been replaced with 1, 2, 3	Formulas, Working with Formulas, R1C1 Reference Style
Unable to drag cell contents; the fill handle[2] is gone	Advanced, Editing Options, Enable Fill Handle and Cell Drag-and-Drop
Unable to edit directly in cell, can only edit in the formula bar	Advanced, Editing Options, Allow Editing Directly in Cells
AutoComplete no longer appears when entering data in a cell	Advanced, Editing Options, Enable AutoComplete for Cell Values; also ensure there are no blank rows separating your new entry and previous entries

TABLE 1.1 (continued)

Situation	Check This Setting
Instead of moving the sheet up/down when you scroll the mouse, the sheet zooms in/out; you want the sheet to zoom in/out when you use the wheel on the mouse	Advanced, Editing Options, Zoom on Roll with the IntelliMouse
Formula bar has disappeared; Hide the formula bar	Advanced, Display, Show Formula Bar or View tab, Show, Formula Bar
Instead of the calculated values, the formulas are showing in the cells	Advanced, Display Options for This Worksheet, Show Formulas in Cells Instead of Their Calculated Results or Ctrl+~
When you double-click to open a workbook, Excel opens, but remains blank	Advanced, General, Ignore Other Applications That Use Dynamic Data Exchange (DDE)

[1] The mini toolbar is the small formatting toolbar that appears when you right-click a cell.

[2] For more information on the fill handle, see "Extending a Series Containing Text," in chapter 3, "Getting Data Onto A Sheet."

Closing Files and Exiting Excel

To close a file opened in Excel, go to File, Close or click the X in the upper-right corner of the window. This only closes the file. If you have multiple files open, you need to close each one before Excel will close.

 TIP If your Excel taskbar buttons are combined, you can quickly close all open Excel files by right-clicking Excel in the Windows taskbar and selecting Close All Windows.

Customizing the Excel Window

If you're using Excel on a tablet, the ribbon can take up a lot of the screen. If you're entering a long formula in a cell, you might not be able to see enough of it in the formula bar. Or perhaps you want a quicker way of getting to the ribbon options you use the most. In any case, Excel offers multiple customizations to make Excel handier for the way you use it.

Changing the Size of the Formula Bar So You Can See More Data

By default, the formula bar shows a single line, and that's probably how you'll want it most of the time, but it can be expanded to show multiple lines. One way is by clicking the down arrow on the far right of the formula bar. This opens the bar to show about three lines of information. Click the arrow again to shrink the field back up to a single line.

The other option allows you more control on how wide the field is. Place the cursor along the bottom of the field until it turns into a double arrow, as shown in Figure 1.6. Press and hold down the mouse button as you drag the field down. Let go of the mouse when you have the field the desired size. To return the field to its normal size, drag it up in the same way you dragged it down or click the arrow on the far right.

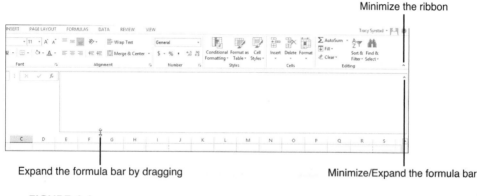

Minimize the ribbon

Expand the formula bar by dragging   Minimize/Expand the formula bar

FIGURE 1.6

You can change the size of the ribbon and formula bar to suit your needs.

TIP   Once you've manually resized the formula bar, that's the size it will open to when using the down arrow.

Minimizing the Ribbon to Show Only the Tab Names

If you're working on a system with a small screen, the ribbon probably takes up too much space on the screen. To toggle the ribbon between being minimized and normal, press Ctrl+F1 on the keyboard. You can also minimize the ribbon area by clicking the arrow in the lower-right corner of the ribbon. To set the ribbon back to normal, click on a tab to open up the ribbon, then click on the pin that now appears where the arrow used to be. When minimized, the ribbon will expand when you select a tab and then minimize when you click your mouse elsewhere.

Showing or Hiding Tabs in the Ribbon

Going to File, Options, Customize Ribbon opens the dialog box shown in Figure 1.7. The dialog box allows you to show or hide existing tabs or create your own tabs and groups. You can also open this dialog box by right-clicking on a tab and selecting Customize the Ribbon.

 TIP When you open the dialog box, the Main Tabs are shown on the right side of the window. To see the context-sensitive Tool Tabs, select Tool Tabs from the drop-down above the list of tabs.

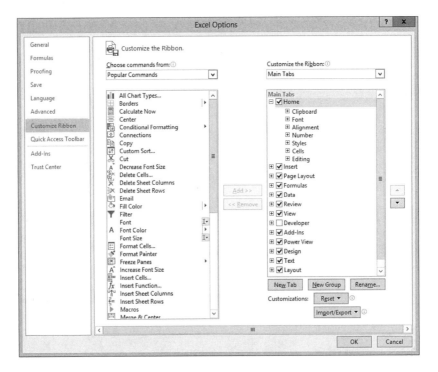

FIGURE 1.7

Use the Customize the Ribbon dialog box to hide tabs you don't feel you need or to create tabs with controls you find most useful.

If you have a narrow screen, you might want to hide some tabs so that others can be more easily accessed. To show or hide a tab, follow these steps:

1. Right-click on any tab and select Customize the Ribbon.

2. The list of existing tabs is on the right side of the Customize the Ribbon dialog box.

3. Select or deselect the tab(s) you want shown or hidden from view and then click OK.

 TIP Selecting a Tool Tab won't change the fact that it is a context-sensitive tab. It will still only appear as needed.

Removing a Group from a Tab

You can't customize the default groups with your own commands, but you can remove the groups, making room for your own custom group on the tab. To remove a group, follow these steps:

1. Right-click on any tab and select Customize the Ribbon.

2. The list of existing tabs is on the right side of the Customize the Ribbon dialog box.

3. Expand the tab containing the group you want to remove.

4. Select the group to remove, right-click it, and select Remove.

 NOTE If you remove a group and later decide you want it back, use the Reset option on the Customize the Ribbon dialog box.

Adding More Buttons to the Ribbon

The default tabs and groups in Excel might not be the ones best for you or for a particular situation. You can insert a custom tab into the Main Tabs group or the Tool Tabs group. Once the tab has been added, you can add the groups and buttons most useful to you.

Inserting a New Tab

To create a custom tab in Excel to which you can add groups and buttons that you find most useful, follow these steps:

1. Right-click on any tab and select Customize the Ribbon.

2. Select where you want your tab to be from the list on the right side of the dialog box. The new tab will be placed below your selection.

3. Click New Tab. Excel creates a new tab with a new group, both with (Custom) after the name.

4. Highlight the new group and click Rename to rename the group.

 NOTE   Though the Rename dialog box shows Symbols, selecting one will not show it in the group.

5. Highlight the new tab and click Rename to rename the tab.

Adding a New Group to a Tab

Although not required, grouping similar buttons together can make them easier to find, especially if you're helping someone else find a specific function. When you create a new tab, Excel automatically adds a new group for you, but you might need another group.

 NOTE   A custom group is the only way to add buttons to a default tab.

To add a custom group to a tab, follow these steps:

1. Right-click on any tab and select Customize the Ribbon.

2. In the list on the right side of the dialog box, navigate to where you want to add a new group. The new group will be placed below your selection.

3. Click New Group. Excel creates a new group.

4. Highlight the new group and click Rename to rename the group.

 TIP   You can also add one of the predefined groups found on the default tabs. These predefined groups are located under the Main Tabs and Tool Tabs commands in the list on the left side of the dialog box.

Adding a New Button

Excel won't allow you to add a button to any of the default groups, but there aren't any such limitations on the custom groups you create. To add a new button to a custom group, follow these steps:

1. Right-click on any tab and select Customize the Ribbon.

2. In the list on the right side of the dialog box, navigate to where you want to add the new button. The new button will be placed below your selection.

3. In the list on the left side of the dialog box, find the button you want to add.

4. Click Add to add the button to the group.

Moving the QAT to Below the Ribbon

You can move the Quick Access Toolbar (QAT) to below the ribbon by clicking on the arrow on the right end of the toolbar and selecting Show Below the Ribbon, as shown in Figure 1.8. If the toolbar is already below the ribbon, the option will be changed to Show Above the Ribbon.

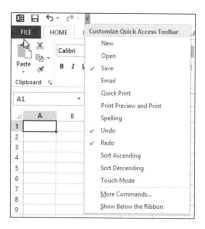

FIGURE 1.8

Almost any command can be added to the QAT and you can also add some selections from within drop-downs.

Customizing the Commands on the QAT

You can create a custom tab if you have a lot of commands to add, but those commands are only available when the tab is active. If you have options you want available at any time, you can add them to the QAT.

Clicking the arrow on the right end of the QAT opens a list of commonly used commands, as shown in Figure 1.8. Click on one of the options to add it to the QAT. If the command you want isn't listed, you can select More Commands, which opens the Customize the Quick Access Toolbar dialog box.

There are three ways to customize the QAT:

*   Click on the drop-down arrow on the right end of the toolbar and select from the predefined commands.

- Right-click a button on the toolbar and select Customize Quick Access Toolbar to open the Customize the Quick Access Toolbar dialog box.
- Right-click on a command or drop-down item in the ribbon. If the option Add to Quick Access Toolbar appears, select it to add the item to the toolbar.

To add a command to the Quick Access toolbar using the Customize the Quick Access Toolbar dialog box, follow these steps:

1. Click on the drop-down arrow on the right end of the toolbar and select Customize Quick Access Toolbar.

2. Navigate the list on the left side of the dialog box, shown in Figure 1.9, to find the command you want to add to the toolbar.

3. Select the command and click Add to copy the command to the Quick Access Toolbar.

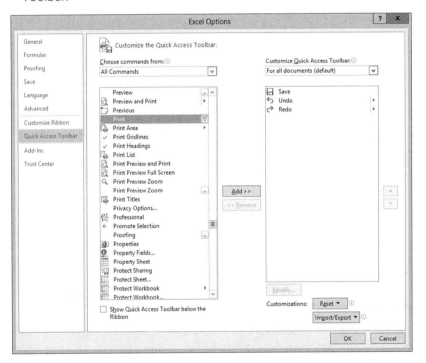

FIGURE 1.9

Add commands you always want available to the QAT.

Customizing the QAT for Just the Current Workbook

You can add commands to the QAT that will appear only when a specific workbook is open. This can be especially useful if your workbook contains macros you want to activate with buttons (for more information on macros, see chapter 15, "An Introduction to Using Macros and UDFs"). To add a macro button to the QAT that only appears when the current workbook is open, follow these steps:

1. Click on the drop-down arrow on the right end of the toolbar and select Customize Quick Access Toolbar.

2. Select the current workbook from the drop-down on the right side of the dialog box.

3. Select Macros from the drop-down on the left side of the dialog box.

4. Select the macro you want to assign to the toolbar and click Add.

5. With the macro selected in the list on the right side of the dialog box, click Modify.

6. Select a symbol for the button and change the Display Name that will appear when the cursor hovers over the button. Click OK.

7. Your custom macro button will appear in the toolbar.

Removing Commands from the QAT

If you decide you no longer require a command on the QAT, you can remove it in one of three ways:

- Click on the drop-down arrow on the right end of the toolbar and deselect the command from the list of predefined commands.

- Click on the drop-down arrow on the right end of the toolbar or right-click any button on the ribbon and select Customize Quick Access Toolbar to open the Customize the Quick Access Toolbar dialog box. Select the command from the list on the right side of the dialog box and click Remove.

- Right-click the command button itself in the Quick Access Toolbar and select Remove from Quick Access Toolbar.

Moving Around and Making Selections on a Sheet

You can move around on a sheet using the mouse or the keyboard, depending on which method is most comfortable for you. To select a cell using the mouse, click on the desired cell. To select a cell using the keyboard, use the navigation arrows on the keyboard. You can also use the number keypad arrows if the NumLock feature is turned off.

Keyboard Shortcuts for Quicker Navigation

Using the navigation arrows on the keyboard can be a little slow, especially if you have a lot of cells between your currently selected cell and the one you want to select. Even using the mouse can take some time to navigate from the top of your data to the bottom. The following list details a few keyboard shortcuts to make navigation a little easier:

- Ctrl+Home jumps to cell A1, located at the upper-left corner of the sheet.

- Ctrl+End jumps to the last row and column in use.

- Ctrl+Left Arrow jumps to the first column with data to the left of the currently selected cell. If there is no data to the left, then it will select a cell in the first column, A.

- Ctrl+Right Arrow jumps to the first column with data to the right of the currently selected cell. If there is no data to the right, then it will select a cell in the last column, XFD.

- Ctrl+Down Arrow jumps to the first row with data below the currently selected cell. If there is no data below the selected cell, it will select a cell in the last row.

- Ctrl+Up Arrow jumps to the first row with data above the currently selected cell. If there is no data above the selected cell, it will select a cell in row 1.

Selecting a Range of Cells

You'll often find yourself needing to select more than a single cell. For example, if you have text on a sheet you want to apply a new font to, instead of selecting one cell at a time and applying the font, you can select all the cells and then apply the font, as shown in Figure 1.10.

 TIP When selecting a range, it doesn't matter if you start at the top or bottom or far left or far right of the range.

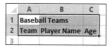

FIGURE 1.10

The ability to select a range is an important skill to have when working on a sheet.

To select a range using the mouse, follow these steps:

1. Select a cell that will be in the corner of your selection.

2. Hold down the mouse button as you drag the mouse to cover the desired cells.

3. When you get to the last cell, let go of the mouse button. You will have selected a range similar to what is shown in Figure 1.10.

4. As long as you don't click elsewhere on the sheet, the range will remain selected.

To select a range using the keyboard, follow these steps:

1. Select a cell that will be in the corner of your selection.

2. Press F8 on the keyboard.

3. Use the arrow keys to navigate to the end of the desired range.

4. Press F8 on the keyboard to stop the selection from extending.

5. As long as you don't select another cell on the sheet, the range will remain selected.

NOTE   Pressing F8 on the keyboard turns on the Extend Selection option in Excel. If you look at the left side of the status bar, you will see Extend Selection. As long as the option is on, selecting different cells will extend the selection.

Installing Optional Components

Additional tools and applications can be added to Excel. Some of these programs automate or expand on existing functionality in Excel. Others can bring new functionality into Excel.

Add-Ins

Add-ins are a special type of Excel file that contain macros, a programming ability built in to Excel. Some add-ins come with Excel, such as the Analysis Toolpak, which provided additional functions not part of Excel, and the Solver add-in, which allows you to run what-if scenarios to find the optimal value for a formula. You can also install your own add-ins. There are many sites available with add-ins available for free or a fee. These add-ins range from functions not available in Excel to simplifiying a series of steps that you manually do in Excel.

 CAUTION If the file has an XLA (Excel 97–2003) or XLAM (Excel 2007–2013) extension, it can be installed as an add-in. But you cannot simply rename a file to turn it into an add-in. It must be saved with the proper extension.

To install a new add-in, follow these steps:

1. Save the add-in in a safe place on your hard drive.

2. In Excel, go to File, Options, Add-Ins.

3. At the bottom of the Add-Ins dialog box, select Excel Add-Ins from the Manage drop-down, and then click Go.

4. Browse to where you saved your add-in and click OK.

5. The add-in will appear in the list of add-ins available. Verify that it is selected.

6. Click OK to return to Excel.

7. Some add-ins will create custom tabs or add a custom command to the Add-Ins tab.

To uninstall an add-in, deselect the add-in from the Add-Ins dialog box.

COM Add-Ins and DLL Add-Ins

COM add-ins and DLL add-ins are programs created outside of Excel that expand on Excel's functionality, similar to the add-ins mentioned in the previous section. They might or might not add custom options to the ribbon. To install a COM add-in or DLL add-in, follow these steps:

1. Go to File, Options, Add-Ins.

2. At the bottom of the Add-Ins dialog box, select COM Add-Ins from the Manage drop-down and then click Go.

3. From the COM Add-Ins dialog box, click Add and browse to the EXE or DLL that you want to install. Click OK.

4. Continue installing the program by following the prompts.

You can also temporarily disable an add-in. You might want to do this if Excel is slower when the add-in is active or if you are trying to troubleshoot performance issues in Excel. To temporarily disable or remove an add-in, return to the COM Add-Ins dialog box and deselect the add-in to temporarily disable it or highlight it and click Remove.

 NOTE These add-ins may also come in an installation package so that you can install and uninstall them as you would normal Windows programs.

Apps for Office

New to Excel 2013 are Apps for Office. These are applications that can provide expanded functionality to a sheet, such as a selectable calendar for inserting dates in cells, or interface with the web, such as retrieving information from Wikipedia or Bing. To add an App for Office to Excel, follow these steps:

1. Go to Insert, Apps, Apps for Office, See All.

2. If an Internet connection is found, the Apps for Office dialog box opens, as shown in Figure 1.11. Select the Featured Apps link in the upper-left corner or search for an app using the Search field on the right.

FIGURE 1.11

Apps for Office can expand the functionality of Excel and provide information from web pages.

3. Click on the desired app and it is installed in Excel. It appears as a task pane on the right side of the Excel window or as a floating window on the sheet, as shown in Figure 1.12.

 NOTE Some apps are free, whereas others are not. To purchase an app, click the Buy button and log into your Microsoft account. Once logged in, you are brought to a webpage where you can purchase the app.

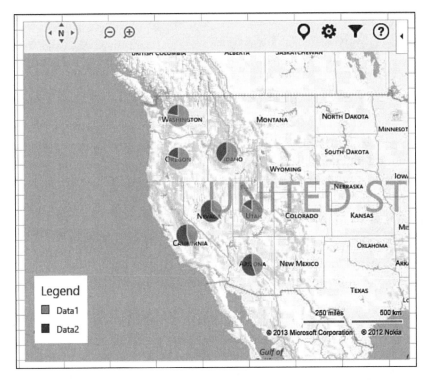

FIGURE 1.12

An app can be a floating window that charts your data to a map (Bing Maps shown).

4. To see your installed apps, return to the Apps for Office dialog box and click on My Apps in the upper-left corner of the dialog box. You will see all the apps from the store that you own.

5. Select an app from the list and click Insert to open the app in Excel.

THE ABSOLUTE MINIMUM

At first glance, Excel may seem a little intimidating with its specific terminology and numerous features. You've taken that first crucial step, though, and hopefully you realize you can master what you need to do in Excel. By now, you should:

- Understand what a cell address is

- Know how to select a single cell and a range

- Know how to add useful buttons to the QAT

2

IN THIS CHAPTER

- Understand the difference between a workbook and a sheet.
- Use a template.
- Insert a new sheet.
- Move Rows, Columns, and Ranges.

WORKING WITH WORKBOOKS, SHEETS, ROWS, COLUMNS, AND CELLS

An Excel file is called a workbook and each workbook can contain one or more sheets. This chapter shows you how to create workbooks from scratch or from templates. It shows you how to add, delete, and move sheets within a workbook or between workbooks.

Even a well-planned-out sheet layout may be missing something, such as a date column. Or you might change your mind in the middle of the design, deciding that you want a table elsewhere on a sheet. Instead of starting over, this chapter shows you how to insert rows or columns and move your tables to a new location on your sheet.

Managing Workbooks

Workbook is another name for an Excel file. It's the workbook you open, save, and close. This section shows you how to create a new workbook, open an existing workbook, and save and close a workbook.

Creating a New Workbook

When you open Excel, it already makes a new workbook available (if the Start screen is disabled) or you can create one by clicking Blank Workbook from the Start screen (if the Start screen in enabled). To create a new workbook if you already have another workbook open, you can click File, New and then click on Blank Workbook, or you can press Ctrl+N.

Opening an Existing Workbook

If the Start screen is turned on, when you open Excel you will see various template icons on the right side of the window and a list of recent workbooks and the option to Open Other Workbooks on the left side of the window, as shown in Figure 2.1.

If you want to open a workbook that was recently open, select it from the list on the left. Notice that the Recent Workbooks list shows the workbook name and its location. See the section "Using the Recent Workbooks list" for information on keeping a workbook in the list.

 TIP By default, Excel shows the most recent 25 workbooks opened on the Recent list. You can change this by clicking File, Options, Advanced; then under Display, change the value for Show This Number of Recent Workbooks.

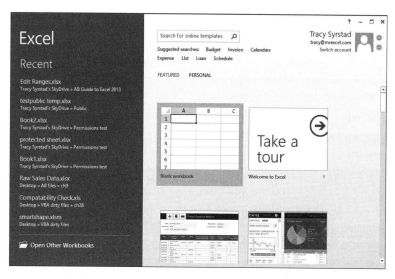

FIGURE 2.1

The left side of the Start screen lists recently opened workbooks. The right side shows various templates you can start working with.

If the workbook you are looking for is not listed, select Open Other Workbooks. A new window opens in which you can choose the place where the workbook is located, as shown in Figure 2.2. The default places are as follows:

- **Recent Workbooks**—The most recently opened workbooks and any workbooks you have pinned to the list

- **Your SkyDrive**—A location on the Internet on Microsoft's SkyDrive server

- **Computer**—Your local computer and any networks attached

- **Add a Place**—A new location you can add, such as a network drive, so it is readily available

The area to the right of the Places list will update to reflect your places selection. For the SkyDrive and Computer options, recent folders will be listed, or you can browse to another folder.

When you select a folder or the Browse option, the Open dialog box, shown in Figure 2.3, appears, allowing you to search for a specific Excel file and offering multiple ways to open it.

In the upper-right corner of the dialog box is a Search field in which you can enter terms to search the current folder and its subfolders. Type in a keyword and press Enter.

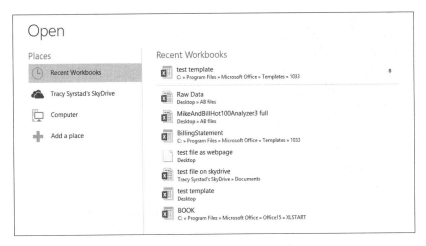

FIGURE 2.2

Excel makes it easy to share your workbook online with access to your SkyDrive and Microsoft's online server, or you can save it to your local drive or network.

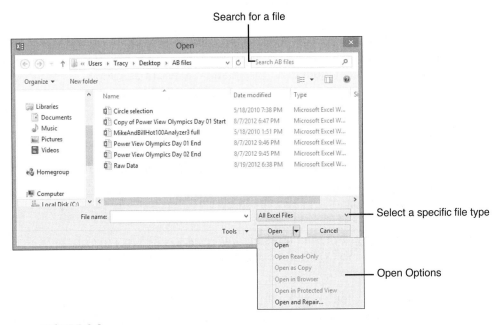

FIGURE 2.3

The Open dialog box offers multiple options to search for a specific file.

Excel can open a variety of files, both Excel files and non-Excel. To change the file type, click All Excel Files and a drop-down of other file types appears.

Once you've found the file you want to open, you can choose how Excel should open it. By default, Excel opens the file normally, but you can also choose to open it as read-only, as a copy, and more:

- **Open**—Opens the workbook normally.

- **Open Read-Only**—Opens a read-only copy of the workbook. You must save the workbook with a different filename if you want to save any changes.

- **Open as Copy**—Opens as a new copy of the workbook. Excel appends "Copy" to the beginning of the filename.

- **Open in Browser**—Opens a workbook saved as a web page in your browser.

- **Open in Protected View**—Opens in Protected view, allowing you to only view the workbook. To make changes, you have to click the Enable Editing button that appears in the alert bar at the top of the sheet.

- **Open and Repair**—Performs checks while opening the workbook and tries to repair any issues it finds. Or, Excel tries to extract the formulas and values.

Using the Recent Workbooks List

When you go to File, Open a list of workbooks recently opened is shown. The Recent Workbooks list makes it easy to open files you're currently working on. A pushpin appears when you place your cursor over a workbook listed under Recent Workbooks. The pushpin points to the left when not in use, but place your cursor over the pushpin and click and the pushpin will face downward and the workbook will be moved to the top section of the list, as shown in Figure 2.2. A workbook with a pin facing down is stuck—that is, the workbook will not be removed from the list of recent workbooks until you unstick it by clicking the pushpin again.

    TIP   A workbook you've deleted or moved may appear in the list for a while. If you've moved the file, you might get confused by seeing the old location in the list. To remove the workbook from the list, right-click on it and select Remove from List.

Saving a Workbook

When you click the File menu, you see two options for saving your workbook: Save and Save As. Selecting Save saves the workbook with the current name, overwriting the existing file. If the workbook is new and doesn't have a filename yet, clicking Save opens the Save As dialog box. The Save As dialog box allows you to save a workbook with a new name in a new location. You would select

Save to create a copy of the workbook for changes, but want to keep the original workbook intact.

When you select Save As, the area to the right of the File menu changes to show various places where the workbook can be saved to. The default places are as follows:

- **Your SkyDrive**—A location on the Internet on Microsoft's SkyDrive server
- **Computer**—Your local computer and any networks attached
- **Add a Place**—A new location you can add, such as a network drive, so it is readily available

The area to the right of the **Places** list updates to reflect recent folders associated with your places selection. You can select from the list or you can browse to another folder, opening the Save As dialog box, as shown in Figure 2.4.

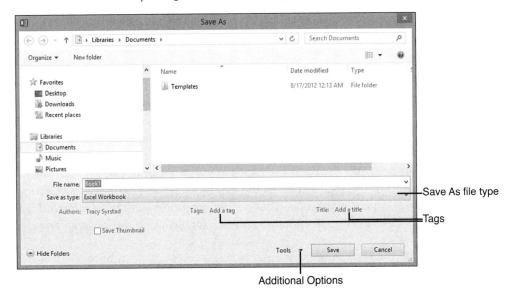

FIGURE 2.4

The Save As dialog box offers multiple options when saving your workbook.

By default, Excel saves your workbook with an XLSX extension. But if you need to share with Excel 97–2003 users or have macros in your workbook, you must choose another Save As file type. Commonly used extensions are as follows:

- **Excel 97–2003 Workbook**—XLS: Excel 97–2003 workbook with or without macros

- **Excel Workbook**—XLSX: Excel 2007–2013 workbook without macros
- **Excel Macro-Enabled Workbook**—XLSM: Excel 2007–2013 workbook with macros
- **PDF**—PDF: A Portable Document Format that can be used to distribute your report but prevent users from making changes

 TIP   If you find yourself often changing the Save As file type to something else, such as Excel 97–2003 Workbook, you can change the default setting by clicking File, Options, Save and changing the Save Files in This Format value. You will still have the ability to select another file type when saving.

Closing a Workbook

When you're done working with a workbook, you need to close it. To close a workbook, click File, Close or click the X in the upper-right corner. Excel prompts you to save changes if changes have recently been made to the workbook, including recalculating formulas, and the workbook hasn't been saved. When the final workbook is closed, Excel closes.

Using Templates to Quickly Create New Workbooks

Templates are a great way for keeping data in a uniform design. You could simply design your workbook and reuse it as needed, but if you accidentally save data before you have renamed the file, your blank workbook is no longer clean. When using a template, there's no risk of saving data in the template because you are working with a copy of the original workbook, not the workbook itself.

Using Microsoft's Online Templates

Microsoft offers a variety of templates, such as budgets, invoices, and calendars, which can help you get a start on a project. You can search for templates to fit your needs either from the Start screen or by clicking File, New and selecting Featured. A selection of templates appears in the window or you can enter your own keywords in the Search field in the upper left. A search returns matches, which you can filter from a list on the right.

TIP When you place your cursor over a template preview, a pushpin appears in its lower-right corner, giving you the option to pin it so that it always appears in the list. If you found your template by searching for it, this is a way to make it easily accessible the next time you need it.

When you click on a template, a preview window opens up, as shown in Figure 2.5. The preview shows a larger example of the template, a brief explanation of its purpose, and how the template has been rated by other users. If you click Create, the template is downloaded (for first-time use) and opened.

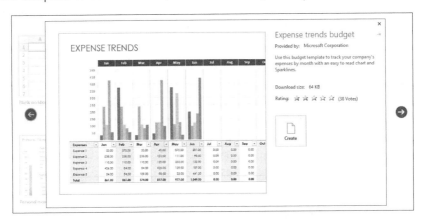

FIGURE 2.5
Use the left and right arrows in the template preview window to scroll through other available templates before opening one.

Opening a Locally Saved Template to Enter Data

There are multiple ways to open a template to enter data and you can use the method that is most convenient to you. To open a template to create a new workbook, use one of the following methods:

- Double-click the file from its saved location.

- From its saved location, right-click the file and select New.

- Click File, New and select the template from the list of online templates.

- Click File, New, Personal and select from the list of templates saved locally. See the "Saving a Template" section for details on how to configure the location. The Personal option will not appear unless the location is set up.

Opening a Locally Saved Template to Make Changes to the Design

If you need to make changes to the design of a template, the previous methods for opening a copy of the template won't work. If you do open a template using one of those methods and make changes, you must use the Save As option and save it as a new template. Instead, to open the original template to make changes, use one of the following methods:

- Right-click the file and select Open.
- Click File, Open, select the file and click Open.

Saving a Template

NOTE   You do not have to save templates to the configured templates location if you plan to use the double-click or right-click method to open a copy of the file.

Before you can use your own template or one provided to you and not downloaded from the Office Store, you have to configure where your templates will be stored. This will be a folder where you will place all your templates you want to access through the File, New, Personal dialog box. To set up the location, click File, Options, Save and enter the path in the Default Personal Templates Location field. Once you have a location configured, Personal will appear to the right of Featured. Featured shows Microsoft's online templates; Personal shows templates in the locally configured location.

CAUTION   The location must exist before you enter it in the field. To make sure you get the path correct, navigate to it in File Explorer, copy the full path from the address bar, then paste it in the Excel field.

Customizing All Future Workbooks

Excel's default template is fine to start with, but what if there are changes you always make, like changing the margins or the font on the sheet? There isn't a template file you can overwrite with your preferred adjustments. But if you design your template and save it with a specific name in a specific location, Excel will use it instead of its own template when you create a new workbook. To change the default template used by Excel, follow these steps:

1. Open a blank workbook and make the desired changes.

2. Click File, Save As, Computer and browse to the XLSTART folder. The location is based on where Office was installed. The default location for 64-bit Office is: C:\Program Files\Microsoft Office\Office15\XLSTART.

 CAUTION You must have the proper permissions to save to this location.

3. Enter **BOOK** in the File Name text box.

4. Select Excel Template as the Save As Type.

5. Click Save. Now, the next time you create a new workbook from scratch, your custom template will be used.

 NOTE If you select the Blank Workbook icon on the Start screen, it uses Excel's default template. To have Excel open directly to a blank workbook based on your template, you'll have to turn the Start screen off. To do this, go to File, Options, General and deselect Show the Start Screen When This Application Starts.

If you prefer to keep the Start screen on, then save a second copy of your template in the template folder configured in the options. The template will then be available when you select Personal from the Start screen.

Working with Sheets and Tabs

A sheet, also known as a spreadsheet or worksheet, is where you enter all your data in Excel. A workbook can have multiple sheets—the number limited only by the power of the computer opening the workbook.

Each sheet has a tab, visible above the status bar, as shown in Figure 2.6. The sheet with data that you're looking at is considered the active sheet. To select another sheet, click on its tab.

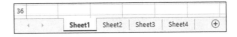

FIGURE 2.6

The font of the sheet tab you are working on, Sheet1, is bold compared with the other sheet tabs.

Inserting a New Sheet

The quickest way to add a new sheet to a workbook is to click on the circle with a plus sign that appears to the right of the rightmost sheet tab. This inserts a new sheet to the right of the active sheet.

To insert a new sheet to the left of a specific sheet, select the sheet (refer to the "Activating Another Sheet" section) and click Home, Insert, Insert Sheet.

A third method is to right-click on the tab to the right of where you want the new sheet to appear. From the menu, select Insert, select Worksheet, and click OK. The new sheet appears to the left of the tab you right-clicked on, as shown in Figure 2.7.

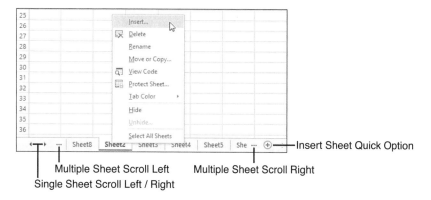

FIGURE 2.7

You can control where a new sheet is inserted by right-clicking on a tab and selecting Insert. In the figure, the new sheet, Sheet8, appears to the left of the selected Sheet2.

Activating Another Sheet

To activate another sheet, click on its tab along the bottom of the Excel window. You can also navigate sheet to sheet using the keyboard. Ctrl+Page Up selects the sheet to the left; Ctrl+Page Down selects the sheet to the right.

If you have more sheets than can fit in the tab area, three small dots will appear on the left and right side of the area, to show there are more sheets available to view, as shown in Figure 2.7. Clicking on the three dots quickly scrolls through multiple sheets. If instead, you need to scroll one sheet at a time, click the left and right arrows located to the left of the sheet tab area.

If you right-click on the left and right arrows instead, a list of all sheets in the workbook appears. You can then select a sheet, click OK, and you'll go straight to that sheet.

Selecting Multiple Sheets

You can select multiple sheets at one time. This doesn't activate them all at once. It groups them together so that an action on one, such as changing the tab color, affects all of them.

To select multiple sheets, select the first one, then while holding down the Ctrl key, select the tabs for the others. As you select each sheet tab, the sheet name will become bold.

To ungroup the sheets, you can either select any sheet other than the active sheet or right-click on any tab and select Ungroup Sheets.

Deleting a Sheet

If you no longer need a sheet, you can delete it, getting it out of your way and reducing the size of your workbook. To delete a sheet, right-click on the sheet's tab and select Delete. You can also delete a sheet by making it your active sheet and clicking Home, Cells, Delete and selecting Delete Sheet from the drop-down. If there is data on the sheet, a prompt appears to verify this is the action you want to take.

 CAUTION Deleting a sheet cannot be undone.

Moving or Copying Sheets Within the Same Workbook

You might want to reorganize sheets within the current workbook to group similar sheets together. Or you might need to copy a sheet to run tests on the data but don't want to change the original. To move a sheet within a workbook, use the Move or Copy Sheet option found under Home, Cells, Format. The dialog box can also be accessed by right-clicking on a sheet tab and selecting Move or Copy.

In the Move or Copy dialog box, shown in Figure 2.8, make sure the To Book field is the current workbook. If you're making a copy of the sheet, select the Create a Copy box. Then, in the Before Sheet dialog box, select the sheet you want the active sheet to be placed in front of (to the left of). You can also reorganize the sheets in a workbook by clicking, holding the mouse button down, and dragging the sheet's tab to a new location. If you want to copy the sheet, hold down the Ctrl key as you move the sheet tab.

FIGURE 2.8

The Move or Copy dialog box allows you to copy or move sheets within a workbook or between two different workbooks.

Moving or Copying Sheets Between Workbooks

Many database programs will export data to an Excel workbook or compatible file but might not let you choose an existing workbook to export to. If you have a report workbook designed in which you need the new data, you can copy or move the exported data from its workbook to your report workbook. To move a sheet to a new workbook, use the Move or Copy Sheet option found under Home, Cells, Format. The dialog box can also be accessed by right-clicking on a sheet tab and selecting Move or Copy.

To move or copy a sheet to another workbook, the second workbook must already be open. Make sure the sheet you want to move or copy is the active sheet. Then, using the Move or Copy dialog box, shown in Figure 2.8, select from the To Book field the workbook to move or copy the sheet to. If you're making a copy of the sheet, select the Create a Copy box. In the Before Sheet dialog box, select the sheet you want the active sheet to be placed in front of (to the left of).

 CAUTION When you move or copy a sheet from one workbook to another, any formulas on that sheet linked to another sheet in the original workbook will remain linked to the sheet in the original workbook unless you also include the linked sheet(s) in the move or copy procedure.

Renaming a Sheet

Excel's sheet names, Sheet1, Sheet2, etc., aren't very descriptive. Also, when you copy a sheet in a workbook that already has a sheet by that name, Excel will copy the sheet name, appending a number to the end of it. For example, if you copy

Sheet1 within the same workbook, Excel renames it to Sheet1 (2). To give a sheet a more meaningful name, go to Home, Cells, Format and select Rename Sheet from the drop-down. Excel selects the current sheet name in the sheet's tab and you can then type in the new name. You can also rename a sheet by right-clicking on the sheet's tab and selecting Rename.

Coloring a Sheet Tab

If you have several sheets you want to visually group together, you can color their tabs. For example, if you have some sheets that are for data input and others for reports, you could color your data input sheet tabs a light yellow and the report tabs a light blue.

To change the color of a tab, go to Home, Cells, Format, and select Tab Color from the drop-down. A selection of colors appears from which you can select the desired color. The tab color of the active sheet appears as a gradient but fills the entire tab for the other sheets. You can also change the tab color by right-clicking the tab and selecting Tab Color.

Working with Rows and Columns

It's hard to create the perfect data table the first time around. There's always something you've forgotten, such as the date column. Or maybe you did remember the date column but put it in the wrong place. Thankfully, you don't have to start over. You can insert, delete, and move entire columns and rows with a few clicks of the mouse.

Selecting an Entire Row or Column

When you select an entire row or column on a sheet, you are selecting beyond what you can see on the sheet. You really do select the entire row or column, and whatever you do to the part you can see affects the entire selection.

To select an entire row, place your cursor on the header until it turns into a single black arrow then click on the header for the row. For example, to select row 5, as shown in Figure 2.9, click on the header 5. To select an entire column, click on the header for the column.

3	2008	2000	123	42	21	0	TRUE	1
4	2008	2000	233	42	26	9	TRUE	1
5	2008	2000	258	30	11	0	TRUE	1
6	2008	2000	264	23	4	0	TRUE	1
7	2008	2000	310	21	12	0	TRUE	1

FIGURE 2.9

Click on the headers to quickly select an entire row or column.

If you need to select multiple, contiguous rows (or columns), click on the first header, then as you hold down the mouse button, drag the mouse down (or up) until you have selected all the rows you need. Let go of the mouse button and perform your desired action on the selection.

If you need to select multiple, noncontiguous rows (or columns), click on the first header, then as you hold down the Ctrl key, carefully click on the headers of the other rows. When done selecting, release the Ctrl key and perform your desired action on the selection.

Inserting an Entire Row and Column

You might want to insert a row if your data table is missing titles over the data. Or, you might need to insert a column if the data table is missing a column of information and you don't want to enter the information at the end (right side) of the table. When you insert a row, Excel shifts the existing data down. When you insert a column, Excel shifts the existing data to the right.

TIP If you select multiple rows or columns, Excel will insert that many rows or columns. For example, if you need to insert five new rows in your data, instead of highlighting one row, right-clicking, selecting Insert, and then repeating this four more times, select five rows, right-click, and select Insert and—Voila!—you have five blank rows. Note that the selection doesn't have to be contiguous. For example, if you've selected several noncontiguous rows, Excel will insert one row beneath each selected row.

To insert a new row or column within an existing data set, select a cell in the row or column where you want the inserted row or column to go. For example, if you need to insert a new row 10, select a cell in row 10. Go to Home, Cells. From the Insert drop-down, select Insert Sheet Rows or Insert Sheet Columns. For a shortcut, you can right-click on the row or column header and select Insert, as shown in Figure 2.10.

NOTE If you don't have the entire row or column selected and you right-click over the selection, Excel displays the Insert dialog box, prompting you to specify whether you want to shift the selected cells right or down, or if you want to insert an entire row or column. See the "Inserting Cells and Ranges" section for more information.

FIGURE 2.10

Right-clicking a header brings up the options to let you quickly insert or delete a row or column.

Deleting an Entire Row and Column

When you import data from another source, you might need to clean it up by deleting rows or columns of data you don't need. When deleting a row, Excel shifts the data below the row up. For example, after deleting row 5, what was in row 6 now appears in row 5. If deleting a column, Excel shifts the data that was to the right of the deleted column to the left.

To delete a row or column, select a cell in the row or column to delete and go to Home, Cells and from the Delete drop-down, select Delete Sheet Rows or Delete Sheet Columns. For a shortcut, you can right-click on the row or column header and select Delete, as shown in Figure 2.10.

 TIP Your selection of rows or columns does not have to be contiguous. Excel will delete what you have selected.

Moving Entire Rows and Columns

You have to be careful when moving rows and columns. Depending on the method you use, you could end up overwriting other cells. To move rows or columns when you aren't worried about overwriting existing data, follow these steps:

1. Select the row or column you want to move.

2. The selection is surrounded by a thick line. Place your cursor over the line until it turns into a four-headed arrow, as shown in Figure 2.11.

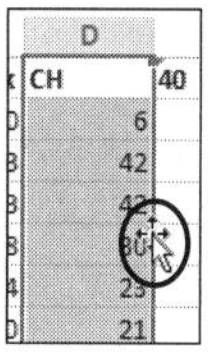

FIGURE 2.11

When the cursor changes to a four-headed arrow, you can click and drag the column to a new location.

3. Click on the line and hold the mouse button down.

4. Drag the selection to a new location and let go.

5. If there is any data in the new location, Excel asks if you want to overwrite it. If you say No, the move will be canceled.

6. The original row or column will still be there, but it will be empty.

If you need to keep data in the new location intact, you could insert a row or column in the new location, copy the data to be moved, paste it in the inserted rows or columns and then go back to the original location, select it again, and delete it. Or, you could get it done more quickly by selecting and cutting the row or column, right-clicking on the new location, and selecting Insert Cut Cells. Excel moves the data in the new location, inserting the cut data and also deleting the data in the old location.

To perform these actions using the ribbon, after selecting and cutting the row or column, select a cell in the new location and go to Home, Cells, Insert and select Insert Cut Cells from the drop-down.

 TIP With one small addition, you can use both of the previous methods to copy a row to a new location. If using the drag method, hold down the Ctrl key as you drag the row to the other location. If using the menu method, copy the row instead of cutting it and select Insert Copied Cells from the menu.

Working with Cells

Just like you can insert, move, and delete entire rows and columns, you can also insert, move, and delete cells. This section will show you how to quickly jump to a cell you can't currently see on your sheet, select noncontiguous ranges, and insert, move, and delete cells.

Selecting a Cell Using the Name Box

Chapter 1, "Understanding the Microsoft Excel Interface," explained how each cell has an address made up of the column and row it resides in. The basics of navigation were touched upon—you can either click on a cell or use the keyboard to select a cell.

You can also jump to a cell by typing the cell address in the Name box, located above the sheet in the left corner. This is a great way of traveling quickly to a specific location on a large sheet.

To use this method, you must enter the cell address properly—that is, the column then the row. For example, if you want to jump to cell AA33, you must type in AA33; you can't type in 33AA. After typing the address, press Enter and the currently selected cell will move to cell AA33.

TIP If you have R1C1 notation turned on—you'll have numbers instead of letters in the column header—A1 notation won't work. You will have to enter the cell address using the R1C1 system of addressing cells. See the section "Using R1C1 Notation to Reference Cells" in chapter 5, "Using Formulas" for more information on R1C1 notation.

Selecting Noncontiguous Cells and Ranges

In Chapter 1, you were introduced to the basics of cell and range selection in the section "Selecting a Range of Cells." In this section, you learn how to select multiple, noncontiguous ranges, as shown in Figure 2.12.

FIGURE 2.12

You can select noncontiguous cells by holding down the Ctrl key as you select each range.

You don't always want to select cells right next to each other. For example, you might want to select only the cells with negative values and make them bold. You could select each cell one at a time and apply the bold format, or you could hold down the Ctrl key and select each cell. Once all the cells are selected, then you let go of the Ctrl key and select your desired format (or other action).

CAUTION Once a cell has been selected using the Ctrl key method, you cannot deselect it. If you make a mistake in your cell selection, you have to start over.

Inserting Cells and Ranges

When you insert or delete rows and columns, Excel shifts all the data on the sheet. If you don't want all the data shifted, select a specific range, then either right-click over the selection and choose Insert or go to Home, Cells, Insert and select Insert Cells from the drop-down. A prompt will appear, asking you in which direction you want to shift your existing data, as shown in Figure 2.13. If you want to insert rows, choose Shift Cells Down. If you want to insert columns, choose Shift Cells Right.

	Year	Decade	Yearly Rank	CH	40	10	InTop10	PK	High	Artist
2	2008	2000	50	6					1	58 Ashley Tisda
3	2008	2000	123	42					1	13 Taylor Swift
4	2008	2000	233	42					1	6 Finger Eleve
5	2008	2000	258	30					1	26 Paramore
6	2008	2000	264	23					1	37 Billy Ray Cyr
7	2008	2000	310	21					1	25 Good Charlo
8	2008	2000	319	28					2	12 Wyclef Jean
9	2008	2000	332	26					2	16 Taylor Swift
10	2008	2000	336	20					2	56 Seether
11	2008	2000	345	18	0	0	TRUE		1	70 Last Goodni

Insert ? ×

Insert
○ Shift cells right
● Shift cells down
○ Entire row
○ Entire column

OK   Cancel

FIGURE 2.13

You can control how much of a row or column is inserted by selecting a specific range beforehand.

Deleting Cells and Ranges

When you delete a range, you remove the cells from the sheet, shifting other data over to fill in the empty space. If you aren't careful, you can ruin the careful layout of your sheet, for example, moving data from the credit column to the debit column. If what you really wanted was to delete the data in the cells, leaving the cells intact, Excel calls this clearing the contents. For specifics on clearing contents, see the section "Clearing the Contents of a Cell," in Chapter 3, "Getting Data onto a Sheet."

To delete a range from a sheet, select the range and go to Home, Cells, Delete and select Delete Cells from the drop-down. From the Delete dialog box that opens, choose whether you want to Shift Cells Left or Shift Cells Up. You can also open the dialog box by right-clicking on the selected range and choosing Delete from the menu.

Moving Cells and Ranges

You have to be careful when moving a range—you could end up overwriting other cells. If you need to move rows or columns and aren't worried about overwriting existing data, use the following method. If you don't want to overwrite existing data in the new location, you need to use the Insert Cells method explained in the section "Inserting Cells and Ranges." To move rows or columns when you aren't worried about overwriting existing data, follow these steps:

1. Select the range you want to move.

2. The selection is surrounded by a thick line. Place your cursor over the line until it turns into a four-headed arrow, as shown in Figure 2.14.

3. Click on the line and hold the mouse button down.

4. Drag the selection to a new location and let go.

5. If there is any data in the new location, Excel asks if you want to overwrite it. If you select No, the move will be canceled. Select Yes to complete the move and clear the contents of the original range.

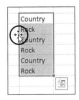

FIGURE 2.14

Be careful when dragging your selection to a new area as it will overwrite anything there.

THE ABSOLUTE MINIMUM

You don't always have to start from scratch when creating a workbook—you can use templates offered online at Microsoft or create your own. Nor are you limited to a single sheet. You can add sheets as needed, for example one for your data and one for your report on that data.

You know how to insert new rows and delete columns. With what you've learned in this chapter, you're ready to learn how to enter data on a sheet and put those inserting, deleting, and moving skills to the test.

GETTING DATA ONTO A SHEET

Data entry is one of the most important functions in Excel—and one of the most tedious, especially when the data is repetitive. This chapter shows you tricks for copying down data, fixing entered data, and helping your users enter data correctly by providing a predefined list of entries.

Types of Data You Enter into Excel

It's important to differentiate types of data because Excel treats each differently. You tell Excel what kind of data is in a cell by how you type it into the cell or by how you format the cell. Data in Excel can fall into one of four categories.

- **Numbers**—Numeric data that can be used for calculation purposes.

- **Text**—Alphabetic *or* numeric data that is not used for calculation purposes. Examples of numeric text are phone numbers or Social Security numbers.

- **Dates and Times**—Although dates and times may be considered alphanumeric, there are occasions where you might want to perform calculations on the values, so it is important to identify the data correctly to Excel.

- **Formulas and Functions**—It's important that Excel knows you're entering a formula or it will treat what you enter like text. This topic is covered in detail in Chapter 5, "Using Formulas."

You can't combine types of data in a cell. You can type "5 oranges," but Excel will see that as text. It won't separate the "5" as a number and the "oranges" as text. If you want to deal with the 5 as a number, then you need to enter it into its own cell.

Entering Different Types of Data into a Cell

How you intially type data into a cell affects how Excel interprets it. You can save yourself some time if you let Excel format your data, but it will only do so properly if it can understand what you want. The following sections will help you help Excel understand what you want.

Typing Numbers into a Cell

Numbers are the simplest thing to type into a cell. You select a cell, type in a number, press Enter or Tab, and you're done.

Typing Text into a Cell

If you simply select a cell and start typing without any forethought, you might get unexpected results. For example, select a cell and type the ZIP Code for Chester, MA, which is 01011, and press Enter or Tab. The beginning 0 disappears and all you see is 1011, as shown in Figure 3.1.

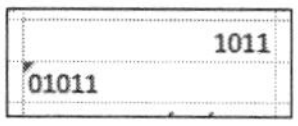

FIGURE 3.1

Excel tries its best to decipher the data you enter, but sometimes you have to help it out.

The reason this happens is because Excel assumes you are typing in a number, and numbers do not start with zeros. Although ZIP Codes are numeric, they aren't numbers—that is, you don't do any math with them. You need to plan ahead—know that you are entering numeric data that should be treated like text, and you need to let Excel know this. To let Excel know that you are entering a number that should be treated like text, type an apostrophe before you type the number.

Select another cell and this time type '01011 and then press Enter or Tab. You'll notice that the beginning zero remains. But you don't see the starting apostrophe. Also, the ZIP Code is aligned to the left side of the cell instead of the right. This is another default action Excel takes when you enter data—it aligns the values for numbers, dates, and times to the right and text to the left.

 NOTE   You'll also notice a small green triangle in the upper-left corner of the cell. This is an Error Checking option covered in more detail later in this chapter.

When you type alphabetic characters into a cell, you don't need to worry about a leading apostrophe. Nor do you need to worry about the apostrophe if you are mixing numbers and letters in the cell. But if you do have an apostrophe because it's habit, that's OK because Excel ignores leading apostrophes. However, if you need an apostrophe at the beginning of a cell, then enter two apostrophes—only the second one will show.

Typing Dates and Times into a Cell

Dates and times are another category in which it's important for Excel to know what you are typing in. But in this case, the important thing to remember is to *not* put an apostrophe or other character before your date or time. Excel is very smart about date and time entry, and if you simply type it in, it does a very good job of deciphering your data.

Excel uses the system-configured date format. For example, in the United States, when entering numeric dates, the month comes first. For example, May 14, 2012 is written as 5/14/12.

If you enter only a month and day, Excel will append the current year. But this also means that if you enter a fraction that could be interpreted as a date, such as 3/4, Excel will convert it to a date, 3/4/12. To enter a fraction, you must format the cell as Fraction before entering it.

Dates must always include a day, month, and year, even if not all three will appear when the cell is formatted (see Chapter 4, "Formatting Sheets and Cells," for more details on how formatting affects what you see but not actually what's in the cell).

When entering times, you must enter it using a 24-hour clock, also known as military time or include the a.m. or p.m.

When entering a date, the time is included. But you might not see the part you didn't type in until the cell is formatted to show it.

Controlling the Next Cell Selection

If you're typing a single column list into Excel, you might get frustrated as the next selection moves to the next cell to the right when you want it to go *down* to the next cell. Or if your list has multiple columns, you find the next cell selection going down instead of to the *right*. You don't have to put up with how Excel moves to the next cell selection. You can use several tricks to control what cell you enter data into next.

 TIP   Although Enter and Tab are commonly used to exit out of a cell, you can also use the navigation keys on the keyboard. Another option is Ctrl+Enter, which exits the cell but keeps it selected, allowing you to continue working with the cell, like when applying a format to it.

Entering Data in a Multicolumn List

Normally, when you press the Enter key as you enter data, the active cell moves directly down the column. If instead you want the selection to move to the right, you use the Tab key.

You can take advantage of these default actions to enter data in a multicolumn list, having Excel smoothly move from column to column to the next row. To make this happen, you must use the Tab key to move from one column to the next. When you get to the end of your data entry row, press Enter. Excel keeps track of which column you started your data entry on and returns you there, making it easier to start the next row of data.

Changing the Next Cell Direction when Pressing Enter

If you don't want to use both Tab and Enter, you can go to File, Options, Advanced, After Pressing Enter, Move Selection, and change the Direction from Down to Right. But Excel will no longer move the selection to the next row when you get to the last column as explained in the previous section—because it doesn't realize you are at the last column.

Preselecting the Data Range

If you have the selection set to move right when you press Enter, you can tell Excel when to go down to the next row by selecting the range into which you are entering data before you begin the data entry. In this way, Excel knows when you've reached the last column and will move down to the next row.

Using a Named Range to Indicate Data Entry Cells

If the data you need to fill in isn't in consecutive columns or rows, such as the form shown in Figure 3.2, you can configure Excel to jump around to the different cells as you press the Enter key. You do this by setting up the data entry cells in a *named range*.

FIGURE 3.2

You can jump quickly from one highlighted cell to the next by setting those cells to be a named range.

To set up a named range to assist in data entry, follow these steps:

1. Ignore the first data entry field, and select the second field.

2. Hold down the Ctrl key and select each data entry field in the order you want to enter the data.

3. After all the other data entry fields have been selected, while still holding down the Ctrl key, select the first field.

4. Type a name for the selected range in the Name box and press Enter.

5. The next time you need to enter data in the fields, select the named range from the Name box drop-down and the fields will be highlighted, as shown in Figure 3.2. Begin entering data in the first field and press Tab or Enter to automatically go to the next field, repeating until you are done.

Using Copy, Cut, Paste, Paste Special to Enter Data

You can copy or cut data from different sources, such as other workbooks, Word documents, or web pages, and paste the information onto a sheet. Depending on how the data appeared in the original source, you might have to modify it after you paste it in Excel.

One of the ways you can clean up data copied or cut from another source is to use the Paste Special command instead of just Paste. To access this special command, go to Home, Clipboard and click the arrow on the Paste button or right-click on a cell. Various Paste Special options will appear. If you place your cursor over one of the icons, a tip appears, as shown in Figure 3.3. You can access more options by clicking Paste Special at the bottom of the drop-down.

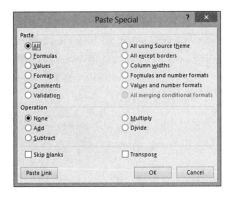

FIGURE 3.3

The Paste Special drop-down provides quick access to the more commonly used options. Click Paste Special at the bottom of the list to access the full dialog box.

Using Paste Special with Ranges

Figure 3.3 shows the Paste Special options available if pasting a range copied or cut from within Excel. The Paste area of the dialog box has different paste options you can choose from. For example, if you select Values, you will only paste the value of what you copied. The formatting and formulas will not be pasted. If you do want the original formatting but also the values, select Values and Number Formats. If you want a combination of values and comments, then you need to use Paste Special twice, selecting Values once and then Comments the second time.

The Operation area allows you to perform simple math on the selected range. For example, if you have a list of prices that need to go up by 1.5%, type .015 in a cell and copy the cell. Select your range of prices and bring up the Paste Special dialog box. From the dialog box, select Values (so you don't lose any formatting you have on your prices) from the Paste area and Multiply from the Operation area. Click OK. Your prices will have increased by 1.5%.

Using Paste Special with Text

If you copy or cut data within a cell (versus the entire cell) or from a non-Excel source, such as a Word document or web page, the Paste Special options are limited. Depending on the source, text, or graphic, you may get the options shown in Figure 3.4.

 NOTE The options available depend on the original source. For example, if you copied text from within a cell (versus the entire cell), you would only see pasting options for Unicode Text and Text. You wouldn't have the option of pasting the text as a Word document object because it didn't originate from Word.

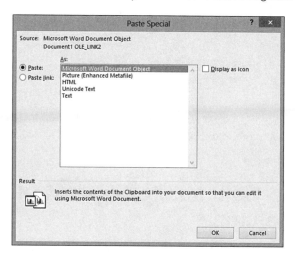

FIGURE 3.4

When doing a Paste Special with text, there are fewer options available.

As you select an option in the As list box, an explanation appears in the Result area at the bottom of the dialog box. If you select the Paste Link option to the left of the list, you'll also be able to link the pasted data to its original source.

If available, the Display as Icon option lets you paste an icon instead of the text. Double-clicking on the icon opens the text in an editing application (for example, if pasting text from a Word document, you can edit the text in Word).

Using Paste Special with Images and Charts

When pasting images and charts, the dialog box is similar to that shown in Figure 3.4, but the As list box options differ, listing various image types. The different types can affect image resolution and workbook size.

Using Paste to Merge a Noncontiguous Selection in a Row or Column

If you try to copy/paste a noncontiguous selection from different rows and columns, an error message appears. But if the selection is in the same row or column, Excel allows you to copy and paste the data. When the data is pasted, though, it is no longer separated by other cells, as shown in Figure 3.5. You can use this method to create a table of specific values copied from another table.

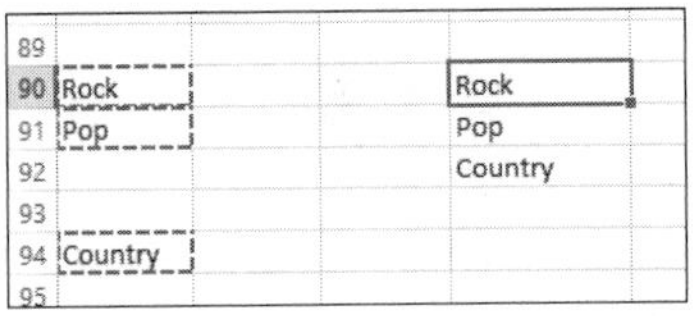

89				
90	Rock		Rock	
91	Pop		Pop	
92			Country	
93				
94	Country			
95				

FIGURE 3.5

Data from rows 90, 91, and 94 was copied from the table on the left to create the list on the right using the method explained in this section.

Using Text to Columns to Separate Data in a Single Column

Data, Data Tools, Text to Columns can be used to separate data in a single column into multiple columns, such as if you have full names in one column and need a column with first names and a column with last names. When you select the command, a wizard dialog box opens to help you through the process. In step 1 of the wizard, select whether the text is Delimited or Fixed Width (see the next sections for definitions of Delimited and Fixed Width). In step 2, you provide more details on how you want the text separated. In step 3, you tell Excel the basic formatting to apply to each column.

If you have data in the columns to the right of the column you are separating, Excel overwrites the data. Be sure to insert enough blank columns to not overwrite your existing data before beginning Text to Columns. See the section "Inserting an Entire Row & Column" in chapter 2, "Working with Workbooks, Sheets, Rows, Columns, and Cells," for instructions on how to insert columns.

Working with Delimited Text

Delimited text is text that has some character, such as a comma, tab, or space, separating each group of words that you want placed into its own column. To separate delimited text into multiple columns, follow these steps:

1. Highlight the range of text to be separated.

2. Go to Data, Data Tools, Text to Columns. The Convert Text to Columns Wizard opens.

3. Select Delimited from step 1 of the wizard, as shown in Figure 3.6, and click Next.

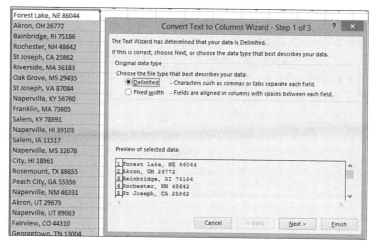

FIGURE 3.6

Select the Delimited option to separate text joined by delimiters, such as commas, spaces, or tabs.

4. Select one or more delimiters used by the grouped text, as in Figure 3.7, and click Next.

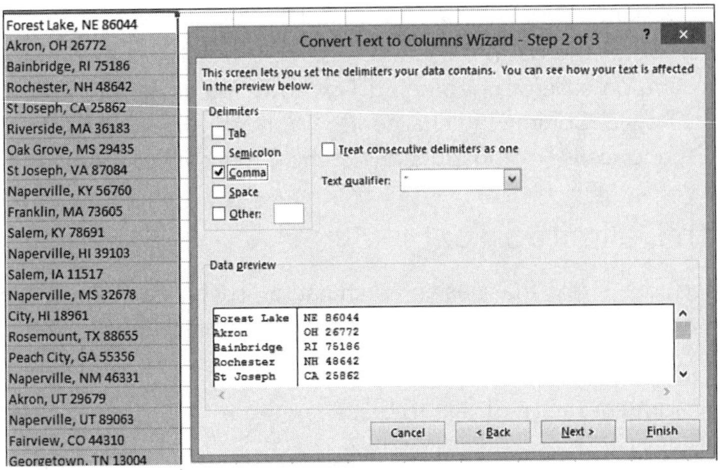

FIGURE 3.7

Select the Delimited option to use the comma as a delimiter between the city, state, and ZIP Code.

If you need more than one delimiter but one of the delimiters is used normally in the text, such as the space between city names and the space between a state and ZIP Code (Sioux Falls, SD 57057), consider running Text to Columns twice: once to separate the city (Sioux Falls) from the state ZIP Code (SD 57057) and again to separate the state and ZIP Code.

5. For each column of data, select the data format. For example, if you have a column of ZIP Codes, you need to set the format as Text so any leading zeros are not lost. But be warned—setting a column to Text prevents Excel from properly identifying formulas entered into that column.

6. Click Finish. The text is separated, as shown in Figure 3.8.

Forest Lake	NE 86044
Akron	OH 26772
Bainbridge	RI 75186
Rochester	NH 48642
St Joseph	CA 25862
Riverside	MA 36183
Oak Grove	MS 29435

FIGURE 3.8

Using Text to Columns with a comma delimiter separated the city from the state and ZIP Code. Run the wizard again on the state ZIP Code column with a space as a delimiter to split up that data.

Working with Fixed-Width Text

Fixed-width text describes text where each group is a set number of characters. You can draw a line down all the records to separate all the groups, as shown in Figure 3.9. If your text doesn't look like it's fixed width, try changing the font to a fixed-width font, such as Courier. It's possible that it's fixed-width text in disguise.

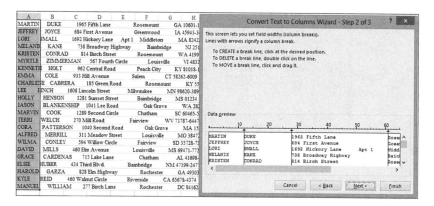

FIGURE 3.9

Use the Fixed Width option when each group in the data has a fixed number of characters.

To separate fixed-width text into multiple columns, follow these steps:

1. Highlight the range of cells that includes text to be separated.

2. Go to Data, Text to Columns.

3. Select Fixed Width from step 1 of the wizard and click Next.

4. Excel will guess at where the column breaks should go, as shown in Figure 3.9. You can move a break by clicking and dragging it to where you want it, insert a new break by clicking where it should be, or remove a break by double-clicking it. Click Next.

   Don't worry about leading spaces—Excel will remove them for you.

5. For each column of data, select the data format. For example, if you have a column of ZIP Codes, you need to set the format as Text so any leading zeros are not lost, as shown in Figure 3.10. But be warned—setting a column to Text prevents Excel from properly identifying formulas entered into that column.

6. Click Finish.

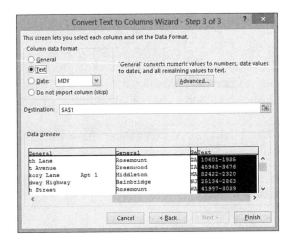

FIGURE 3.10

In step 3 of the wizard, set the format of each column. If you have numeric text, such as ZIP Codes, make sure you configure the wizard to treat the column as text so you don't lose any leading zeros.

Inserting Symbols and Equations into a Cell

Sometimes you need more than the symbols available on the keyboard, such as a copyright or registered trademark symbol. Some people have the Alt+number combination memorized, but if you're like me, you don't. No worries, though—if you go to the Insert tab, the Symbols group has commands for inserting equations and symbols.

First, select the cell where you want the symbol to appear. Next, select the Symbol option, and a window appears where you can search for the symbol you want. Once you find it, double-click on it, or click on it once and then click the Insert button. The symbol appears in the cell. The dialog box remains open in case you want to enter more symbols.

 TIP   If the symbol you need is after another word, start typing your text and when you get to the point where the symbol needs to go, don't press Enter or Tab to get out of the cell. Instead, leave the cursor where it is and click the symbol command. When you insert your symbol, it will appear at the cursor's location.

An **equation** isn't the same as a formula. The formulas entered in Excel are meant to do calculations on the sheet. An equation doesn't perform a calculation. Instead, it shows how a calculation is performed, using variables instead of numbers, like E=mc². If you click on the down arrow of the Equation button, a list of popular equations appears. If you don't see the one you want, click the Equation button itself. A frame with Type Equation Here will appear on your sheet. Also, two new ribbons will appear—Drawing Tools and Equation Tools. Use the commands on the Equation Tools, Design tab to create your equation. Use the commands on the Drawing Tools, Format tab to format the frame in which the equation appears. When you're done with the equation, just click elsewhere on the sheet.

Using Web Queries to Get Data onto a Sheet

A web query allows you to link a range to text from a web page. As the web page updates, the data on the sheet also updates. To retrieve data from a web page, follow these steps:

1. Go to Data, Get External Data, From Web. The New Web Query dialog box opens.

2. From the Address field at the top, navigate to the desired web page and it will load. If Excel is able to retrieve data from the web page, a yellow box with a black arrow appears near the data.

3. Place your cursor over the box and a frame appears around the data that box is tied to. Not all areas of a web page are retrievable. If you find a box that has the data you want, click the box and it turns into a green box with a black check mark.

4. Select as many sections as you need, then click the Import button at the bottom of the dialog box.

5. From the Import Data dialog box, select the cell where you want the data to appear. If you don't like the current cell address shown, you can click on the sheet and the dialog box updates with a new sheet address. Click OK.

6. After a few seconds, depending on your Internet connection, the data appears on the sheet.

By default, the data refreshes every 60 minutes. You can refresh manually by clicking Data, Connections, and from the Refresh All drop-down, select Refresh. Or you can configure the automatic refresh time by going to Data, Connections, Properties or right-clicking the data and selecting Data Range Properties. Either way opens the External Data Range Properties dialog box where you can set the refresh time by selecting Refresh Every x Minutes and changing the value in the field, as shown in Figure 3.11.

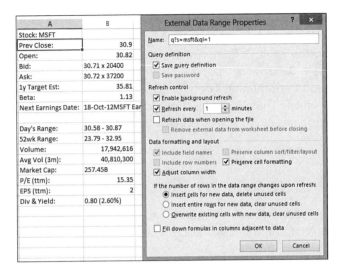

FIGURE 3.11

Use a web query to return an automatically updating summary of stock information for MSFT.

Using Series to Quickly Fill a Range

The fill handle, shown in Figure 3.12, can speed up data entry by completing a series for you. Excel comes with several preconfigured series, such as months, days of the week, and quarters. You can also add your own series, as described in the "Creating Your Own Series" section later in this chapter.

Fill Handle

FIGURE 3.12

Use the fill handle to quickly fill in a series.

Extending a Series Containing Text

To extend a series containing text, enter the text you want the series to start with and press Ctrl+Enter to exit the cell, but keep it selected. Place your cursor over the lower-right corner of the cell until a black cross appears. Click the mouse button and as you hold it down, drag the fill handle.

You don't need to start at the beginning of the series. You can start anywhere in the series and Excel will continue it, starting over if you drag the handle long enough. For example, if you begin a series in A1 with Sunday and drag the fill handle to A8, Sunday will appear again, repeating the series.

CAUTION   If the text series contains a numerical value, Excel instead copies the text and extends the numerical portion. For example, if you try to extend Monday 1, you get Monday 2, not Tuesday 2. But if you type in Jan 1 and extend that text, Excel extends the numerical portion until Jan 31, then switches to Feb 1. It does this because dates are actually numbers. Seeing the date as Jan 1 is a matter of formatting.

Extending a Numerical Series

If you try to fill numerical series based off of a single cell entry, Excel just copies the value instead of filling the series. There are four ways to get around this:

- Enter at least the first two values of the series before dragging the fill handle.

- Hold down the Ctrl key while dragging the fill handle.

- If there is a blank column to the left or right of the numerical column, include that column in your selection when dragging the fill handle down. For example, if you enter 1 in A1 then select A1:B1 (B1 is blank); when you drag the fill handle down, the series in column A is filled down.

- Hold the right mouse button down while dragging the fill handle and select Fill Series from the context menu that appears when you release the mouse button.

CAUTION   If you hold the Ctrl key while trying to extend a text series, Excel copies the values instead of filling in the series.

Creating Your Own Series

You can teach Excel the lists that are important to you so that you can take advantage of the series capabilities in Excel. You can take almost any list of items on a sheet and create a custom list for use in filling or sorting.

To create a custom list, follow these steps:

1. Create your list on the sheet and select the range.

2. Go to File, Options, Advanced, General, Edit Custom Lists.

3. The range you selected is already in the Import List from Cells field at the bottom of the Custom Lists dialog box, so click Import.

4. The list is added to both the Custom Lists and List Entries list boxes, as shown in Figure 3.13. The next time you type an item from your list and drag the fill handle, Excel fills in the rest of the series for you.

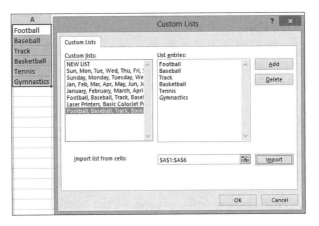

FIGURE 3.13

Create a custom list for use in filling in a series.

Editing Data

Now that you know how to enter data into a blank cell—how do you edit data already in a cell? If you select a cell and start typing, you'll overwrite what was originally in the cell. You have three methods to choose from:

- **Double-click**—When you place your cursor over a cell and it's a big white cross, double-click and the cursor appears wherever you double-clicked at, so you can go directly to a word or between numbers.

- **Formula bar**—Select the cell and then click where you want to edit in the formula bar.

- **F2**—Select the cell and press F2. The cursor appears at the right end of data in the cell.

When you're done making changes, press Enter or whatever method you prefer to exit out of the cell and save your changes. If you change your mind about the changes while you're still in the cell, press Esc and you'll exit the cell without saving your changes.

Editing Multiple Sheets at One Time

You can change the exact same range on multiple sheets at the same time by grouping the sheets and making the change to one of the sheets. For example, you can enter the word *Sales* in cell A1 of all the selected sheets. Or you can apply a bold format to cell C2 in a group of sheets.

To make a change to multiple sheets by just changing one sheet, follow these steps:

1. Go to one of the sheets you need to change.

2. While holding down the Ctrl key, select the tabs of the other sheets you want to make the same change to. This groups the sheets together.

3. Make the changes to the active sheet.

4. To ungroup the sheets, select another sheet, or right-click on a sheet tab and select Ungroup Sheets.

Clearing the Contents of a Cell

To clear the data from a range, leaving the cells otherwise intact, such as the formatting, select the range and press the Delete key or right-click over the selection and choose Clear Contents.

CAUTION   You may be tempted to use the spacebar to clear a cell. DON'T! While you can't see the space in the cell, Excel can. That space can throw off Excel's functions because to Excel, that space is a character.

Clearing an Entire Sheet

To clear a sheet of all data, but leave any formatting intact, click the intersection between the headers, shown in Figure 3.14, and press Delete or right-click and choose Clear Contents.

To clear a sheet of all data and formatting, select the entire sheet using the intersection between the headers, right-click and select Delete, or go to Home, Cells, Delete.

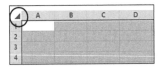

FIGURE 3.14

Clicking the intersection of the row and column headers selects all the cells on the sheet.

Working with Tables

When you enter information in multiple columns on a sheet, it is often referred to as a table, as in a table of data. But Excel also has a special term for a setting you can apply to a data table, imbuing it with special abilities and rules. This term is also *Table*. When your data table is defined as a Table, additional functionality in Excel is made available. For example, with Excel's intelligent Tables, the following additional functionality becomes available:

- AutoFilter drop-downs, shown in Figure 3.16, are automatically added to the headings.

- You can apply predesigned formats, such as banded rows or borders.

- You can remove duplicates based on the values in one or more columns.

- You can toggle the total row on and off.

- Adding new rows or columns automatically extends the table.

- You can take advantage of automatically created range names.

 NOTE Throughout this book, when I am referring to this special kind of Table, the T will be capitalized. A normal table that does not have the additional functionality, will have a lowercase t.

Defining a Table

For your data to convert to a Table, it must be set up properly. This means that, except for the headings row (row 1 in Figure 3.15), each row must be one complete record of the data set—for example, a customer or inventory item—as shown in Figure 3.15. Column headers are not required, but if they are included, they must be at the top of the data. If your data does not include headers, Excel inserts some for you.

	A	B	C	D	E	F	G
1	Region	Product	Date	Customer	Quantity	Revenue	COGS
2	East	XYZ	1/1/2012	Exclusive Shovel Trader	1000	22810	10220
3	Central	DEF	1/2/2012	Bright Hairpin Company	100	2257	984
4	East	DEF	1/	Create Table	800	18552	7872
5	East	XYZ	1/		400	9152	4088
6	East	ABC	1/	Where is the data for your table?	400	8456	3388
7	East	DEF	1/	=$A$1:$G$15	000	21730	9840
8	Central	ABC	1/9		800	16416	6776
9	Central	XYZ	1/10	☑ My table has headers	900	21438	9198
10	Central	ABC	1/12		800	6267	2541
11	East	XYZ	1/14	OK Cancel	100	2401	1022
12	East	ABC	1/15/2012	Bright Hairpin Company	500	9345	4235
13	East	ABC	1/16/2012	Appealing Calculator Co	600	11628	5082
14	West	DEF	1/19/2012	Bright Hairpin Company	100	2042	984
15	East	ABC	1/21/2012	Best Vegetable Compar	800	14440	6776

FIGURE 3.15

Set up your data properly to define it as a Table. Make sure the Create Table dialog box includes your entire data set and properly reflects the existence of headers.

After your data is set up properly, you can define the Table with one of the following methods. Select a cell in the data set and then do the following:

1.   Go to Insert, Tables, Table.

2.   Go to Home, Styles, Format as Table, and select a style to apply to the data.

3.   Press Ctrl+T.

4.   Press Ctrl+L.

When you use any one of the preceding methods, Excel determines the range of your data by looking for a completely empty row and column. The Create Table dialog box opens, showing the range Excel has defined. You can accept this range or modify it as needed. To modify it, you can click on the sheet and, holding down the mouse button, drag to create a box enveloping your entire data set. You can also modify it by editing the cell addresses in the Create Table dialog box.

If Excel was able to identify headers, the My Table Has Headers dialog box will be selected, so make sure that Excel has correctly identified whether your data has headers and click OK. If there were no headers, make sure the box is unselected and click OK. Your table will be formatted with AutoFilter drop-downs in the headers, as shown in Figure 3.16.

NOTE With the creation of the Table, a new tab Table Tools, Design has appeared in the ribbon. Whenever you select a cell in a Table, this tab appears. It contains functionality and options specific to Tables.

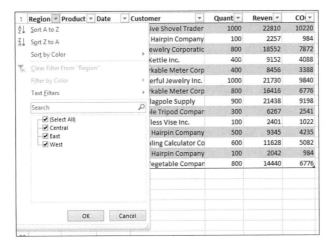

FIGURE 3.16

A Table automatically has AutoFilter drop-downs in the headers.

Expanding a Table

After your data is defined as a Table, the Table automatically expands as you add adjacent rows and columns. If you don't want the new entry to be part of the Table, you can tell Excel by clicking the lightning bolt icon that appears and then selecting either Undo Table AutoExpansion or Stop Automatically Expanding Tables, as shown in Figure 3.17.

FIGURE 3.17

If you don't want a new row or column to be part of the Table, instruct Excel to undo or stop the autoexpansion.

 CAUTION When adding new rows to the bottom of a Table, make sure the total row is turned off; otherwise, Excel cannot identify the new row as belonging with the existing data. The exception is if you tab from the last data row, Excel inserts a new row and moves the total row down.

To manually resize a Table, click and drag the angle bracket icon in the lower-right corner of the Table. You can also select a cell in the Table and go to Table Tools, Design, Properties, Resize Table. Specify the new range in the Resize Table dialog box that opens.

Adding a Total Row to a Table

When you go to Table Tools, Design, Table Style Options, Total Row, Excel adds a total row to the bottom of the active Table. By default, Excel adds the word Total to the first column of the Table and sums the data in the rightmost column, as shown in Figure 3.18. If the rightmost column contains text, Excel returns a count instead of a sum.

Total							73006 ▾
							None
							Average
							Count
							Count Number
							Max
							Min
							Sum
							StdDev
							Var
							More Function

FIGURE 3.18

Selecting the Total Row check box adds a total row to the bottom of the Table. Use the drop-downs in each cell in this row to add or change the function used to total the data in the above column.

Each cell in the total row has a drop-down of functions that can be used to calculate the data above it. For example, instead of the sum, you can calculate the average, max, min, and more. Just make a selection from the drop-down and Excel inserts the formula in the cell.

 TIP The functions listed in the drop-down are calculated using variations of the SUBTOTAL function. For more information on this function, see Chapter 10, "Subtotals and Grouping."

Fixing Numbers Stored as Text

Sometimes when you import data or receive data from another source, the numbers might be converted to text. When you try to sum them, nothing works. That is because Excel will not sum numbers stored as text.

When numbers in a sheet are being stored as text, Excel lets you know by placing a green triangle in the cell (if File, Options, Formulas, Error Checking, Enable

Background Error Checking is selected). When you select the cell and click the warning sign that appears, Excel informs you that the number is being stored as text, as shown in Figure 3.19. It then gives you options for handling the number, such as Convert to Number or Ignore Error.

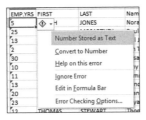

FIGURE 3.19

With Background Error Checking enabled, Excel informs you if a number is being stored as text.

If you have a worksheet with thousands of cells, it will take a long time to convert them all to numbers. Three options for doing a larger-scale conversion are covered in the next sections.

Using Convert to Number on a Range

One option for converting multiple cells into numbers is to use the information drop-down that Excel has provided:

1. Select the range consisting of all the cells you need to convert (making sure that the first cell in the range needs to be converted). The range can include text and other numerical values, as long as it doesn't include cells you do not want to be converted to numbers.

2. Click the warning symbol in the first cell.

3. From the drop-down, select Convert to Number, and all cells in the selected range will be modified, turning the numbers to true numbers.

Using Paste Special to Force a Number

If you have the Background Error Checking disabled and don't see the green warning triangle, try this method for converting cells to numbers:

1. Enter a **1** in a blank cell and copy it.

2. Select the cells containing the numbers, right-click and select Paste Special, Paste Special.

3. From the dialog box that opens, select Multiply, and click OK.

The act of multiplying the values by 1 forces the contents of the cells to become their numerical values.

TIP   You can also copy a blank cell and use the Add option instead of Multiply.

Using Text to Columns to Convert Text to Numbers

In step 3 of the Text to Columns wizard, you select the data type of a column. You can use this functionality to also correct numbers being stored as text. To convert a column of numbers stored as text to just numbers, follow these steps:

1. Highlight the range of text to be converted.

2. Go to Data, Text to Columns.

3. Click Finish. The numbers are no longer considered numbers stored as text.

NOTE   For more information on the Text to Columns wizard, refer to the section "Working with Delimited Text" earlier in this chapter.

Spellchecking Your Sheet

Just like Word, Excel has a spellchecker included. To access it, go to Review, Proofing, Spelling. It reviews all text entries on the sheet. You can configure the options, such as Ignore Words in Uppercase, by clicking the Options button in the Spelling dialog box, or by going to File, Options, Proofing.

If you click the AutoCorrect Options button in the Excel Options dialog box, the AutoCorrect dialog box opens, allowing you to configure how you want the AutoCorrect to work, including automatically replacing text as you type. For example, if you like to abbreviate department as dept. but need it spelled out, you can configure that from this dialog box. Type dept. in the Replace field and department in the With field and click Add. Next time you type dept. in Excel, after you press the spacebar, it will be corrected to department.

Finding Data on Your Sheet

If you press Ctrl+F or go to Home, Editing, Find & Select and select Find from the drop-down, the Find and Replace dialog box opens. Through this dialog box, you can find data anywhere on the sheet or in the workbook. Click on the Replace tab and you can quickly replace the found data.

Click the Options button and the Find dialog box opens up, showing several options to aid in your search, as shown in Figure 3.20:

FIGURE 3.20

Click the Options button to open up the full search potential of the Find and Replace dialog box.

- **Within**—You can search just the active Sheet or the entire Workbook. You can also narrow Excel's search by selecting the range before bringing up the dialog box.

- **Search**—To have the search go down all the rows of one column before going on to the next column, set this to By Rows. To have the search go across all columns in a row before going on to the next row, select By Columns.

- **Look In**—By default, Excel looks in Formulas, that is, the true value of the data in a cell. When you've applied formulas or formatting to a sheet, what you see in a cell might not be what is actually in the cell. Look at Figure 3.21. The value 22.81 is obviously at the top of the column, but a search in Excel does not find it because the value in the cell was calculated. To search for the value, change the drop-down to Values. You can also choose to search in Comments.

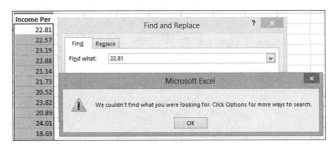

FIGURE 3.21

If Excel can't find the number you know is on the sheet, check your settings. If set to Formulas, change to Values and vice versa.

CAUTION The settings in the Find and Replace dialog box are stored throughout an Excel session. This means that if you change them in the morning for a search and then try a search again later in the afternoon without having closed Excel at all during the day, the settings changes you've made are still active, even if you're searching a different workbook.

Performing a Wildcard Search

What if you don't know the exact text you're looking for? For example, you're doing a search for Jon Smith but don't know if Jon was entered correctly. To do a wildcard search, you can use an asterisk (*) to tell Excel there might or might not be additional characters between the n, like this: Jo*n Smith. In this case, Excel would return John Smith, Jon Smith, and Jonathan Smith.

If you have a list of part numbers and can remember all but one of the characters, you can use a question mark (?) to replace the unknown character. Use a ? for each unknown. So if you aren't sure of the first and last characters, do this: ?482?. This tells Excel that there is definitely one character in each of those positions.

If you need to include a * or ? as part of your search—not as a wildcard, but as actually part of the search text, then precede the symbol with a tilde (~). Doing this tells Excel that the * or ? is not a wildcard character but an actual text character to use in the search.

Using Data Validation to Limit Data Entry in a Cell

Data validation, found under Data, Data Tools, Data Validation, allows you to limit what a user can type in a cell. For example, you can limit users to whole numbers, dates, a list of selections, or a specific range of values. Custom input and error messages can be configured to guide the user entry.

The available validation criteria are as follows:

- **Any Value**—The default value allowing unrestricted entry.

- **Whole Number**—Requires a whole number be entered. You can select a comparison value (Between, Not Between, Equal To, and so on) and set the Minimum and Maximum value.

- **Decimal**—Requires a decimal value be entered. You can select a comparison value (Between, Not Between, Equal To, and so on) and set the Minimum and Maximum value.

- **List**—Requires user to select from a predefined list, as shown in Figure 3.22. The source can be within the Data Validation dialog box or can be a vertical or horizontal range on any sheet.

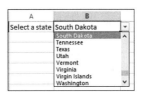

FIGURE 3.22

Provide users with a list of entries to choose from.

- **Date**—Requires a date be entered. You can select a comparison value (Between, Not Between, Equal To, and so on) and set the Minimum and Maximum value.

- **Time**—Requires a time be entered. You can select a comparison value (Between, Not Between, Equal To, and so on) and set the Minimum and Maximum value.

- **Text Length**—Requires a text value be entered. You can select a comparison value (Between, Not Between, Equal To, and so on) and set the Minimum and Maximum number of characters.

- **Custom**—Uses a formula to calculate TRUE for valid entries or FALSE for invalid entries.

Limiting User Entry to a Selection from a List

Data validation allows you to create a drop-down in a cell, restricting the user to selecting from a predefined list of values, as shown in Figure 3.22. To set up the source range and configure the data validation cell, follow these steps:

1. Create a vertical or horizontal list of the values to appear in the drop-down. You can place these values in a sheet different from where the drop-down will actually be placed, then hide the sheet, preventing the user from changing the list.

2. Select the cell you want the drop-down to appear in.

3. Go to Data, Data Tools, Data Validation. The Data Validation dialog box opens.

4. From the Allow field of the Settings tab, select List.

5. Place your cursor in the Source field.

6. Select the list you created in step 1, as shown in Figure 3.23. If your list is short, instead of the separate list you created in step 1, you can enter the values separated by commas directly in the Source field. For example, you could enter Yes, No in the source field (no quotes, no equal sign).

FIGURE 3.23

The source for the validation list can be a different sheet. You can then hide the sheet from users.

7. If you want to provide the user with an input prompt, go to the Input Message tab and fill in the Title and Input Message fields.

8. If you want to provide the user with an error message, go to the Error Alert tab and fill in the Style, Title, and Error Message fields.

9. Click OK.

 NOTE The font and font size of the text in the drop-down is controlled by your Windows settings, not Excel.

THE ABSOLUTE MINIMUM

By now, you should have a good idea on how to enter data in Excel. You can even design a form with drop-downs to guide your users on what entries are allowed in a cell. You've also learned some tricks for quickly entering data by using the fill handle to copy cells or fill in a series. If you receive a sheet with numbers that won't add up, you don't need to go back to the originator and tell them to try again—instead, you know how to use Text to Columns to fix those numbers.

Now that you have your data on the sheet, you probably want to sharpen it up, make a professional looking report or table, drawing the user's eye to something specific or downplaying other parts. The next chapter teaches you how to format your data, including setting things up so that the formatting changes automatically based on what is entered in the cell.

- Add icons in cells to represent their value with an image.
- Quickly copy a format from one range to another.
- Switch between number formats.
- Create your own custom number format.

4

FORMATTING SHEETS AND CELLS

Now that you have your data on a sheet, you need to format it so that it's easy to decipher and readers can quickly make sense of it. From simple font formatting, wrapping text, and merging cells to placing icons in cells so it's obvious how one number compares with another, Excel has the tools you need to make reports visually interesting.

Adjusting Row Heights and Column Widths

If you can't see all the data you enter in a cell or the data in a column doesn't use up very much of the column width, you can adjust the column width as needed. Several methods are available for adjusting column widths on a sheet. Each method described here also works for adjusting row heights:

- **Click and drag the border between the column headings**—Place your cursor on the border between two column headings, as shown in Figure 4.1. Once the cursor turns into a two-headed arrow, you can click and drag to the right to make the column to the left wider or drag to the left to make the column narrower. The advantage of this method is you have full control of the width of the column. The disadvantage is that it affects only one column.

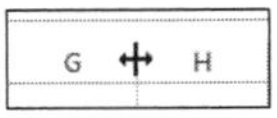

FIGURE 4.1

The border between columns is the key to quickly adjusting the column width.

- **Double-click the border between the column headings**—Excel automatically adjusts the left column to fit the widest value in that column. The advantage of this method is that the column is now wide enough to display all the contents. The disadvantage is if you have a cell with a very long entry, the new width may be impractical.

- **Select multiple columns and drag the border for one column**—The width of all the columns in the selection adjusts to the same width as the one you just adjusted.

- **Select multiple columns and double-click the border for one column**—Each column in the selection adjusts to accommodate its widest value.

- **Apply one column's width to other columns**—If you have a column with a width you want other columns to have, you can copy that column and paste its width over the other columns by using the Column Widths option of the Paste Special dialog box.

- **Use the controls on the ribbon**—Select the column(s) to adjust. Go to Home, Cells, Format, Column Width. Enter a width and click OK.

- **AutoFit a column to fit all the data below a title row**—If you have a long title and need to fit the column to all the data below the title, double-clicking the border between column headings won't work as this adjusts the column width based on the title. Instead, select the data in the column, without the title, and use the AutoFit Column Width option under Home, Cells, Format.

Using Font Size to Automatically Adjust the Row Height

The default row height is based on the largest font size in the row. For example, if cell F2 has a font size of 26, even if there is no other text in the row, the row automatically adjusts to approximately 33. You can take advantage of this to set the height of a row, instead of manually setting the row height. The advantage is that when a user tries autofitting the row height, your setting won't change.

Changing the Font Settings of a Cell

Changing font aspects allows you to add emphasis to a selected range. There are multiple ways of accessing the font-changing tools in Excel. You can open the Format Cells dialog box by right-clicking a cell and selecting Format Cells, by pressing Ctrl+1 (the number one), or by going to Home, Cells, Format and from the drop-down, selecting Format Cells. The options are also available on the Mini toolbar in Excel, shown in Figure 4.2, and from the Font group on the Home tab.

Mini toolbar

Format Cells dialog

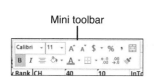

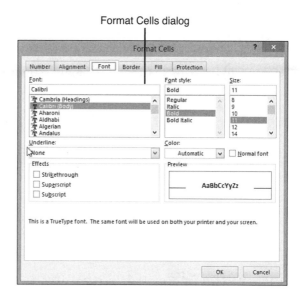

FIGURE 4.2

The Format Cells dialog box and the Mini toolbar, which appears above the context menu when you right-click over a cell, are just two ways you can change font settings.

Selecting a New Font Typeface

The default font in Excel is Calibri, but many others are available. To change the font, select the range, and then select a new font from the drop-down in the Font group, as shown in Figure 4.3. If your cell is viewable, you can preview the selection in the selected range as you move your cursor through the list.

FIGURE 4.3

If your cell is viewable, you can preview the font selection in the selected range as you move your cursor through the list.

Increasing and Decreasing the Font Size

To change the font size, select the range, and then select a new size from the drop-down. The ribbon and Mini toolbar have two additional buttons next to the Font Size drop-down, shown in Figure 4.4. To increase the font size by one point (two after 12 point), click the A with the up arrow (A^); to decrease the font size by one point (two after 12 point), click the slightly smaller A with the down arrow (Av).

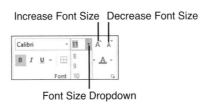

FIGURE 4.4

The Increase Font Size and Decrease Font Size buttons allow you to change the font size of the selected range with one click.

Applying Bold, Italic, and Underline to Text

The three icons for bold, italic, and underline toggle the property on and off. The Bold icon is a bold letter **B**. The Italic icon is an italic *I*. The Underline icon, which is a drop-down, is either an underlined U̲ or a double-underlined D̲. To apply formatting, select the range and click the desired formatting button.

Applying Strikethrough, Superscript, and Subscript

The strikethrough, superscript, and subscript effects are available only in the Effects group on the Font tab of the Format Cells dialog box. To apply the formatting, select the cell or specific characters in the cell, right-click over the selection, and select Format Cells to bring up the dialog box and select the desired formatting option.

Changing the Font Color

In the ribbon and Mini toolbar, the Font Color drop-down is the button with the A underscored by a thick red line, which changes when you select a different color from the available colors. In the Format Cells dialog box, the Font Color drop-down is found on the Font tab. Any color in the drop-down can be applied to a cell.

TIP To quickly return to the default color, usually black, select the Automatic option at the top of the Font Color drop-down.

Formatting a Character or Word in a Cell

All of the previous methods can also be applied to a single character or word in a cell, not just the entire cell contents. To change the formatting of just part of a cell, highlight the desired characters and use your preferred method of formatting.

NOTE The Mini toolbar changes to show only the available formatting options when formatting only part of a cell. Also, a modified Format Cells dialog box opens instead of the one shown in Figure 4.2.

Aligning Text in a Cell

The Alignment group on the Home tab consists of tools that affect how a value is situated in a cell or range. You can also access these controls from the Alignment tab of the Format Cells dialog box (refer to the beginning of the "Changing the Font Settings of a Cell" section for the various methods to open the dialog box).

There are six alignment buttons in the Alignment group, representing the most popular settings for how a value is situated in a cell. Top Align, Middle Align, and Bottom Align describe the vertical placement of the value in the cell. Align

Text Left, Center, and Align Text Right describe the horizontal placement of the value in the cell. More options are available in the Format Cells dialog box on the Alignment tab. The Mini toolbar only has one button for horizontal alignment, which centers the text of the selected cell.

Merging Two or More Cells

Merging cells takes two or more adjacent cells and combines them to make one cell. For example, if you are designing a form with many data entry cells and need space for a large comment area, resizing the column might not be practical as it will also affect the size of the cells above it. Instead, select the range you want the comments to be entered in and merge the cells. Any text other than that found in the upper-left cell of the selection is deleted as the newly combined cell takes on the identity of this first cell.

On the Alignment tab in the Format Cells dialog box, there is a check box for Merge Cells. In the upper-right corner of the Mini toolbar is a toggle button (Merge/Unmerge) to merge and center the text of the selected range.

The Merge & Center drop-down in the Alignment group on the Home tab offers several options to merge cells in different ways:

- **Merge & Center**—This is the default action of the drop-down button. The selected cells will be merged and the text will be centered.

- **Merge Across**—If you have several rows where you want to merge the adjacent cells in the same row, you can select all the rows (and their adjacent columns to merge) and select Merge Across. See Figure 4.5.

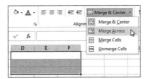

FIGURE 4.5

Notice that although several rows are selected, using Merge Across kept the separate rows intact.

- **Merge Cells**—Equivalent to the check box in the Format Cells dialog box, the selected range will be merged, retaining the alignment of the upper-left cell in the selection.

- **Unmerge Cells**—Use this option to unmerge the selected cells.

Use caution when merging cells because it can lead to potential issues:

- Users will be unable to sort if there are merged cells within the data.

- Users will be unable to cut and paste unless the same cells are merged in the pasted location.

- Column and row AutoFit won't work.

- Lookup type formulas will return a match only for the first matching row or column.

 TIP   For an alternative to merging to get a title centered over a table, refer to the section "Centering Text Across a Selection."

Centering Text Across a Selection

As noted in the earlier section "Merging Two or More Cells," merging cells can cause problems in Excel, limiting what you can do with a table. If you need to center text over several columns, instead of merging the cells, center the text across the multiple columns. To center a title across the top of a table without merging the cells, as shown in Figure 4.6, follow these steps:

1. Type your title in the leftmost cell to the table.

2. Select the title cell and extend the range to include all cells you want the title centered over.

3. Press Ctrl+1 or go to Home, Cells, Format, Format Cells to open the Format Cells dialog box.

4. Go to the Alignment tab.

5. From the Horizontal drop-down, select Center Across Selection.

6. Click OK.

Wrapping Text in a Cell to the Next Line

When you type a lot of text in a cell, it continues to extend to the right beyond the right border of the cell if there is nothing in the adjacent cell. You can widen the column to fit the text, but sometimes that may be impractical. If that's the case, you can set the cell to wrap text, moving any text that extends past the edge of the column to a new line in the cell.

A1		▼	⋮	×	✓	f_x	January Product Revenue	

	A	B	C	D	E
1		**January Product Revenue**			
2	Region	Product	Date	Customer	Quantity
3	East	XYZ	1/1/2012	Exclusive Shovel Trader	1000
4	Central	DEF	1/2/2012	Bright Hairpin Company	100

FIGURE 4.6

Use Center Across Selection instead of merging cells to center a title on a report.

Normally, when you wrap a cell, the row height automatically adjusts to fit the text. If it doesn't, make sure you don't have the cell merged with another; Excel will not autofit merged cells. If there are merged cells, unmerge them and manually force an autofit (see the "Adjusting Row Heights and Column Widths" section). The row height will begin to automatically adjust again.

To turn on text wrapping, select the cell and go to Home, Alignment, Wrap Text or from the Format Cells dialog box, select Wrap Text on the Alignment tab. There is no option on the Mini toolbar.

CAUTION   If you manually adjust the row height anytime before pasting, the height won't adjust automatically. To reset the row so it does adjust automatically again, double-click the border between the desired row and the one beneath.

TIP   Refer to the "Reflowing Text in a Paragraph" section if you don't want to wrap text in a single cell and would prefer to have each line on its own row.

Indenting Cell Contents

By default, text entered in a cell is flush with the left side of the cell, while numbers are flush to the right. To move a value away from the edge, you might be tempted to add spaces before or after the value. If you change your mind about this formatting at a later time, it can be quite tedious to remove the extraneous spaces.

Instead, use the Increase Indent and Decrease Indent buttons to move the value about two character lengths over. Increase Indent moves the value away from the edge it is aligned with. Decrease Indent moves the value back toward its edge.

TIP If you use these buttons with a right-aligned number, the number will become left-aligned and adjust from the left margin. This does not occur with right-aligned text. To correct this, go to the Alignment tab of the Format Cells dialog box, set the Horizontal alignment to Right and then set the Indent value.

When adjusting the Indent from the Format Cells dialog box, the Alignment tab uses a single Indent field with a number to indicate the number of indentations. The Mini toolbar does not offer options for indenting.

Changing the Way Text Is Oriented

Vertical text can be difficult to read, but sometimes limited space makes it a requirement. The Orientation button, which looks like ab written at a 45-degree angle, has five variations of Vertical Text, Angle Counterclockwise, Angle Clockwise, Vertical Text, Rotate Text Up, and Rotate Text Down. The Orientation section in Format Cells, Alignment offers more precise control (see Figure 4.7). There is no option on the Mini toolbar.

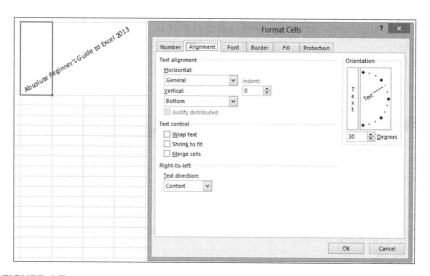

FIGURE 4.7

Use the Orientation settings to rotate the contents of a cell.

Reflowing Text in a Paragraph

There's a very handy tool that's not found with the other formatting tools. It is hidden in the Editing group on the Home tab. The button is the Fill button (a blue down arrow) and the option within it is Justify.

The **Justify** option reflows the text in a paragraph to fit a certain number of columns. For example, if you paste a paragraph directly into a cell with Wrap Text on, the height of the cell increases, but the column width is unaffected. Use Fill, Justify to reflow the text.

Be careful when selecting the range, because if you do not have enough empty rows available for the text to flow into, Excel will, after warning you, overwrite the rows below the selection.

To reflow text in a paragraph to fit a certain number of columns, follow these steps:

1. Ensure that the text is composed of one column of cells. The sentences can extend beyond one column, but the left column must contain text and the remaining columns must be blank.

2. Select a range as wide as the finished text should be. Ensure that the upper-left cell of the selection is the first line of text, as shown in Figure 4.8.

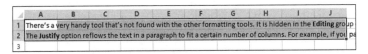

FIGURE 4.8

The number of columns selected determines the width of the final result.

3. From the Home tab, select Editing, Fill, Justify. You may receive a prompt that the text will reflow into more rows than selected. Click OK to continue. The text reflows so that each line is shorter than the selection range, as shown in Figure 4.9.

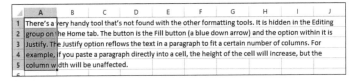

FIGURE 4.9

The text flows to the width of the original selection and down the number of rows it needs to.

CAUTION If any text in the cell has formatting applied to it, such as the word "Justify" in Figure 4.8, the formatting will be lost when the text is reflowed (see Figure 4.9).

Applying Number Formats with Format Cells

The way you see number data in Excel is controlled by the format applied to the cell. For example, you may see the date as August 21, 2012, but what is actually in the cell is 41142. Or you may see 10.5%, but the actual value in the cell is 0.105. This is important because when doing calculations, Excel doesn't care what you see. It deals only with the actual values.

There are only a few formatting options on the Home tab in the Number group. This section reviews the formatting options available in the Format Cells, Number dialog box. To apply a number format, select the range, select the desired format from the dialog box, and click OK.

For a review of the Number Format drop-down and the Increase Decimal and Decrease Decimal buttons in the ribbon, see the "The Number Group on the Ribbon" section.

General

General is the default format used by all cells on a sheet when you first open a workbook. Decimal places and the negative symbol are shown if needed. Thousand separators are not.

Number

By default, the **Number** format uses two decimal places but does not use the thousands separator. You can change the number of decimal places, turn on the thousands separator, and choose how to format negative numbers, as shown in Figure 4.10.

Currency

The default **Currency** format displays the system's currency symbol, two decimal places, and a thousands separator. You can change the number of decimal places, change the currency symbol, and select a format for negative numbers.

Accounting

Accounting is similar to **Currency** but automatically lines up the currency symbols on the left side of the cell and decimals points to the right side of the cell. The default Accounting format displays the system's currency symbol, two decimal places, and a thousands separator. You can change the number of decimal places and the currency symbol.

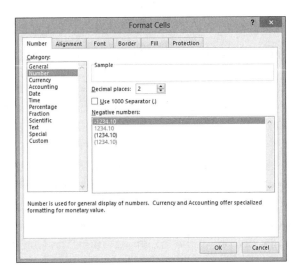

FIGURE 4.10

Additional options may be available when you select a format to apply.

Date

There is no default **Date** format. Sometimes Excel reformats the date you enter; sometimes it keeps it the way you entered it. You can select a date format from the list in the Type box, which also contains date and time formats.

The date formats vary from short dates, such as 4/5, to long dates, such as Monday, April 5, 2010. When selecting a date format, look at the sample above the Type list. It will help you differentiate between the format 14-Mar, which is March 14, and the format Mar-01, which is March 2001, not March 1.

Time

There is no default **Time** format. You can select a time format from the list in the Type box, which also contains two date and time formats.

Excel sees times on a 24-hour clock. That is, if you enter 1:30, Excel assumes you mean 1:30 a.m. But if you enter 13:30, Excel knows you mean 1:30 p.m.

If you need to display times beyond 24 hours, such as if you're working on a timesheet adding up hours worked, use the time format 37:30:55, as shown in Figure 4.11.

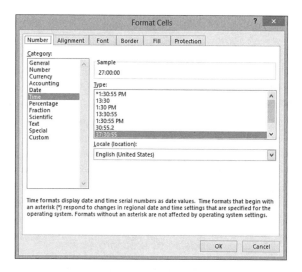

FIGURE 4.11

There are various time formats available.

Percentage

The default **Percentage** format includes two decimal places. When you apply this format, Excel takes the value in the cell, multiplies it by 100, and adds a % at the end. When you use the cell in a calculation, the actual (decimal) value is used. For example, if you have a cell showing 90% and multiply it by 1,000, the result will be (in General format) 900 (0.9*1,000).

If you include the % when you type the value in the cell, in the background Excel converts the value to its decimal equivalent, but the Percentage format is applied to the cell.

Fraction

The **Fraction** category rounds decimal numbers up to the nearest fraction. You can select to round the decimal to one, two, or three digits, or to round to the nearest half, quarter, eighth, sixteenth, tenth, or hundredth.

Scientific

The default **Scientific** category displays the value in scientific notation accurate to two decimal places. You can change the number of decimal places.

Text

There are no controls for the **Text** category. Setting this format to a cell forces Excel to treat the numbers in the cell as text, and you view exactly what is in the cell. If you set this format before typing in a number, the number becomes a number stored as text and may not work in some calculations.

Special

The **Special** category provides formats for numbers that do not fall in any of the preceding categories because the values are not actually numbers. That is, they aren't used for any mathematical operations and instead are treated more like words.

The four special types are specific to U.S. formatting:

- **ZIP Code**—Ensures that East Coast cities do not lose the leading zeros in their ZIP Codes.

- **ZIP Code + 4**—Ensures that East Coast cities do not lose the leading zeros in their ZIP Codes and formats the +4 in ZIP codes.

- **Phone Number**—Formats a telephone number with parentheses around the area code and a dash after the exchange.

- **Social Security Number**—Uses hyphens to separate the digits into groups of three, two, and four numbers.

Creating a Custom Format

Despite all the options available in the preceding categories, not all the possible situations are covered. For example, you need to remove the - symbol from negative numbers and instead color the negative numbers red. Yet for calculation purposes, you still want the values to be negative. Or you need to add text, such as kg, to a cell without actually having the text in the cell, which would interfere with calculations. That's why there's the option of **Custom** formats, allowing you to create a format specific to your situation.

Custom formats are saved with the workbook they are created in.

Understanding the Four Sections of a Number Format

A custom format can contain up to four different formats, each separated by a semicolon.

You should keep several things in mind when creating a custom format:

- Use semicolons to separate the code sections.

- If there is only one format, it applies to all numbers.

- If there are two formats, the first section applies to positive and zero values. The second section applies to negative values.

- If there are three formats, the first section applies to positive values, the second section applies to negative values, and the third section applies to zero values.

- If all four sections are used, they apply to positive, negative, zero, and text values, respectively.

Figure 4.12 shows a custom number format using all four sections. The table in C9:D13 displays how the formats would be applied to different values. The \M in in the first and second sections adds an M to the numerical values. The @ in the fourth section is a placeholder for any text the user types into the cell. Note the value in cell D11 is red, and a zero, not a blank, must be entered in cell C12 for "No Sales" to appear.

Using Text and Spacing in a Custom Number Format

Excel can't perform mathematical calculations on cells with text in them. For example, if you have a mileage chart and wanted to have "miles" in each cell, you wouldn't be able to also sum those cells because the "miles" would throw Excel off. Instead of typing the text in the cells, you can apply a custom number format that would make it look like the word "miles" is in the cell. As shown in Figure 4.12, you can display both text and numbers in a cell using a custom format. To do this, enclose the text in double quotation marks. If you need only a single character, you can omit the quotation marks and precede the character with a backslash (\). Some characters don't need quotes or a backslash. These special characters are: $ - + / ( ) : ! ^ & ' ~ { } = < > and the space character.

If you're using the fourth section of the number format, include the @ sign where you want to display any text in the formatted cell. If the @ is omitted from the format, text entered in the cell will not be displayed.

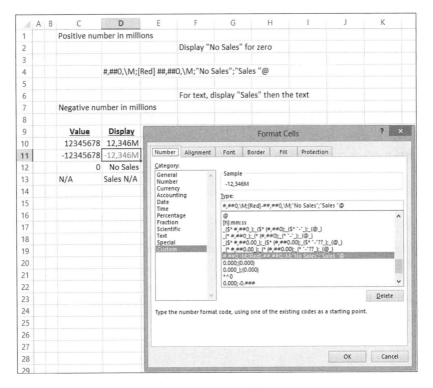

FIGURE 4.12

Use the four sections of a custom format to design formatting for positive, negative, zero, and text values.

To have Excel add space to a format, such as having Excel line up the decimals in a column on negative and positive numbers where the negative numbers are wrapped in parentheses, use an underscore followed by a character. In Figure 4.13, the format in column B doesn't include the _) in the positive section of the format, and so the positive value in the cell is flush with the right margin. In contrast, the format in column C does include the _) and the decimal points beneath are lined up. It's like having an invisible) in the cell.

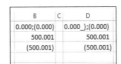

FIGURE 4.13

Use an underscore to instruct Excel to add a specific amount of space to a format.

To fill unused space in a cell with a repeating character, use an asterisk followed by the character to repeat. The repeating character can appear before or after the value in the cell. For example *-0 fills the leading space in the cell with dashes, whereas 0*^ fills in the trailing space with carets.

Using Decimals and the Thousands Separator in a Custom Number Format

Zeros are used as placeholders in a format when you need to force the place to be included, such as if you need to format all numbers with exactly three decimal places. If there aren't enough digits to fill in the required decimal places, Excel adds zeros to the end of the value.

If you would like to display up to three decimal places, but it is not necessary, use the pound (#) sign as the placeholder. Excel shows a maximum of three decimal places, but if there are only two, it won't fill in the third with a zero.

Use a question mark (?) on either side of a decimal to replace insignificant zeros if you will be using a fixed-width font (such as Courier) and want the decimal points to line up.

For example, to format the positive section to always show three decimal places and the negative section to show only what's entered, use this custom format: 0.000;-0.###. Positive values will display exactly three decimal places, including a filler zero if needed, and negative values will display up to three decimal places, as shown in Figure 4.14.

To include a thousands separator, use a comma in the format, such as #,###.0. To scale a number by thousands, as shown in Figure 4.15, include a comma at the end of the numeric format for each multiple of 1,000.

Using Color and Conditions in a Custom Number Format

You can use eight text color codes in a format: red, blue, green, yellow, cyan, black, white, and magenta. You place the color in square brackets, such as [cyan]. It should be the first element of a numeric formatting section.

You can use conditions in conjunction with colors to create number formats that apply only when specific conditions are met. The colors and conditions can only be applied to the first two sections of the number format, but the other sections can still be used. For example, to color values greater than or equal to 50 in green, less than 50 in red, a blank for zeros, and have "Sales" joined to any existing text, use this format: [Green][>=50];[Red][<50];"";"Sales "@.

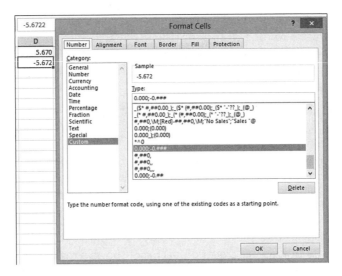

FIGURE 4.14

Create a custom format to treat positive and negative values differently.

Format	Display
Number	1,000,000,000
#,##0,	1,000,000
#,##0,,	1,000
#,##0,,,	1

FIGURE 4.15

Use a comma as a thousands multiplier to change how a value is displayed.

Using Symbols in a Custom Number Format

You can include various currency symbols, percent signs, and scientific notations in the number format.

If formatting with the exponent codes (E-,E+) and the format has a zero or pound sign (#) to the right of the code, Excel displays the number in scientific format and inserts an E or e. The number of zeros or pound signs to the right of the code determines the number of digits in the exponent. Code E+ places a minus sign by negative exponents and a plus sign by positive exponents. Code E- places a minus sign by negative exponents. Figure 4.16 shows the results of 0.00E+00 and 0.00E-00 on different numbers.

Value	Result	Format
1563	1.56E+03	0.00E+00
1563	1.56E03	0.00E-00
-1563	-1.56E+03	0.00E+00
-1563	-1.56E03	0.00E-00
0.1563	1.56E-01	0.00E+00
0.1563	1.56E-01	0.00E-00

FIGURE 4.16

The use of E+ or E- makes a difference in how the scientific notation is formatted.

Formatting a Cell to Show the Cent (¢) Symbol

Normally when you apply a currency format, you get the dollar sign ($), but if the value is less than a dollar, you don't get the cent symbol. To format a cell to show the cent symbol when the value is less than 1 and to show the dollar sign for values of 1 or greater, follow these steps:

1. Right-click over the cell to format and select Format Cells.

2. On the Number tab, select Custom from the Category list.

3. In the Type field, enter `[<1]0.00¢;$0.00_¢` and click OK. To get the cent symbol, hold down the Alt key and type `0162` on the numeric keypad.

4. Values less than 1 will display with a ¢ at the end, such as 0.23¢. Values 1 or greater will display with the $ at the beginning, such as $12.23. A note of caution—negative values are technically less than zero and so a value such as -12.23 would format with the cent symbol (-12.23¢), but this format would work well on a sales column.

Using Dates and Times in a Custom Number Format

Date and Time formats have the greatest variety of codes available when it comes to creating number formats. Whereas there's no real difference between the codes ## and ###, the difference between formatting a date cell mm or mmm are more obvious, as shown in Table 4.1.

TABLE 4.1 Date and Time Formats

To Display This	Use This Code
Months as 1–12	m
Months as 01–12	mm
Months as Jan–Dec	mmm
Months as January–December	mmmm
Months as the first letter of the month	mmmmm
Days as 1–31	d
Days as 01–31	dd
Days as Sun–Sat	ddd
Days as Sunday–Saturday	dddd
Years as 00–99	yy
Years as 1900–9999	yyyy
Hours as 0–23	H
Hours as 00–23	hh
Minutes as 0–59	m
Minutes as 00–59	mm
Seconds as 0–59	s
Seconds as 00–59	ss
Hours as 4 AM	h AM/PM
Time as 4:36 PM	h:mm AM/PM
Time as 4:36:03 P	h:mm:ss A/P
Elapsed time in hours; for example, 25.02	[h]:mm
Elapsed time in minutes; for example, 63:46	[mm]:ss
Elapsed time in seconds	[ss]
Fractions of a second	h:mm:ss.00

There are a couple of things to keep in mind when creating date and time formats:

- If the time format has an AM or PM in it, Excel bases the time on a 12-hour clock. Otherwise, Excel uses a 24-hour clock. See the previous section "Time" for more information on entering times in Excel.

- When creating a time format, the minutes code (m or mm) must appear immediately after the hour code (h or hh) or immediately before the seconds code (ss) or Excel displays months instead of minutes.

When Cell Formatting Doesn't Seem to Be Working Right

Most of the time, you can type in a number and then set the formatting, and the cell will reflect the formatting. This works about 99% of the time. But there is that 1% of cases that can cause a headache until you understand what is going on.

You've spent hours designing your sheet, copying ranges from various workbooks, and moving data around. You have a column of numbers and add a SUM function at the bottom. A few things may happen:

- The data sums, but the number doesn't look correct.

- After pressing Enter, you see the formula exactly as you typed it in. It doesn't sum the selected range.

- You see #### in a cell.

Check the format of the cell in question. If you were using the cell for something else earlier, it might still retain that format, such as text. If you're looking at the formula cell, change the format to General. You still see the formula. That's because the format has been applied to the cell, but not the contents of the cell. You need to force the format by entering the cell (F2, or double-click) and then pressing Enter.

If the issue is the range being summed, you can either go to each cell and force the formatting onto the contents as described previously, or refer to the section "Fixing Numbers Stored as Text" in Chapter 3, "Getting Data onto a Sheet."

If you see ### in a cell, try increasing the size of the column. Sometimes Excel doesn't automatically adjust the column width for an entered number.

The Number Group on the Ribbon

The Number group on the Home tab has several quick formatting options. The Number Format drop-down in the Number group of the Home tab has 11 formatting options available. Figure 4.17 shows an example of each format.

FIGURE 4.17

The Number Format drop-down offers many quick formatting options.

Below the Number Format drop-down is a drop-down button with a dollar sign ($) on it, the **Accounting Number** format. This button applies the accounting format to the selected range. From the drop-down, you can select different currency symbols.

Also beneath the drop-down are buttons for applying the **Percent Style (%)** and **Comma Style (,)** formats to a selection.

Use the Increase Decimal and Decrease Decimal buttons on the Home tab in the Number group (see Figure 4.18) to quickly increase and decrease the number of decimal places shown in number formats that use decimals. The Increase Decimal button has an arrow pointing left, whereas the Decrease Decimal button has an arrow pointing right.

Adding a Border Around a Range

The Borders drop-down in the Font group on the Home tab includes 13 of the most popular border options. These borders are applied to the selected cell or range, either the inside borders or the outside borders, depending on your selection. For more options, go to the Borders tab in the Format Cells dialog box.

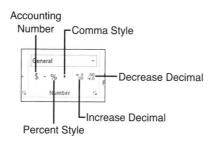

FIGURE 4.18

The Number Format drop-down offers many quick formatting options.

When applying a border, Excel sees the entire selection as one object and applies the border you select to the selection, not the individual cells that make it up. For example, if you select a range consisting of five rows and apply the Bottom Border, the border appears only in the last cell, not at the bottom of each cell in the selection.

 TIP   The Format Cells, Border tab dialog box has more options for applying borders, including different border styles and colors. When using the dialog box, select the desired color and style before making selections in the Border drawing box.

Formatting a Table with a Thick Outer Border and Thin Inner Lines

You can apply multiple border formats on top of each other. For example, if you want your table to have a Thick Box Border with thin inner lines, that option doesn't existing in the drop-down. Instead, you have to apply the following steps to create a table that has a thick outer border and a thin border around each inner cell, as shown in Figure 4.19:

FIGURE 4.19

You can apply multiple selections from the Borders drop-down to a selected range to get the desired design.

1. Select the range to format.

2. From the Borders drop-down, select the All Borders option.

3. Return to the Borders drop-down and select the Thick Box Border option.

Coloring the Inside of a Cell

Fill Color refers to the color applied inside of a cell; it is represented by a paint bucket on its button in the Font group of the Home tab and on the Mini toolbar. When you click the button, a drop-down of available colors opens up. As you move your cursor over the colors, the selected range automatically updates to reflect the color your cursor is currently over. When you've decided on the color you want, click the color; the drop-down closes and the range is colored as specified.

 NOTE Don't be surprised if one day you open the color drop-down of a workbook and see a different set of colors. In a new, blank workbook, you get the standard color scheme. But Excel allows custom color schemes, called themes, to be created and shared. Themes are a good way to ensure uniformity of color in an organization (see the section "Using Themes to Ensure Uniformity in Design" for more information).

The Format Cells, Fill tab dialog box offers additional **Fill Effects**, such as patterns, styles, and gradient fills. **Pattern Color** and **Pattern Style** work together to fill a cell with a pattern (various dots, lines) in the selected color. This effect is placed on top of the **Background** color. A gradient fill is when a color slowly changes from one color to another within a cell.

Applying a Two-Color Gradient to a Cell

Instead of filling a cell with a single solid color, you can apply a two-color gradient to a range by following these steps:

1. Select one or more cells. If you select a range, the gradient will repeat across the range.

2. Press Ctrl+1 to open the Format Cells dialog box.

3. Go to the Fill tab.

4. Click the Fill Effects button. The Fill Effects dialog box, shown in Figure 4.20, opens.

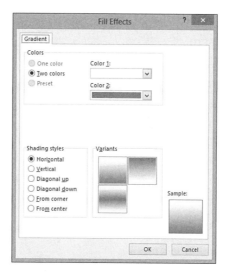

FIGURE 4.20

The Fill Effects dialog box offers more options for applying color inside of a cell.

5. Select a color from the Color 1 drop-down.

6. Select a different color from the Color 2 drop-down.

7. Select a shading style from the Shading Styles section.

8. Make a selection from the Variants section. The Sample box updates to reflect your selection.

9. Click OK twice.

Creating Hyperlinks

Hyperlinks allow you to open web pages in your browser, create emails, and jump to a specific cell on a specific sheet in a specific workbook. For web and email addresses, Excel automatically recognizes what you've typed in and applies the format accordingly, turning the cell into a clickable link.

If you want to link to a sheet, you have to go through the Insert Hyperlink dialog box, shown in Figure 4.21. You can open the dialog box by right-clicking on a cell and selecting Hyperlink or clicking Insert, Links, Hyperlink.

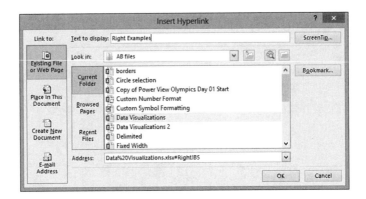

FIGURE 4.21

Use hyperlinks to help users quickly jump to sheets and specific ranges.

Creating a Hyperlink to Another Sheet

Being able to create a hyperlink to a sheet can be useful if you want to create a table of contents for a large workbook or a series of workbooks.

If you select just a sheet, Excel defaults to cell A1 on the sheet, but you can link to any specified cell. To create a hyperlink to a specific sheet, follow these steps:

1. Select the cell where you want the link.

2. Go to Insert, Links, Hyperlink and the Hyperlinks dialog box opens.

3. Browse to the workbook you want to link to. If you want to link to a cell in the current workbook, click the Place in This Document button.

4. If linking to an external workbook, click the Bookmark button to open the Select Place in Document dialog box. If linking to the active workbook, continue to step 5.

5. Select the sheet from the Cell Reference list. If you have a specific cell address you want the link to go to, enter it in the Type the Cell Reference field. Or, if you have a name assigned to the cell, select it from the Defined Names list. In that case, you don't have to enter a cell reference.

6. Click OK.

7. If the cell selected in step 1 is blank, the Text to Display field at the top of the dialog box shows the destination for the hyperlink. You can type in new text if desired.

8. Click OK. The next time you click on the cell, you will follow the link.

Quick Formatting with the Format Painter

The Format Painter is a handy, but tricky, little icon in the Clipboard group on the Home tab. It's handy because it enables you to quickly copy the formatting of one cell to another. It's tricky because whether you single-click or double-click the button affects how it functions. If you click the button once, you can copy the format of the selected range to one other range. If you double-click the button, it remains on, enabling you to copy from the format of the selected range to as many other ranges as needed. Use the Esc key, or click or double-click the button again to turn it off.

To copy a format from a source range to a single destination range, follow these steps:

1. Select the source range.

2. Click the Format Painter button once. The cursor changes to a paintbrush with a plus sign, as shown in Figure 4.22.

FIGURE 4.22

When the Format Painter is activated, the cursor changes to include a paintbrush.

3. Select the cell in the upper-left corner of the destination range if the range is the same size. If the destination range is larger, select the entire range.

4. The operation is complete and the cursor changes back to normal. If you accidentally selected the wrong range, undo and start over.

Dynamic Cell Formatting with Conditional Formatting

An unformatted sheet of just numbers isn't going to grab your audience's attention. But you don't have time to create a colorful report—or do you? Conditional formatting allows you to quickly apply color and icons to data. The quick formatting options consist of the following:

*   **Data Bars**—A data bar is a gradient or solid fill of color that starts at the left edge of the cell. The length of the bar represents the value in the cell compared with other values in the range the format is applied to. The smallest

numbers have just a tiny amount of color, and the largest numbers in the range fill the cell.

- **Color Scales**—A color scale is a color that fills the entire cell. Two or three different colors are used to relay the relative size of each cell to other cells in the range the format is applied to.

- **Icon Sets**—An icon set is a group of three to five images that provide a graphic representation of how the number in a cell compares with the other cells in the range the format is applied to.

The quickest way to apply one of the conditional formats is to select all the cells you want to apply it to, go to Home, Conditional Formatting, click the formatting type, and select one of the formatting options from the submenu that appears, as shown in Figure 4.23. As you move your cursor over the options, your range changes to reflect the connection. When you find the formatting you want, click it, and it will be applied to your range.

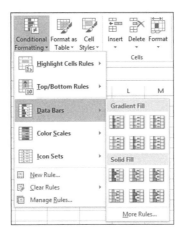

FIGURE 4.23

Quickly apply formatting to your data by selecting one of the prebuilt options in the Conditional Formatting drop-down.

TIP When you select a range of numbers, in the lower-right corner of the very last cell, Excel's Quick Analysis tool will appear with several preset conditional formatting options to choose from.

Applying Multiple Icon Sets

You can mix and match the individual icons. To use a green check mark for values in the top 67%, a red stoplight for items below 33%, and a yellow exclamation point for everything in between, follow these steps:

1. Select the range to which you want to apply the formatting.

2. On the Home tab, go to Conditional Formatting, Icon Sets, More Rules.

3. Click the first drop-down under the Icon heading and select the green check mark, as shown in Figure 4.24.

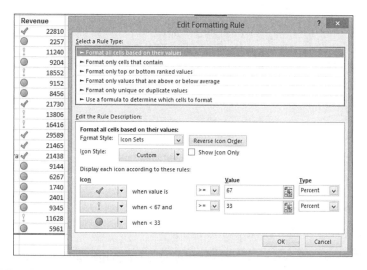

FIGURE 4.24

You can mix and match the conditional formatting icons.

4. To the right of the drop-down, select >= from the drop-down.

5. Enter **67** in the Value field.

6. Select Percent from the Type drop-down.

7. Click the second drop-down under the Icon heading and select the yellow exclamation point.

8. To the right of the drop-down, select >= from the drop-down.

9. Enter **33** in the Value field.

10. Select Percent from the Type drop-down.

11. Click the third drop-down under the Icon heading and select the red stoplight.

12. Click OK.

Conditional Formatting Using the Built-in Rules

Use the preset conditional formats if all you need is to format all the cells in a range based on how they compare with each other. But if your needs are more advanced, such as formatting only the top 10% or only cells that meet a specific condition, then you need to apply formatting using rules.

Under Conditional Formatting, Highlight Cells Rules and Top/Bottom Rules options, you'll find several built-in rules that you can apply to your data. Apply selected formatting to the following:

- Cells containing values greater than, less than, between, or equal to the value you specify
- Cells containing specific text
- Cells containing a date from the last day, two days, and so on
- Cells containing duplicate values
- Cells containing the top or bottom n items
- Cells containing the top or bottom n%
- Cells containing values above or below the average

Mixing Cell Formats with the Built-in Rules

For all of the preceding built-in rules, you can apply one of Excel's preset formats or design your own custom format. To apply a custom format to the top n items in the selected range, follow these steps:

1. Select the range to which you want to apply the formatting.

2. On the Home tab, go to Conditional Formatting, Top/Bottom Rules, Top 10 Items.

3. Enter the number of items you want formatted.

4. From the Format drop-down, select Custom Format.

5. From the Format Cells dialog box that opens, design the format you want applied (see Figure 4.25). You can go to any of the tabs (Number, Font, Border, and Fill) to make your selections. The only change you cannot make is to the font type and size on the Font tab.

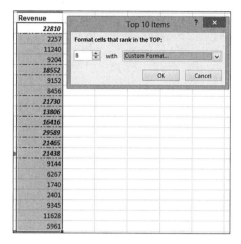

2FIGURE 4.25

The Custom Format option of the Top 10 Items dialog box allowed me to apply a bold italic font and a border around the top 8 items in the range.

Building Custom Conditional Formatting Rules

You can customize any of the prebuilt rules, but if what you need is not listed, you'll want to build your own conditional formatting rule based on a formula. For example, you've set up a data validation drop-down in one section of a sheet, and based on the selection, you want to highlight certain rows in a table in another section. A built-in formula won't do this for you. You'll need to apply a formula to the table that looks at the value in the drop-down then applies conditional formatting.

The formula box, shown in Figure 4.26 has a few rules for writing a formula:

- The formula must start with an equal (=) sign.

- The formula must evaluate to a logical value of TRUE or FALSE or the equivalents of 1 and 0.

- If you use your mouse to select cells on the sheet, Excel inserts the address using absolute referencing. If relative referencing is what you need, press the F4 key three times to toggle away the dollar signs in the formula.

  For more information on absolute versus relative referencing, see the section "Relative Versus Absolute Formulas" in Chapter 5, "Using Formulas."

- The formula you write will apply to the topmost left cell of your selection, so you need to look at the Name box in the formula bar and see what cell is the active cell. If you are writing a relative formula, write the formula as it would appear for the active cell. Excel will apply the formula appropriately to all the other cells you have selected. In Figure 4.26, the first cell in the range the formatting is applied to is cell A5 (29-Jul), which is also referenced in the formula.

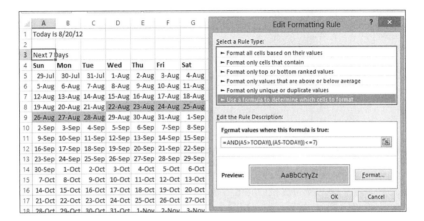

FIGURE 4.26

Use a custom formula to highlight the next seven days in your calendar.

- By default, the keyboard navigation keys (up arrow, down arrow, left arrow, right arrow, Page Up, Page Down, Home) are tied to the sheet and won't work in the Formula field. If you try to use the arrow keys to change your cursor position while typing in the Formula field, Excel will instead place the cell address you just selected. To work around this behavior, press F2 before using the navigation keys. You can verify what mode you are in by looking in the lower-left corner of the status bar. There are three modes:

  - **Enter**—The default mode for entering a formula in the Formula field. Using the navigation keys changes the selection on the sheet.

  - **Edit**—The mode for using the navigation fields to move through the Formula field.

  - **Point**—The mode for selecting cells on the sheet. Excel automatically switches to this mode when selecting cells on the sheet.

To set up a conditional format based on a formula, select the range it applies to and, from the Home tab, go to Conditional Formatting, New Rule, and select Use a Formula to Determine Which Cells to Format from the Select a Rule Type box. Enter your logical formula in the Formula field and set the desired Format.

Combining Conditional Formatting Rules

You can have multiple conditions evaluate to True and as each condition is met, the format is applied to the cell. For example, one rule sets the fill color to gray and another rule italicizes the contents, as shown in Figure 4.27. If both rules are met, the cell is formatted in italic with a gray fill. If a cell meets one condition, only the corresponding format is applied. If the formatting of the rules is conflicting, for example the first rule applies a red font and the second rule applies a blue font, the formatting of the first rule, the red font, is applied.

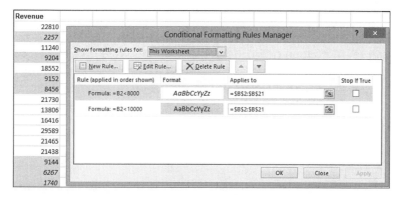

FIGURE 4.27

Setting up multiple rules can apply multiple formatting to cells.

Stopping Further Rules from Being Processed

Because rules are applied starting at the top, you might want to prevent further rules from being applied if a certain condition is met. In that case, check the Stop If True option in the Conditional Formatting Rules Manager for the rule you want to be the last if the condition is true. For example, in Figure 4.28, values below 8,000 were italic with a gray fill. But if you want to differentiate between items below 8,000 and those between 8,001 and 10,000 (without setting up a rule referencing the specific range), you would check the Stop If True for the first rule, as shown in Figure 4.28.

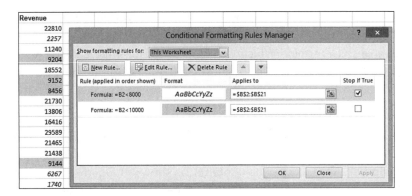

FIGURE 4.28

Check the Stop If True check box to prevent further rules from being applied to the data.

Clearing Conditional Formatting

You can set more than one conditional formatting rule on a range, so if you want to replace a format with another, you need to clear the previous rule. Or, you might want to clear all the formatting on a sheet. To clear conditional formatting, go to Home, Conditional Formatting, Clear Rules. From the drop-down that appears, you can select from the following options:

- Clear Rules from Selected Cell

- Clear Rules from Entire Sheet

- Clear Rules from This Table

- Clear Rules from This PivotTable

You can also select Clear Format from the Quick Analysis tool, which appears in the lower-right corner of a multiple cell selection.

Editing Conditional Formatting

Whether you've applied one of Excel's quick apply formats or created your own, there might come a time when you need to edit the conditional formatting, whether it be the formatting you applied or the range you applied it to.

To edit conditional formatting, select Manage Rules from the Conditional Formatting drop-down. From the Show Formatting Rules For drop-down at the top, select which formatting rules you want to view. You can then select the rule and click Edit Rule.

Using Cell Styles to Quickly Apply Formatting

You're probably used to using styles in Word but never realized that styles are also available in Excel. Select a range in Excel and go to Home, Styles, Cell Styles. Move your cursor over the predefined styles and watch your range update to reflect the styles.

You aren't limited to these predefined styles. You can create and save your own style for use throughout the workbook it's saved in. To quickly create a custom style in the active workbook, follow these steps:

1. Select a cell with all the formatting styles needed.

2. Go to Home, Styles, Cell Styles, New Cell Style.

3. If there is any type of formatting you do not want as part of the style, such as the alignment, unselect that style option.

4. Enter a name for the style in the Style Name field and click OK.

Using Themes to Ensure Uniformity in Design

Themes are collections of fonts, colors, and graphic effects that can be applied to a workbook. This can be useful if you have a series of company reports that need to have the same color and fonts. Only one theme can affect a workbook at a time.

Excel includes several built-in themes, which you can access from the Themes drop-down under Page Layout, Themes. You can also create and share themes you design.

A theme has the following components, which you can apply individually, instead of applying an entire Theme package:

- **Fonts**—A theme includes a font for headings and a font for body text.

- **Colors**—There are 12 colors in a theme: 4 for text, 6 for accents, and 2 for hyperlinks.

- **Graphic effects**—Graphic effects include lines, fills, bevels, shadows, and so on.

Applying a New Theme

The Themes group on the Page Layout tab has four buttons:

- **Themes**—Allows you to switch themes or save a new one
- **Colors**—Allows you to select a new color palette from the available built-in themes
- **Fonts**—Allows you to select a new font palette from the available built-in themes
- **Effects**—Allows you to select a new effect from the available built-in themes

Before applying a theme, arrange the sheet so you can see any themed elements such as charts or SmartArt. Then go to Page Layout, Themes and watch the elements update as you move your cursor over the various themes in the Themes drop-down. When you find the one you like, click it, and it will be applied to the workbook.

If you just want to change a theme component, make a selection from the component's drop-down in the same way you would a theme.

Creating a New Theme

To create a new theme, you need to specify the colors and fonts and select an effect from the respective component's drop-down. Then, under the Themes drop-down, choose Save Current Theme to save the theme.

To create a new theme, follow these steps:

1. Select Page Layout, Themes, Colors, Customize Colors.
2. To change an item's color, such as Accent 5 in Figure 4.29, choose its drop-down to open the color chooser.
3. When you find the desired color, click it to apply it to your theme.
4. Repeat steps 2 and 3 for each color you want to change.
5. In the Name field at the bottom, type a name for your color theme.
6. Click Save.
7. Select Page Layout, Themes, Fonts, Customize Fonts.
8. To change the Heading font, choose its drop-down to open the list of available fonts.

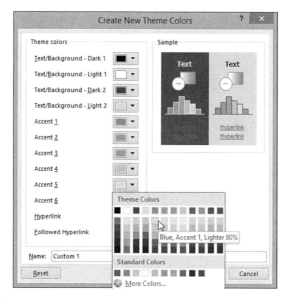

You can customize different aspects of a theme. As you select an item and change the color, the Samples on the right side of the dialog box will update.

9. When you find the desired font, click it to apply it to your theme. The Sample box on the right updates to reflect your selection, as shown in Figure 4.30.

Create a custom theme using your organization's specific font type.

10. Repeat steps 8 and 9 for the Body font.

11. In the Name field at the bottom, type a name for your font theme.

12. Click Save.

13. Select Page Layout, Themes, Effects.

14. Select an effect from the gallery of built-in effects, shown in Figure 4.31.

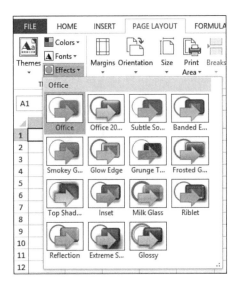

FIGURE 4.31

Select an Effect theme to change the default design of objects you insert, such as shapes.

15. Go to Page Layout, Themes, Save Current Theme.

16. Browse to where you want to save the theme, type a name for it, and click Save.

Sharing a Theme

To share a theme with other people, you must send them the *.thmx file you saved when you created the theme.

When they receive the file, they should save it to either their equivalent theme folder or some other location and use the Browse for Themes option under Page Layout, Themes, Browse for Themes.

THE ABSOLUTE MINIMUM

Excel offers a lot of options to format your data. You can change fonts, add color, or add conditional formatting icons to your data. You can design styles and themes for reuse in other reports, making it easier to maintain uniformity between them. Now that you're creating eye-catching reports, it's time to expand their usefulness by applying formulas to the data.

IN THIS CHAPTER

- Learn how to enter a formula into a cell.

- Simplify formulas by using Names to refer to ranges instead of cell addresses.

- Use absolute and relative referencing properly to copy formulas to other cells instead of retyping them.

- Convert formulas to values.

- Troubleshoot formula issues.

5

USING FORMULAS

Excel is great for simple data entry, but its real strength is its capability to perform calculations. After you design a sheet to perform calculations, you can easily change the data and watch Excel instantly recalculate. This chapter not only shows you how to enter a formula, but also teaches you fundamental basics, such as the difference between absolute and relative referencing, which is important when you want to copy a formula to multiple cells, and how to use a Name to refer to a cell instead of having to memorize a cell address. You'll take the formula basics you learn here and apply them later in Chapter 6, "Using Functions," to really crank up the calculating power of your workbook.

The Importance of Laying Out Data Properly

Except for when using certain functions, such as VLOOKUP, Excel doesn't really care how you lay out your data. For example, you can lay out your data as shown in Figure 5.1, with dates across the top. But if you later decide you want to use a pivot table (a function of Excel that quickly summarizes data. See chapter 12, "PivotTables and Slicers," for more information) or certain functions, your options are limited. You'll have fewer limitations if you lay out your data in the optimal fashion, shown in Figure 5.2, with a column assigned to each type of information entered. Start getting into the habit now of laying your data out in this fashion whenever possible so you can take full advantage of the power of Excel.

		1/1/2012	1/2/2012	1/3/2012	1/4/2012
Bright Hairpin Company	Quantity			100	
Bright Hairpin Company	Revenue			2257	
Bright Hairpin Company	COGS			984	
Bright Hairpin Company	Profit			1273	
Cool Jewelry Corporation	Quantity				800
Cool Jewelry Corporation	Revenue				18552
Cool Jewelry Corporation	COGS				7872
Cool Jewelry Corporation	Profit				10680
Exclusive Shovel Traders	Quantity	1000			
Exclusive Shovel Traders	Revenue	22810			
Exclusive Shovel Traders	COGS	10220			
Exclusive Shovel Traders	Profit	12590			

FIGURE 5.1

Laying out data with dates across the top may make sense when you want to see the data by date, but it can make it more difficult to apply simple formulas or functions.

Date	Customer	Quantity	Revenue	COGS	Profit
1/1/2012	Exclusive Shovel Traders	1000	22810	10220	12590
1/2/2012	Bright Hairpin Company	100	2257	984	1273
1/4/2012	Cool Jewelry Corporation	800	18552	7872	10680
1/4/2012	Tasty Kettle Inc.	400	9152	4088	5064
1/7/2012	Remarkable Meter Corporat	400	8456	3388	5068
1/9/2012	Remarkable Meter Corporat	800	16416	6776	9640
1/15/2012	Bright Hairpin Company	500	9345	4235	5110
1/16/2012	Appealing Calculator Corpor	600	11628	5082	6546

FIGURE 5.2

Providing a column field for each data type allows you to take full advantage of Excel's functionality, such as pivot tables and functions like VLOOKUP and SUMIF.

Adjusting Calculation Settings

By default, Excel calculates and recalculates whenever you open or save a workbook or make a change to a cell used in a formula. At times, this isn't convenient—such as when you're working with a very large workbook with a long recalculation time. In times like this, you will want to control when calculations occur.

The Calculation group on the Formulas tab has the following options:

- **Calculation Options**—Has the options Automatic, Automatic Except for Data Tables, and Manual

- **Calculate Now**—Calculates the entire workbook

- **Calculate Sheet**—Calculates only the active sheet

The calculation options under File, Options, Formulas include the same Calculation Options as the preceding list, but the Manual option allows you to turn on/off the way Excel recalculates a workbook when saving it.

Viewing Formulas Versus Values

You can't tell the difference between a cell containing numbers and one with a formula just by looking at it on the sheet. To see whether a cell contains a formula, select the cell and look in the formula bar. If the formula bar contains just a number or text, the cell is static. But if the formula bar contains a formula, which always starts with an equal sign (=), as shown in Figure 5.3, you know the value you're seeing on the sheet is a result of a calculation.

 NOTE If you see a cell starting with "+=" most likely the person who entered the formula used to use Lotus 1-2-3, another spreadsheet program. Excel accepts the "+=," but it is not required.

G2			f_x	='Movie Data'!$H2<11			
	A	B	C	D	E	F	G	H
1	Year	Decade	Yearly Rank	CH	40	10	InTop10	PK
2	2008	2000	50	6	0	0	TRUE	
3	2008	2000	123	42	21	0	TRUE	

FIGURE 5.3

The formula bar reveals whether a cell, in this case cell G2, contains a number or a formula.

Another way to view formulas on a sheet is to make them all visible. That is, Excel shows all formulas instead of the calculated values. There are several ways to toggle between viewing values and formulas:

- Press Ctrl+~.

- Go to Formulas, Formula Auditing, Show Formulas on the ribbon.

- Go to File, Options, Advanced and under Display Options for This Worksheet, select Show Formulas in Cells Instead of Their Calculated Results.

If you just want to see what cells have formulas, but don't need to see the formulas themselves, you can use the Formulas option in the Go to Special dialog box. Press Ctrl+G and click Special to open the dialog box, or go to Home, Editing, Find & Select, Go To Special. Select Formulas and click OK and all formulas on the sheet will be selected, as shown in Figure 5.4.

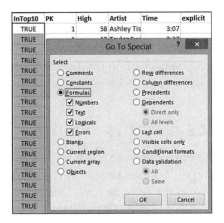

FIGURE 5.4

Using the Formulas option of the Go to Special dialog box highlights all the formulas on the sheet. Once selected, you can modify the cells, such as ensuring they are protected or applying a fill to them.

Entering a Formula into a Cell

Entering a basic formula is straightforward. Select the cell, enter an equal sign, type in the formula, and press Enter. Typing the formula is very similar to entering an equation on a calculator, with one exception. If one of the terms in your formula is already stored in a cell, you can point to that cell instead of typing in the number stored in the cell. The advantage of this is that if that other cell's value ever changes, your formula automatically updates.

To enter a formula that includes a pointer to another cell, follow these steps:

1. Select the cell you want the formula to be in.

2. Type an equal sign. This tells Excel you are entering a formula.

3. Type the first number and an operator, as you would on a calculator. There's no need to include spaces in the formula.

NOTE   See the section "Mathematical Operators" for more information on the operators you can use.

4. Select the cell you want to include in the formula. The cell can even be on another sheet or in another workbook.

5. Press Enter. Excel calculates the formula in the cell.

TIP   If you select the wrong cell, as long as you haven't typed anything else, such as a "+," you can select another cell right away and Excel replaces the previous cell address with a new one. If you have typed something else, you need to highlight the incorrect cell address before you select the correct one.

Of course, there's no need to have any numbers in a formula. It can consist entirely of cell addresses, as shown in Figure 5.5. The table in the figure calculates the total value of inventory by multiplying the cost (column B) by the quantity (column C). To enter the formula, after typing the equal sign, select the first cell, type an operator, then select the second cell. After pressing Enter, copy the formula down to the other rows using the fill handle.

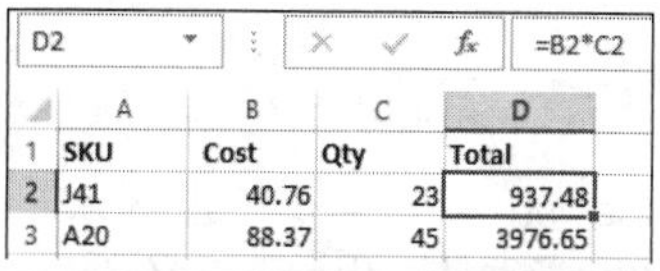

| D2 | | ▾ | : | ✕ | ✓ | f_x | =B2*C2 |

⊿	A	B	C	D
1	SKU	Cost	Qty	Total
2	J41	40.76	23	937.48
3	A20	88.37	45	3976.65

FIGURE 5.5

Using cell addresses in formulas, instead of values, means the value in cell D2 automatically updates when those other cells, B2 and C2, are updated.

NOTE   For information on using the fill handle to extend a series, see Chapter 3, "Getting Data onto a Sheet," or refer to the section "Copying a Formula Using the Fill Handle" later in this chapter.

Three Ways of Entering a Formula's Cell References

After typing the equal sign to start a formula, you have three options for entering the rest of the formula:

- Type the complete formula.

- Type numbers and operator keys, but use the mouse to select cell references.

- Type numbers and operator keys, but use the arrow keys to select cell references.

 NOTE See the section "Mathematical Operators" for more information on the operators you can use.

The method you use depends on what you find most comfortable. Some users consider the first method the quickest because they never have to move their fingers off the main section of the keyboard. For others, using the mouse makes more sense, especially when selecting a large range for use in the formula.

Relative Versus Absolute Formulas

When you copy a formula, such as =B2*C2, down a column, the formula automatically changes to =B3*C3, then =B4*C4, and so on. Excel's capability to change cell B2 to B3 to B4 and so on is called *relative referencing*. This is Excel's default behavior when dealing with formulas, but it might not always be what you want to happen. If the cell address must remain static as the formula is copied, you need to use *absolute referencing*. This is achieved through the strategic placement of dollar signs ($) before the row or column reference, as shown in Table 5.1.

TABLE 5.1 Relative Versus Absolute Reference Behavior

Format	Copied Down	Copied Across
A1	A2—the row reference updates	B1—the column reference updates
$A$1	$A$1—neither reference updates	$A$1—neither reference updates
$A1	$A2—the row reference updates	$A1—neither reference updates
A$1	A$1—neither reference updates	B$1—the column reference updates

Using a Cell on Another Sheet in a Formula

When writing a formula, not all the cells you need to use have to be on the same sheet. As a matter of fact, it might be a better design to have different types of information on different sheets and then pull them together on one sheet using formulas. For example, if you have to periodically import data from another source, instead of possibly messing up the layout of your calculation table by sharing the sheet with the imported data, import the table to a separate sheet and use linked formulas to reference the required cells. Another use could be a lookup table that you allow users to update, but the sheet with the calculations is protected, allowing users to only view that information, not edit it.

To reference a cell on another sheet, navigate to the sheet and then select the cell, as you would if the cell were on the same sheet as the formula. If you have more cells to select, enter your operator and continue to select cells, returning to the formula sheet if needed. If the last cell you need is on a different sheet, press Enter when you are done and Excel returns you to the sheet with the formula.

Figure 5.6 shows a sales sheet that calculates the tax for each record (row). Instead of placing the tax rate in the formula itself, it is placed in another cell on a sheet named Lookups. The tax formula uses an absolute reference to the tax rate cell (Lookups!$B$1), but a relative reference to the cost of the item (D2), as shown in Figure 5.6. When the formula is copied down, all records reference not only the tax rate cell, but their own item cost. And, if the tax rate needs to be modified, you only have to change it in the one cell (Lookups!$B$1) to update all the records.

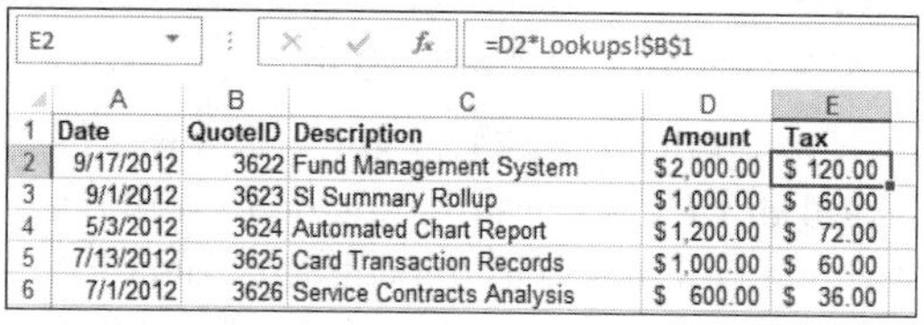

	A	B	C	D	E
			fx	=D2*Lookups!$B$1	
1	Date	QuoteID	Description	Amount	Tax
2	9/17/2012	3622	Fund Management System	$2,000.00	$ 120.00
3	9/1/2012	3623	SI Summary Rollup	$1,000.00	$ 60.00
4	5/3/2012	3624	Automated Chart Report	$1,200.00	$ 72.00
5	7/13/2012	3625	Card Transaction Records	$1,000.00	$ 60.00
6	7/1/2012	3626	Service Contracts Analysis	$ 600.00	$ 36.00

FIGURE 5.6

A separate sheet is often used to store lookup values, like the Lookups sheet in this formula. This is a good idea because it makes layout changes to the data sheet easier.

Using R1C1 Notation to Reference Cells

The default setting in Excel is A1 notation. R1C1 notation is another reference style for cells. To turn it on, go to File, Options, Formulas and in the Working with Formulas section, select R1C1 Reference Style. When you do this, your sheet column headers change from letters to numbers, as shown in Figure 5.7.

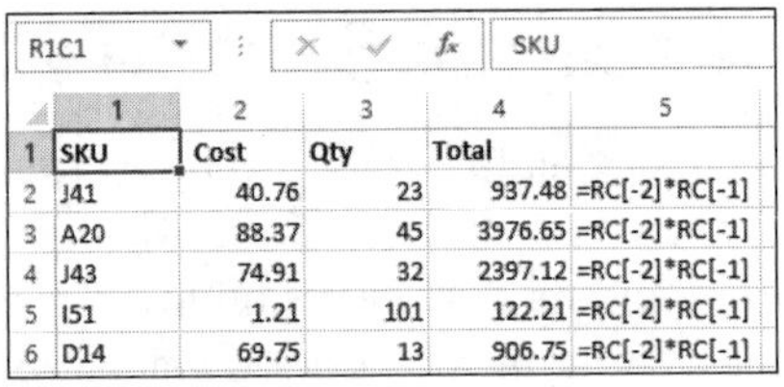

FIGURE 5.7

R1C1 notation is very different from the A1 reference style.

Instead of A1 in the Name box when you select the top leftmost cell on a sheet, you see R1C1, which stands for Row 1 Column 1, the reverse of A1 style where we have column (A) then row (1). There are three basic rules to R1C1 notation:

- If there's no number next to the letter, then it's the current row or column.

- If the number is right next to the letter, then it's an absolute reference.

- If there are brackets around the number, then it's a relative reference.

In R1C1 notation, the reference RC refers to the current cell. If the R or C does not have a number next to it, then the reference is to the row or column in which the formula appears. For example, if you type =RC5 in cell B26, when you revert to A1 style, =$E26 now appears in the cell. The R does not have a number next to it, so it refers to the row in which the formula is typed (26). Notice the column reference in this example is absolute (has a $). That's because in the R1C1 notation, the number (5) appears right next to the C. Whereas in A1 notation you use a dollar sign ($) to denote absolute referencing, the lack of anything separating the letter and number denotes absolute referencing in R1C1 style.

To indicate relative referencing in R1C1 style, you modify RC by adding or subtracting the number of rows or columns representing the location of the cell in reference to the active cell. Keep in mind these rules for relative referencing:

- The numbers must be enclosed in square brackets.

- When referring to a cell above or to the left of the active cell, the number is negative.

- When referring to a cell below or to the right of the active cell, the number is positive.

For example, if you have a formula in cell G8 and use the reference R[-1]C[3], you are referring to a cell one row above and 3 columns to the right of G8, which is J7.

CAUTION Despite the fact that I have mixed reference styles in the previous paragraphs, Excel does not allow you to type R1C1 notation while the sheet is in A1 mode and vice versa.

In Figure 5.7, all the formulas are the same because the formula is based off the cell the formula is in. Note the formulas shown are actually the formulas in the Total column. The formula multiplies the value in the cell two columns to the left (Cost) by the value one column to the left (Qty) of the formula cell (Total). Both references are to a cell in the same row as the formula, so there is no number by the row reference.

Using F4 to Change the Cell Referencing

When you type in a formula and select a cell or range, Excel uses the relative reference. If you need the absolute reference, you will probably either type in the address manually or go back and change the address after you are done with the whole formula. Another option is to change the reference to what you need while typing in the formula. You can do this by pressing the F4 key right after selecting the cell or range. Each time you press the F4 key, it changes the cell address to another reference variation, as shown in Figure 5.8.

When you enter the formula:	
	=B2
Press F4 once:	
	=$B$2
Press F4 again:	
	=B$2
Press F4 again:	
	=$B2

FIGURE 5.8

Use F4 to toggle through the variations of relative to absolute referencing.

TIP If you need to change a reference after you've already entered the formula, you can still place your cursor in the cell address and use the F4 key to toggle through the references.

For example, to change the cell address in a formula to a column fixed reference as you type it in, follow these steps:

1. Select the cell you want the formula to be in.

2. Type an equal sign.

3. Type the first number and operator, as you would on a calculator.

4. Select the cell you want to include in the formula.

5. Press F4 once and the address changes to absolute referencing. Press F4 again and it becomes a Row Fixed Reference. Press F4 a third time and it becomes a Column Fixed Reference.

 TIP If you miss the reference you need to use the first time, continue pressing F4 until it comes up again.

6. Press Enter. Excel calculates the formula in the cell.

Mathematical Operators

Excel offers the mathematical operators listed in Table 5.2.

TABLE 5.2 Mathematical Operators

Operator	Description
+	Addition
-	Subtraction
/	Division
*	Multiplication
^	Exponents
()	Override the usual order of operations
-	Unary minus (for negative numbers)
=	Equal to
>	Greater than
<	Less than
>=	Greater than or equal to
<=	Less than or equal to
<>	Not equal to
&	Join two values to produce a single value
,	Union operator
:	Range operator
(space)	Intersection operator

Order of Operations

Excel evaluates a formula in a particular order if it contains many calculations. Instead of calculating from left to right like a calculator, Excel performs certain types of calculations, such as multiplication, before other calculations, such as addition.

You can override this default order of operations using parentheses. If you don't, Excel applies the following order of operations:

1. Unary minus

2. Exponents

3. Multiplication and division, left to right

4. Addition and subtraction, left to right

For example, if you have the formula

=6+3*2

Excel returns 12, because first it does 3*2, then adds the result (6) to 6. But, if you use parentheses, you can change the order:

=(6+3)*2

produces 18 because now Excel will do the addition first (6+3) and multiply the result (9) by 2.

Copying a Formula to Another Cell

You can use four ways to enter the same formula in multiple cells:

- Copy the entire cell and paste it to the new location.

- Enter the formula in the first cell and then use the fill handle to copy the formula.

- Preselect the entire range for the formula. Enter the formula in the first cell and press Ctrl+Enter to simultaneously enter the formula in the entire selection.

- Define the range as a Table. Excel automatically copies new formulas entered in a Table. See the section "Inserting Formulas into Tables" for more information.

Copying a Formula Using the Fill Handle

This method is useful if you need to copy your formula across a row or down a column. To copy a formula by dragging the fill handle, follow these steps:

1. Select the cell you want the formula to be in.

2. Type the formula in the first cell.

3. Press Ctrl+Enter to accept the formula and keep the cell as your active cell. If you press Enter instead, that's fine—just reselect the cell.

4. Click and hold the fill handle, which looks like a little black square in the lower-right corner of the selected cell. When the cursor is positioned correctly, it turns into a black cross, as shown in Figure 5.9.

5. Drag the fill handle to the last cell that needs to hold a copy of the formula.

6. Release the mouse button. The first cell is copied to all the cells in the selected range.

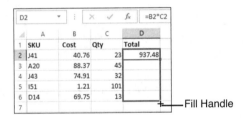

FIGURE 5.9

Clicking and dragging the fill handle is a quick way to copy a formula a short distance.

Copying a Formula by Using Ctrl+Enter

If you have a large range to copy a formula into, and the range isn't a single column or single row, this method might be useful. It copies the formula into the columns and/or rows of the selection, such as a rectangle or even a selection of noncontiguous cells. To copy a formula using Ctrl+Enter, follow these steps:

1. Select the range, or noncontiguous cells, you want the formula to be in.

2. Type the formula in the first cell, ensuring your cell referencing is correct.

3. Press Ctrl+Enter. Excel copies the formula to all cells in the selected range.

Copying Formulas Rapidly Down a Column

If you need to copy a formula into just a few rows, using the fill handle is fine. But if you have several hundred rows to update, you could zoom right past the last row. And if you have thousands of rows, using the fill handle can take quite some time.

One solution is to copy the formula, select the range, and paste the formula into the range. But it can still be a bit tricky to select the entire range you need to paste to.

If you have a data set without any completely blank rows, you can double-click the fill handle and have it quickly fill the formula down the column to the last row of the data set.

To quickly fill the formula down the column to the last row of the data set, follow these steps:

1. Enter your formula in the first cell of the column.

2. Verify that your data set is contiguous without any blank rows or columns. To do this, select the cell from step 1 and press Ctrl+A. Excel selects all the cells of the data set until it runs into a blank row and column. If you see any blank columns or rows interfering with the desired selection, add some temporary text and then try the selection again.

3. Once you've verified that the data set is contiguous, place your cursor on the fill handle until it turns into a black plus sign, as shown in Figure 5.9.

4. Double-click and the formula will be copied down the sheet until it reaches the end of the data set (a fully blank row).

 TIP   If you don't get the fill handle, it's possible you have the option turned off. Go to File, Options, Advanced and ensure Enable Fill Handle and Cell Drag-and-Drop is selected.

Using Names to Simplify References

It can be difficult to remember what cell you have a specific entry in, such as a tax rate, when you're writing a formula. And if the cell you need to reference is on another sheet, you have to be very careful writing out the reference properly, or you must use the mouse to go to the sheet and select the cell.

It would be much simpler if you could just use the word TaxRate in your formula—and you can, by applying a Name to the cell. After a Name is applied to a cell, any references to the cell or range can be done by using the Name instead of the cell address. For example, where you once had =B2*$H$1, you could now have =B2*TaxRate, assuming H1 is the cell containing the tax rate.

There are only a few limitations to remember when creating a Name:

- The Name must be one word. You can use an underscore (_), backslash (\), or period (.) as spacers.

- The Name cannot be a word that might also be a cell address. This was a real problem when people converted workbooks from legacy Excel to Excel 2007 or newer because some names, such as TAX2009, weren't cell addresses before. Now in Excel 2007 and newer, such Names cause problems when opening a legacy workbook. So Name carefully!

- The Name cannot include any invalid characters, such as ? ! or -. The only valid special characters are the underscore (_), backslash (\), and period (.).

- Names are not case sensitive. Excel will see "sales" and "Sales" as the same name.

- You should not use any of the reserved words in Excel. These are Print_Area, Print_Titles, Criteria, Database, and Extract.

Applying and Using a Name in a Formula

To apply a Name to a cell, select the cell, type the Name in the Name box, and press Enter. As long as the Name has not been applied to another cell in the workbook, it replaces the cell address of the selected cell. But if the Name has been applied elsewhere in the workbook, Excel takes you to that cell.

To apply a name to a cell and then use the name in a formula, follow these steps:

1. Select the cell or range you want to apply the Name to.

2. In the Name field, type in the Name, as shown in Figure 5.10.

Name field

FIGURE 5.10

After you select a cell or range, you can type a Name for it in the Name field.

3. Press Enter for Excel to accept the Name.

4. Go to the cell containing the formula that should reference the Name.

5. Replace the cell or range address with the Name you just created, or type in a new formula from scratch using the Name where you would use the cell or range address, as shown in Figure 5.11.

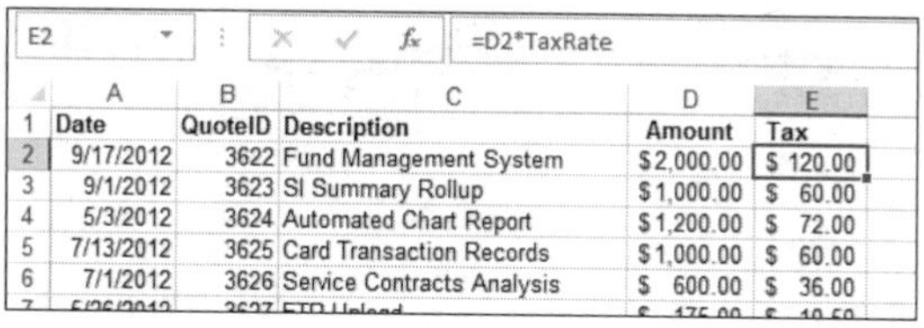

E2			⨯	✓	*fx*	=D2*TaxRate		

	A	B	C	D	E
1	Date	QuoteID	Description	Amount	Tax
2	9/17/2012	3622	Fund Management System	$2,000.00	$ 120.00
3	9/1/2012	3623	SI Summary Rollup	$1,000.00	$ 60.00
4	5/3/2012	3624	Automated Chart Report	$1,200.00	$ 72.00
5	7/13/2012	3625	Card Transaction Records	$1,000.00	$ 60.00
6	7/1/2012	3626	Service Contracts Analysis	$ 600.00	$ 36.00
7	5/26/2012	3627	FTP Upload	$ 175.00	$ 10.50

FIGURE 5.11

Using Names can simplify entering formulas.

If you can't remember the Name assigned to a range, you can look it up by clicking the drop-down in the Name field or by selecting Formulas, Defined Names, Use in Formula, which opens up a drop-down of available Names. You can also go to Formulas, Defined Names, Name Manager, which not only lists the defined Names but shows the range they apply to.

Global Versus Local Names

Names can be *global*, which means they are available anywhere in the workbook. Names can also be *local*, which means they are available only on a specific sheet. With local Names, you can have multiple references in the workbook with the same name. Global Names must be unique to the workbook.

The Name Manager dialog box (shown in Figure 5.12 and found in the Defined Names group on the Formulas tab), lists all the Names in a workbook, even a Name that has been assigned to both the global and local levels. The **Scope** column lists the scope of the Name, whether it is the workbook or a specific sheet such as Sheet1. When you create a Name, by default it is global. To make the Name local, you have to include the sheet name followed by an exclamation point (!) before typing the Name. If the sheet name is more than one word, then you have to wrap the sheet name in single quotes. For example, if the sheet name is "SD Sales" and you're creating the TaxRate name to use just on that sheet, the Name you type would be: 'SD Sales'!TaxRate.

CAUTION   If you have both a local and global reference with the same Name, when you create a formula on the sheet with the local reference, a tip box will appear, letting you choose which reference you want to use.

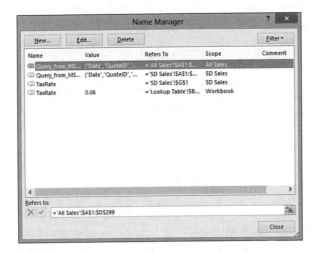

FIGURE 5.12

The Name Manager dialog box lists all local and global names.

Inserting Formulas into Tables

 NOTE   See the "Defining a Table" section in Chapter 3 for information on defining a Table.

When your data has been defined as a Table, Excel automatically copies new formulas created in adjacent columns down to the last row in the Table.

To add a new calculated column to a Table, follow these steps:

1. Type a field header in row 1 of the column adjacent to the rightmost column of the Table. Excel extends any Table formatting to the new column.

2. Select the first data cell in the column. This is cell H2 in Figure 5.13.

3. Type your formula for the selected cell.

4. Press Enter and Excel copies the formula down the column.

Customer	Quantit⌄	Reven⌄	COGS ⌄	Profit ⌄
Alluring Shoe Company	500	11240	5110	=F2-G2
Alluring Shoe Company	400	9204	4088	
Alluring Shoe Company	900	21465	9198	
Alluring Shoe Company	400	9144	4088	
Alluring Shoe Company	500	10445	4235	

FIGURE 5.13

Type a formula in the first cell of a Table column and Excel copies it down the rest of the column. Note that if you select the columns instead of typing in the cell references, your resulting formula will look quite different.

After entering the formula, a lightning bolt drop-down appears by the cell. If you don't want the automated formula copied, select Undo Calculated Column or Stop Automatically Creating Calculated Columns.

 NOTE If you select the cells instead of typing the cell address, you will see Names in the formula instead of the cell address. Refer to the next section "Using Table Names in Table Formulas" to understand why.

Using Table Names in Table Formulas

Names are automatically created when you define a Table. A name, or a specifier, for each column and the entire Table is created. Just like you can use Names to simplify references in your standard formulas, you can use these names to simplify references to the data in your Table formulas. A formula using [@Quantity] is easier to understand than E2.

To create a Table formula using column specifiers instead of cell addresses, you can type in the column name preceded by @ and surrounded by square brackets or you can use the mouse or keyboard to select the desired cell in the Table. To add a new calculated column to a Table, follow these steps:

1. Type a field header in row 1 of the column adjacent to the rightmost column of the Table. Excel extends any Table formatting to the new column.

2. Select the first data cell. This is cell H2 in Figure 5.14.

3. Enter your formula. Instead of typing in cell addresses, use the keyboard or mouse to select the cells. You will notice that column specifiers appear instead of cell addresses.

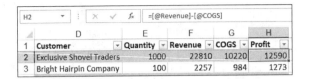

⊿	D	E	F	G	H
1	Customer ▾	Quantity ▾	Revenue ▾	COGS ▾	Profit ▾
2	Exclusive Shovel Traders	1000	22810	10220	12590
3	Bright Hairpin Company	100	2257	984	1273

FIGURE 5.14

The use of specifiers in Table formulas makes it much easier to interpret what fields are used in the calculation.

 NOTE If you select a cell in a different row than that of the formula cell, you will see a cell address. Excel expects formulas in a Table to reference the same row or an entire column or Table.

4. Press Enter and Excel copies the formula down the column.

After entering the formula, a lightning bolt drop-down appears by the cell. If you don't want the automated formula copied, select Undo Calculated Column or Stop Automatically Creating Calculated Columns.

In Figure 5.14, look at the formula in the formula bar. Notice the column specifiers are preceded by @. This is to specify that the formula is referring to the value of the specifier in that column. If the @ is dropped, then the formula would be referring to the entire column. For more information on @ and other specifiers, see the next section "Writing Table Formulas Outside the Table."

Writing Table Formulas Outside the Table

 NOTE Although you can apply the information in this section to formulas in a Table, the specifiers are more commonly used outside of the Table because their strength lies in summarizing data.

To find the name of the Table, select a cell in the Table and go to Table Tools, Design, Properties. The name of the Table appears in the Table Name field. You use this name in formulas to reference the entire Table.

In addition to the Table and column specifiers, Excel provides five more to make it easier to narrow down a particular part of a Table:

- **#All**—Returns all the contents of the Table or specified column
- **#Data**—Returns the data cells of the Table or specified column

- **@ (This Row)**—Returns the current row

- **#Headers**—Returns all the column headers or that of a specified column

- **#Totals**—Returns the total rows or that of a specified column

To access these specifiers from a drop-down, you must first type the Table name followed by the left square bracket. After the bracket is entered, a drop-down of all specifiers appears, as shown in Figure 5.15. For example, to return the sum of the entire Profit column in Table1, the formula would be:

=SUM(Table1[Profit])

If you wanted to return the profit made from a specific company, Alluring Shoe Company, from the same Table, the formula would be:

=SUMIF(Table1[Customer],"Alluring Shoe Company",Table1[Profit])

FIGURE 5.15

You can manually type in a specifier, or when the drop-down appears, arrow down to the desired specifier and click Tab to add it to the formula.

NOTE SUMIF is a function that allows you to sum data from one column based on a specific value in another column. For other functions that summarize data based on criteria, see chapter 6.

Another user would not need to see the Table. As long as the Table name and field name are known, the user can write any desired formula.

The following are rules for writing formulas that refer to Tables:

- The reference to the Table must start with the Table name. If the formula is within the Table itself, you can omit the Table name.

- Specifiers, such as a column name or the total row, must be enclosed in square brackets, like this: TableName[Specifier].

- If using multiple specifiers, each specifier must be surrounded by square brackets and separated by commas. The entire group of specifiers used must be surrounded by square brackets, like this: TableName[[Specifier1], [Specifier2]].

- If no specifiers are used, the Table name refers to the data rows in the Table. This does not include the headers or total rows.

- The @ (This Row) specifier must be used with another specifier, like this: TableName[[@Specifier]].

Figure 5.16 shows examples of using specifiers.

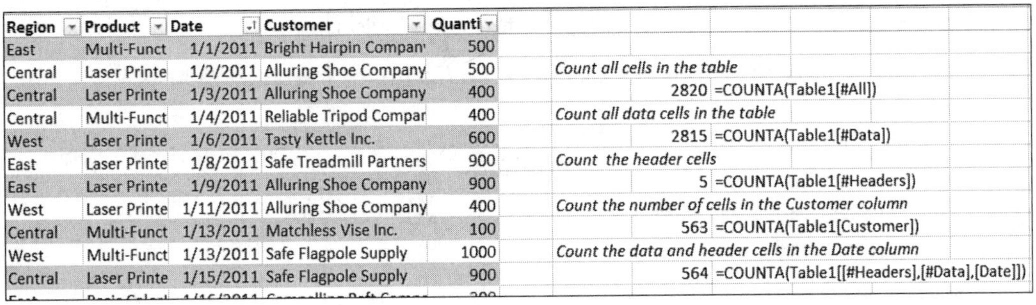

Region	Product	Date	Customer	Quanti		
East	Multi-Funct	1/1/2011	Bright Hairpin Compan	500		
Central	Laser Printe	1/2/2011	Alluring Shoe Company	500	Count all cells in the table	
Central	Laser Printe	1/3/2011	Alluring Shoe Company	400	2820	=COUNTA(Table1[#All])
Central	Multi-Funct	1/4/2011	Reliable Tripod Compar	400	Count all data cells in the table	
West	Laser Printe	1/6/2011	Tasty Kettle Inc.	600	2815	=COUNTA(Table1[#Data])
East	Laser Printe	1/8/2011	Safe Treadmill Partners	900	Count the header cells	
East	Laser Printe	1/9/2011	Alluring Shoe Company	900	5	=COUNTA(Table1[#Headers])
West	Laser Printe	1/11/2011	Alluring Shoe Company	400	Count the number of cells in the Customer column	
Central	Multi-Funct	1/13/2011	Matchless Vise Inc.	100	563	=COUNTA(Table1[Customer])
West	Multi-Funct	1/13/2011	Safe Flagpole Supply	1000	Count the data and header cells in the Date column	
Central	Laser Printe	1/15/2011	Safe Flagpole Supply	900	564	=COUNTA(Table1[[#Headers],[#Data],[Date]])
East	Basic Salad	1/16/2011	Compelling Raft Corner	300		

FIGURE 5.16

Column I has examples of using specifiers to return Table information.

Using Array Formulas

An array holds multiple values individually in a single cell. An array formula allows you to do calculations with those individual values.

It's hard to imagine, but three keys on your keyboard can turn the right formula into a *super* formula. Three keys can take 10,000 individual formulas and reduce them to a single formula. These three keys are Ctrl+Shift+Enter. Enter the right type of formula in a cell, but instead of just pressing Enter, press Ctrl+Shift+Enter and the formula becomes an array formula, also known as a CSE formula.

For example, with an array formula you can do the following:

- Multiply corresponding cells together and return the sum or average, as shown in Example 2.

- Return a list of the top nth items in a list, while calculating the value by which you are judging their rank, as shown in Example 3.

- Sum (or average) only numbers that meet a certain condition, such as falling between a specified range.

- Count the number or records that match multiple criteria.

You can tell if a formula is an array formula because it's surrounded by curly braces ({}). These braces are not typed in. They appear after pressing Ctrl+Shift+Enter. If you edit the formula, the braces will go away and you'll have to press the CSE combination to get them to come back, or press Esc to exit the cell and undo any changes.

Example 1

Look at Figure 5.17. The ROW function returns the row number of what is in the parentheses. When you have a range, such as $1:$10, the function holds all the numbers 1 to 10. In columns A and B, you see the result of a normally entered ROW function looking at rows 1:10—1s all the way down because the formula can only return the first value it holds. In columns C and D, you see the same formula, but entered as an array formula. This time, you can see each value held in the function—the numbers 1 through 10.

	A	B	C	D
1		Normal Formula		Array Formula
2		1 =ROW($1:$10)		1 {=ROW($1:$10)}
3		1 =ROW($1:$10)		2 {=ROW($1:$10)}
4		1 =ROW($1:$10)		3 {=ROW($1:$10)}
5		1 =ROW($1:$10)		4 {=ROW($1:$10)}
6		1 =ROW($1:$10)		5 {=ROW($1:$10)}
7		1 =ROW($1:$10)		6 {=ROW($1:$10)}
8		1 =ROW($1:$10)		7 {=ROW($1:$10)}
9		1 =ROW($1:$10)		8 {=ROW($1:$10)}
10		1 =ROW($1:$10)		9 {=ROW($1:$10)}
11		1 =ROW($1:$10)		10 {=ROW($1:$10)}

FIGURE 5.17

Normally, the formula in B2:B11 would return only a single value. But enter the same formula as an array formula, and range C2:C11 shows the individual values held in the array formula.

Excel returns the value corresponding to the cell's position in the entire range the array is applied to. To let Excel know what the range is, you select the range before you type the formula in. In this case, C2:C11 was selected, the formula typed into C2, then CSE was pressed, applying the array to the range.

Example 2

Figure 5.18 goes to the next step, multiplying each value in the array by 2, as shown in columns H and I. Cell H10 includes the SUM function in the array formula, which not only multiplies each value in the array by 2 but also adds the results. Imagine if you had a sheet with 10,000 quantities and prices. Instead of multiplying each row into a new column and then summing that column, you just have one cell that does the entire calculation. And because you have fewer formulas, the workbook is smaller.

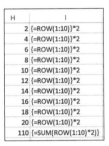

H	I
2	{=ROW(1:10)}*2
4	{=ROW(1:10)}*2
6	{=ROW(1:10)}*2
8	{=ROW(1:10)}*2
10	{=ROW(1:10)}*2
12	{=ROW(1:10)}*2
14	{=ROW(1:10)}*2
16	{=ROW(1:10)}*2
18	{=ROW(1:10)}*2
20	{=ROW(1:10)}*2
110	{=SUM(ROW(1:10)*2)}

FIGURE 5.18

The array formula in cell H11 multiplies each value in the array and sums the results.

NOTE Just like in Example 1, range H1:H10 was selected before entering the formula in cell H1. But the SUM array is standalone, so only that cell was selected when entering the formula.

Example 3

An array formula can also calculate and return multiple values. These values are placed within the range selected before entering the formula.

For example, if you want to return the region, product, and date of the top three revenue generators for the data in Figure 5.19, use a formula like this (explained in more detail after the figure):

=INDEX(A1:A46 & "-" & B1:B46 & " on " &

TEXT(C1:C46,"mm/dd/yy"),MATCH(LARGE(D2:D46*E2:E46,{1;2;3}),(D1:D46*E 1:E46),0))

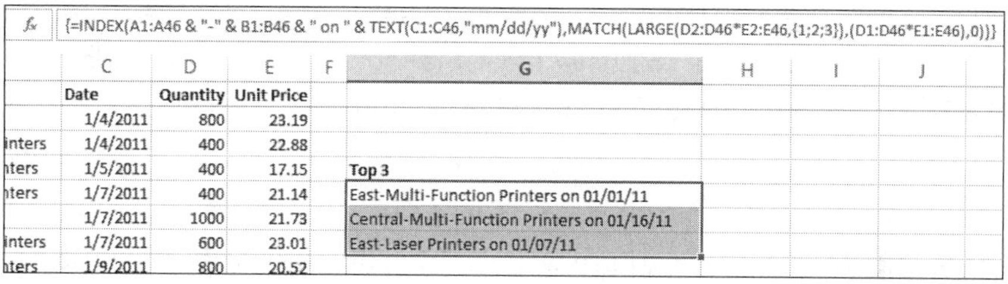

| f_x | {=INDEX(A1:A46 & "-" & B1:B46 & " on " & TEXT(C1:C46,"mm/dd/yy"),MATCH(LARGE(D2:D46*E2:E46,{1;2;3}),(D1:D46*E1:E46),0))} |

	C	D	E	F	G	H	I	J
	Date	**Quantity**	**Unit Price**					
	1/4/2011	800	23.19					
inters	1/4/2011	400	22.88					
nters	1/5/2011	400	17.15		**Top 3**			
nters	1/7/2011	400	21.14		East-Multi-Function Printers on 01/01/11			
	1/7/2011	1000	21.73		Central-Multi-Function Printers on 01/16/11			
inters	1/7/2011	600	23.01		East-Laser Printers on 01/07/11			
nters	1/9/2011	800	20.52					

FIGURE 5.19

An array formula can be used to return multiple values, such as the top three revenue makers.

1. Look for the three largest revenues at the same time they're being calculated, like this:

   LARGE(D2:D46*E2:E46,{1;2;3})

   LARGE is a function that returns the nth largest value in a range, which we are creating by multiplying corresponding values in columns D and E (D2*E2, D3*E3, and so forth). In this case, we are looking for the top three items and place 1;2;3 in curly braces. By placing the numbers manually in curly braces separated by semicolons (;), we're identifying them as an array.

2. Now that we have the top three values, we have to locate them within the range, like this:

   MATCH(LARGE(D2:D46*E2:E46,{1;2;3}),(D1:D46*E1:E46),0)

   MATCH returns the row numbers of the calculated revenues by matching their location within an array of the calculated revenues. The 0 tells the function we need an exact match to the values.

3. The formula now holds the rows that the three largest values are found in. The INDEX function is then used to look up and return the desired details from those rows.

4. After you select three cells where you want the results of the formula placed, type the entire formula and enter it by pressing Ctrl+Shift+Enter. Excel copies the formula down to each of the three cells. The first cell returns the first answer in the calculated array, the second cell returns the second value in the calculated array, and the third cell returns the third value.

When an array formula is holding more than one calculated value, you must select a range at least the size of the most values it is returning before entering it and pressing the CSE combination. If the range selected is too small, only some of the values will be returned. If the range selected is too large, an error will appear in the extra cells. Because you have the same formula in multiple cells, the workbook is smaller; Excel has to track only a single formula.

Editing Array Formulas

Following are a few rules to use when editing multicell array formulas:

- You cannot edit just one cell of the array formula. A change made to one cell affects them all.

- You can increase the size of the range but not decrease it. To decrease it, you must delete the formula and reenter it.

- You cannot move just a part of the range, but you can move the entire range.

- The range must be continuous—you cannot insert blank cells within it.

Deleting Array Formulas

You cannot delete just one cell of a multicell array formula. The entire range containing the array formula must be selected before you can delete it. The message "You Cannot Change Part of an Array" will appear if you try to delete just a portion of the range containing the formula. You can use Go to Special, Current Array to select the entire array or select one cell in the array, press Backspace, then Ctrl+Shift+Enter and this will clear all the cells in the array.

If you need to resize an array to be smaller, you will have to delete and reenter it. To select an entire array formula and delete it, follow these steps:

1. Select a cell in the array formula.

2. Press Ctrl+G to bring up the Go To dialog box.

3. Click the Special button in the lower-left corner of the dialog box.

4. Select Current Array and click OK.

5. Press Delete on the keyboard to delete the entire array formula range.

Converting Formulas to Values

Formulas take up a lot of memory, and the recalculation time can make working in a large workbook a hassle. At times, you need a formula only temporarily; you just want to calculate the value once and won't ever need to calculate it again. You could manually type the value over the formula cell, but if the result is a long number, or if you have a lot of calculation cells, this isn't convenient. You could copy the range then do a Paste Special, Values, but there's a faster option you can access from a special right-click menu. To access the menu and quickly convert formula to their values, follow these steps:

1. Select the range of formulas.

2. Place your cursor on the right edge of the dark border around the range so that it turns from the white plus sign to four black arrows, as if you were going to move the range to a new location.

3. While holding your right mouse button down, drag the range to the next column and then back to the original column.

 CAUTION Be very careful that you place the range exactly where it was originally. Excel allows you to use this method to place the range in a new location.

4. Let go of the right mouse button.

5. From the context menu that appears, shown in Figure 5.20, select Copy Here as Values Only.

FIGURE 5.20

By placing the cursor on the range's border, holding down the right mouse button and dragging to and fro, a hidden menu appears with various options to apply to the range.

Troubleshooting Formulas

It can be frustrating to enter a formula and have it either return an incorrect value or an error. An important part of solving the problem is to understand what the error is trying to tell you. After you have an idea of the problem you're looking for, you can use several tools to look deeper into the error.

NOTE   For assistance more specific to troubleshooting functions, refer to the "Using the Function Arguments Dialog Box to Troubleshoot Formulas" section in Chapter 6.

Error Messages

After entering a formula, you may run into one of the following errors:

- **#DIV/0!**—Occurs when a number is divided by zero.

- **#N/A**—Occurs when a value isn't available in the formula; for example, if you're doing a lookup function and the lookup value isn't found.

- **#NAME?**—Occurs when a formula includes unrecognizable text.

- **#NULL!**—Occurs when an intersection is specified but the areas do not intersect or if a range operator is incorrect. For example, if you entered =SUM(A1:A10 B1:B10), you would get the error because the comma separating the ranges is missing. The correct formula is =SUM(A1:A10,B1:B10).

- **#NUM!**—Occurs when there is an invalid numeric value in a formula or function.

- **#REF!**—Occurs when a cell reference isn't valid, for example, if the cell has been deleted. This can be difficult to trace because the #REF can occur within the formula itself—for example, =#REF*A2—and there's no direct way to trace back to the original reference.

- **#VALUE!**—Occurs when trying to do math with nonnumeric data; for example, D1+D2 will return the error if cell D1 is the column header.

- **######**—This isn't really an error. It can occur if the column width is not wide enough for the formula result or if you're trying to subtract a later date from an earlier date (you can't have a negative date).

The initial help provided by Excel may help trace the problem. When an error cell is selected, an exclamation icon appears. When you click on the icon, a list of options appears.

The first item in the list is a brief description of the issue, so this will change depending on the error. After that, Excel offers four troubleshooting options:

- **Help on This Error**—Opens the Excel Help dialog box to find more information on troubleshooting formulas.

- **Show Calculation Steps**—Opens the Evaluate Formula dialog box. See the "Using the Evaluate Formula Dialog Box" section later in this chapter for more information.

- **Ignore Error**—Causes the error icon to disappear. It reappears if the formula is edited.

- **Edit in Formula Bar**—Puts you in Edit mode, with your cursor in the formula bar. The cells used in the formula, if on the same sheet, are highlighted so you can see what ranges are being used.

At the bottom of the list, is a link to the Excel Options dialog box, Formulas section, where you can modify how Excel interacts with you when it comes to errors.

Additional troubleshooting options are available in the Formula Auditing group on the Formulas tab.

 TIP   If the error icon is not appearing by cells with errors, it's possible that error checking in Excel has been turned off. To check, and turn it back on, go to File, Options, Formulas and select Enable Background Error Checking. If the option is checked, it's possible that all errors have been ignored. In that case, click the Reset Ignored Errors button.

Using Trace Precedents and Dependents to See What Cells Affect or Are Affected By the Active Cell

When you select a cell containing a formula and press F2, you enter Edit mode and Excel highlights any cells on the sheet that are used by the formula. But it doesn't highlight the cells on other sheets. To do that and more, use the trace precedent and trace dependent auditing arrows.

Use the formula auditing arrows found on the Formulas tab in the Formula Auditing group if you have a cell you want to trace, whether it's to locate other cells used in that cell's formula or what cells reference the selected cell. Just select the cell in question and click a trace button.

There are two types of auditing arrows:

- **Trace Precedents**—If the selected cell contains a formula, blue arrows point to the cells used by the formula.

- **Trace Dependents**—If the selected cell is used in a formula in another cell, red arrows point to the cell containing that formula.

When you click one of the trace buttons, arrows appear linking the cell to other cells that are directly connected to it, as shown in Figure 5.21. Click the trace button again and you will get the next level of cell connections. You can continue to click the button and Excel continues adding tracing arrows to the sheet.

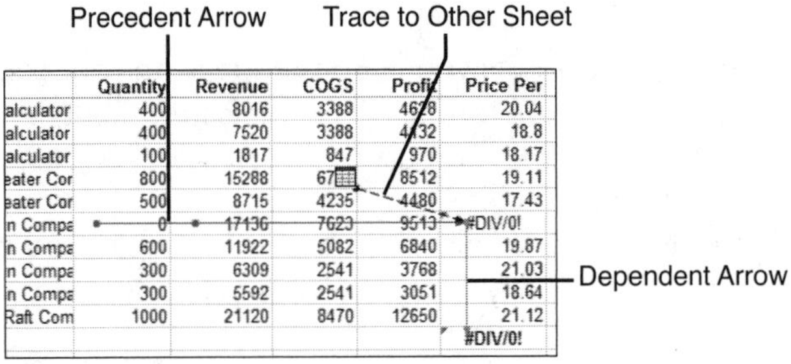

Precedent Arrow   Trace to Other Sheet

	Quantity	Revenue	COGS	Profit	Price Per
alculator	400	8016	3388	4678	20.04
alculator	400	7520	3388	4132	18.8
alculator	100	1817	847	970	18.17
eater Cor	800	15288	67	8512	19.11
eater Cor	500	8715	4235	4480	17.43
n Compa	0	17136	7623	9513	#DIV/0!
n Compa	600	11922	5082	6840	19.87
n Compa	300	6309	2541	3768	21.03
n Compa	300	5592	2541	3051	18.64
Raft Com	1000	21120	8470	12650	21.12
					#DIV/0!

Dependent Arrow

FIGURE 5.21

Use the Trace Precedents and Trace Dependents buttons to locate links to the selected cell, including links to other sheets.

If the connecting cell is on another sheet, Excel displays a dashed arrow pointing to a sheet icon, as shown in Figure 5.21. If you double-click the line (make sure your cursor is a white arrow, not a white plus), the Go To dialog box appears, listing every cell containing a link to the selected cell. You can then double-click one of the listed items in the dialog box and jump directly to the linked cell.

To clear all the arrows, select Formulas, Formula Auditing, Remove Arrows. There is no way to go back just one level or remove one type of arrow.

Using the Watch Window to Track Formulas on Other Sheets

The Watch Window found in the Formula Auditing group of the Formulas tab allows you to watch a cell update as you make changes that will affect it. This can be useful when you have formulas that span multiple sheets and you need to watch a cell on one sheet while you make changes to another. You can double-click a cell in the Watch Window to jump to that cell.

To watch a formula update on another sheet, follow these steps:

1. Select Formulas, Formula Auditing, Watch Window. The Watch Window dialog box opens.

2. Click Add Watch to open the Add Watch dialog box.

3. Select the cell you want to watch update and click Add.

4. Repeat steps 2 and 3 for any additional cells that you want to monitor.

5. Leave the Watch Window open (you can drag it out of the way) and make changes to cells that will affect the watched cells.

6. Whether directly linked or not, if the watched cells are in any way affected by the changes you make, the Watch Window updates to reflect the new value of the cell.

Using the Evaluate Formula Dialog Box

If you want to watch how Excel calculates each part of a formula, you can use Formulas, Formula Auditing, Evaluate Formula.

The Evaluate Formula dialog box, shown in Figure 5.22, has three buttons you can use to investigate a formula. The buttons work only on the underlined portion of the formula:

- **Evaluate**—Replaces the underlined portion of the formula with the value.

- **Step In**—Displays the actual contents of a cell if the underlined portion is a cell address. This may be a value or a formula. If it's a formula, you have the option to continue stepping in until it is resolved.

- **Step Out**—Returns to the previous level of evaluation.

You can continue to evaluate a formula until it is completely resolved.

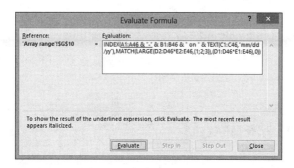

FIGURE 5.22

The Evaluate Formula dialog box is just one tool for troubleshooting formula errors. With this tool, you can watch the results as Excel calculates each portion of a formula.

To see how Excel is calculating each part of a formula, follow these steps:

1. Select the cell with the formula to evaluate.

2. Select Formulas, Formula Auditing, Evaluate Formula. The formula appears in the evaluation window with some part of it underlined, as shown in Figure 5.22.

3. Click the Step In button if it is activated. If it isn't, skip to step 8. A new section appears in the window, showing the result of the underlined portion.

4. Repeat steps 4 and 5 if the Step In button is still active.

5. When the Step In button is no longer active, click the Step Out button to return to the previous level. Each click of the button returns you to the previous level.

6. Click the Evaluate button and Excel evaluates the underlined portion, replacing it in the formula with the returned or calculated value.

7. Continue to click Evaluate or Step In to watch the formula calculate.

8. Excel is done with the evaluation when only the calculated value appears in the Evaluation field. You can either click Restart to go through the steps again, or click Close to return to Excel.

Evaluating with F9

With the Evaluate Formula dialog box, you have to evaluate the formula in the order that Excel calculates the formula. If you want to jump directly to a portion of the formula, you can skip the Evaluate Formula dialog box and instead just highlight that formula portion and press F9 to evaluate to its value.

You should keep two things in mind when using F9 to evaluate a formula:

- When highlighting the portion to evaluate, you must be careful to select the entire portion, including any relevant parentheses.

- You must press Esc to leave the cell. If you don't, Excel replaces your formula with the value you just evaluated to.

THE ABSOLUTE MINIMUM

Although Excel is a great tool for organizing data, formulas is where the real power within the program starts. By now, you should know the difference between A1 and R1C1 notation and have a grasp on using absolute and relative referencing in either style. With this knowledge, you can write a variety of formulas, including array formulas. You know how to create formulas to interact with a Table, and when it's all done, you can replace the formulas with values.

Now that you have the basics down, it's time to step it up and learn about the functions in Excel that you can include in your formulas, making them smarter and more powerful.

IN THIS CHAPTER

- Search Excel's library of over 400 functions.
- Use multiple criteria to look up values.
- Calculate overtime in timesheets.
- Create formulas using multiple functions.
- Troubleshoot formulas.

USING FUNCTIONS

A function is like a shortcut for using a long or complex formula. If you've ever summed cells like this: =A1+A2+A3+A4+A5, you could have instead used the SUM function like this: =SUM(A1:A5). Excel offers more than 400 functions. These include logical functions, lookup functions, statistical functions, financial functions, and more.

This chapter shows you how to look up functions available in Excel and reviews some functions helpful for everyday use. Another useful tool, Goal Seek, is also introduced.

 TIP Only a handful of Excel's functions are reviewed here. For a more in-depth review of functions and possible scenarios you'd use them in, see *Microsoft Excel 2013 In Depth*, by Bill Jelen (ISBN 978-0-7897-4857-7).

Breaking Down a Function

A function consists of the name used to call it and might or might not include arguments, which are variables used in the calculation. In the formula =SUM(A1:A5), SUM is the function and A1:A5 is the argument.

Normally, the syntax of a function is like this:

FunctionName(Argument1, Argument2, ...)

But there are some functions that have no arguments or the argument is optional. There are a few rules to keep in mind when using functions:

- Arguments must be entered in the order required by the function.

- Arguments must be separated by commas.

- Arguments can be cell references, numbers, logicals, or text.

- Some arguments are optional. Optional arguments are placed after the required ones.

- If you skip an optional argument to use one after it, you still have to place a comma for the one you skipped.

- Some functions, such as NOW(), do not require arguments, but the parentheses must still be included in the formula.

Finding Functions

You can always search Excel's Help to find a function, but you might get more than just the function information you're looking for. Instead, narrow down the results by using tools provided specifically for searching functions.

The Formulas tab has a Function Library group with drop-downs grouped by function type. Selecting any function listed in a drop-down opens it up in the Formula Wizard.

If you aren't sure which function you need, or if you need more help in using a function, there are several ways to open the Insert Function dialog box, which helps you find the required function:

- Select the More Functions link at the bottom of the AutoSum drop-down on the Home or Formulas tab.

- Select the Insert Function link at the bottom of one of the other function library drop-downs on the Formulas tab.

- Click the Insert Function button in the Function Library group on the Formulas tab.

- Click the fx button by the formula bar.

When you click Insert Function, the dialog box shown in Figure 6.1 opens. You can enter a search term in the Search for a Function field or select a category from the drop-down. Results appear in the list box. When you select a function from the list box, the arguments and a brief description of the function appear. When you find the function you want to use, highlight it and click OK. The function appears in the active cell and the Function Arguments dialog box opens, ready to help you fill in the rest of the arguments.

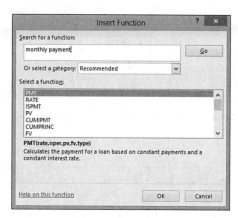

FIGURE 6.1

The Insert Function dialog box helps search through Excel's more than 400 available functions.

Entering Functions Using the Function Arguments Dialog Box

Once you've entered a function in a cell, the Function Arguments dialog box shown in Figure 6.2 opens. It assists in entering the arguments for the selected function. Other than from beginning with the Insert Function dialog box as explained in the previous section, you can also open the dialog box by selecting a cell with a function already in it and using any of the methods listed in the "Finding Functions" section.

A field exists for each argument. If the function has a variable number of arguments, like the SUM function, a new field is automatically added when needed.

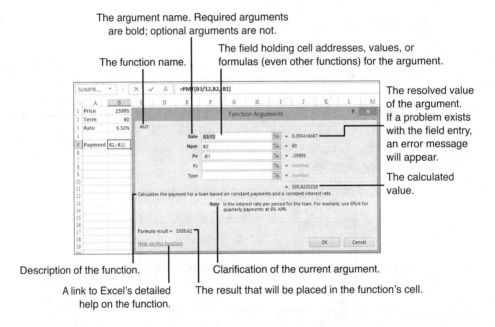

The argument name. Required arguments are bold; optional arguments are not.

The function name.

The field holding cell addresses, values, or formulas (even other functions) for the argument.

The resolved value of the argument. If a problem exists with the field entry, an error message will appear.

The calculated value.

Description of the function.

Clarification of the current argument.

A link to Excel's detailed help on the function.

The result that will be placed in the function's cell.

FIGURE 6.2

The Function Arguments dialog box helps with the arguments of the selected function.

Figure 6.2 shows the PMT function being used to calculate the monthly payment for a loan. The loan amount is in cell B1, the number of months in cell B2, the APR in cell B3. The function is in cell B5. To insert the function and select its arguments, follow these steps:

1. Select the cell that will hold the formula (cell B5).

2. Go to Formulas, Insert Function. In the Search field, type **PMT** and click Go.

3. PMT should appear in the list of functions. Highlight it and click OK. The Function Arguments dialog box should appear. If the dialog box is covering the values on the sheet (B1:B3), then click the title of the dialog box and drag it out of the way.

4. The first argument is **Rate,** the interest rate. When you click in the field and look at the description, notice it says this is the interest rate per period. Because your value is the annual rate, you need to divide it by 12. But first, you need to select it on the sheet. Click cell B3 and the cell address will appear in the Rate field with the cursor blinking at the end of it. Type in **/12** to get the monthly rate.

5. The second argument is the **Nper,** number of payments for the loan. First click the field in the dialog box, then select cell B2 on the sheet.

6. Click in the **Pv** field (present value of the loan) in the dialog box. Before selecting the cell on the sheet, enter a – (a minus sign) so that when you do click the cell on the sheet, you are making the value negative. You do this because of the way the function works. If you didn't make this value negative, the payment itself would be negative.

7. **Fv** (future value after the last payment is made) and **Type** (when the payment is made—1 at the beginning of the period, 0 at the end of the period) are both optional arguments and can be left blank.

8. If you do not see any error messages in the calculated value in the dialog box, click OK to have the cell accept the formula.

Entering Functions Using In-Cell Tips

If you are already familiar with the function you need, you can begin typing it in the cell or formula bar directly. After you enter an equal sign and select the first letter of the function, Excel drops down a list of possible functions, narrowing down the list with each letter entered. You can also select from the list using the arrow and Tab keys.

After the function is selected, an in-cell tip appears, as shown in Figure 6.3. The current argument will be in bold. Optional arguments appear in square brackets. If you want to use the **Function Arguments** dialog box, press Ctrl+A after typing the function name in the cell. For more help with the function, click the function name in the tip, and Excel's detailed Help file for the function appears.

SUMPR...	▼	:	×	✓	*fx*	=PMT(

▲	A	B	C	D	E	F
1	Price	25995				
2	Term	60				
3	Rate	6.50%				
4						
5	Payment	=PMT(				
6		PMT(**rate**, nper, pv, [fv], [type])				

FIGURE 6.3

If you're already familiar with the function, you can use the in-cell help to guide you in filling out the arguments.

 TIP If the in-cell help is in the way, place your cursor on the tip until it turns into a four-headed arrow and then click and drag it out of your way.

To type a function, such as SUM, directly into a cell, follow these steps:

1. Select the cell that will hold the formula.

2. Type an equal sign.

3. Begin typing the name of the function. When the drop-down list appears, you can continue typing or scroll the list to highlight the function and press Tab.

4. Enter the first argument. The argument can be a cell address (you can type it in or select it on the sheet), a value, or a formula.

5. If there is another argument, type a comma and then enter the next argument. Repeat this step for each argument. As you enter each argument, notice that the argument becomes bold in the in-cell tip, showing you your position in the function.

6. When you're finished entering all the arguments, type the closing parenthesis and press Enter or Tab for the cell to accept the formula.

 TIP You don't always have to enter the closing parenthesis; sometimes Excel will do it for you. But because the location and need is a guess by Excel, it's best to be in the habit of doing it yourself.

Using the AutoSum Button

Excel provides one-click access to the SUM function through the AutoSum button found under Home, Editing and Formulas, Function Library. You can apply the AutoSum function to a range of cells in a variety of ways:

- Select a cell adjacent to the range and click the AutoSum button.

- Highlight the range including the adjacent cell where you want the formula placed, and then select the AutoSum button.

- If you need to sum multiple ranges, select the entire table, including the adjacent row or column where you want results to appear, and then click the AutoSum button.

Unless you select the range you want to calculate, Excel guesses which cells you are trying to sum and highlights them. If the selection is correct, press Enter to accept the solution. If the selection is incorrect, make the required changes and then press Enter to accept the solution.

 TIP If you can catch Excel's incorrect selection before you accept the formula, the range Excel wants to use should still be highlighted. If it is, then select your desired range right away. If the selection is not highlighted, you'll have to highlight it first.

You should keep an eye out for a couple of things when using the AutoSum function:

- Be careful of numeric headings (like years) when letting Excel select the range for you. Excel cannot tell that the heading isn't part of the calculation range, and you need to correct the selection before accepting the formula.

- Excel looks for a column to sum before summing a row. In Figure 6.4, the default selection by Excel is the numbers above the selected cell, instead of the adjacent row of numbers.

	Q1	Q2	Q3	Q4	Total	
East	2396	3239	4765	2181	12581	
Central	4338	2008	2558	2959	11863	
West	3026	4174	4956	1613	=SUM(F9:F10)	
Total					SUM(number1, [number2], ...)	

FIGURE 6.4

Excel defaults to calculating columns before rows. I wanted to sum the West data, but Excel selects the totals from East and Central instead.

SUM Rows and Columns at the Same Time

You can SUM multiple ranges at the same time, including rows and columns. In Figure 6.5, the totals in column F and row 6 were all calculated at the same time. This was done by selecting the entire table, including the Total row and column before clicking the AutoSum button. You could also have a single row and column selection, for example, just Q1 (column B) and East (row 3) data. To do so, follow these steps:

1. Select B3:B6.

2. While holding down the Ctrl key, select B3:F3.

3. Click the AutoSum button.

4. Excel calculates and inserts the corresponding totals in the total cells.

	Q1	Q2	Q3	Q4	Total
East	2396	3239	4765	2181	12581
Central	4338	2008	2558	2959	11863
West	3026	4174	4956	1613	13769
Total	9760	9421	12279	6753	38213

FIGURE 6.5

Excel is smart enough to determine that you want to sum each individual row and column.

Other Auto Functions

The default action of the AutoSum button is the SUM function, but several other functions are available. To access these other functions, click the drop-down arrow:

- **Sum**—Adds the values in the selected range (the default action)

- **Average**—Averages the values in the selected range

- **Count Numbers**—Returns the number of cells containing numbers

- **Max**—Returns the largest value in the selected range

- **Min**—Returns the smallest value in the selected range

These other options work on a range in the same way as the SUM function, but you have to select them from the drop-down, whereas with SUM, you can just click the button.

Using the Status Bar for Quick Calculation Results

If you just need to see the results of a calculation and not include the information on a sheet, Excel offers six quick calculations, listed in Figure 6.6, that appear in the status bar when the data is selected.

CAUTION Changes to the status bar affect the application, not just the active workbook or sheet.

To see the list of functions and be able to edit the values shown in the status bar, you must first select some data on a sheet. Next, right-click on the status bar and the **Customize Status Bar** menu, shown in Figure 6.6, appears. You can toggle the check mark next to the functions you want to show or hide in the status bar. Once you have selected the functions you want, whenever you select data, the resulting calculations will appear in the status bar.

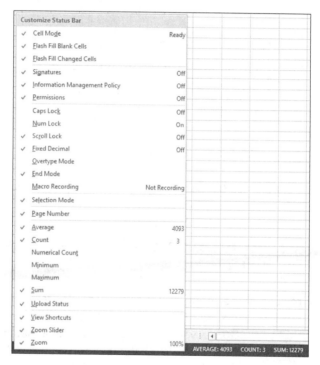

FIGURE 6.6

You can modify the status bar to show the results of calculations done to selected data.

 TIP Use the status bar to quickly verify all numbers in a range are indeed numbers. Select the range and if the resulting sum isn't correct, then at least one cell holds a number as text.

Using Quick Analysis for Column Totals

When you select multiple adjacent cells, the Quick Analysis icon, shown in Figure 6.7, appears in the lower-right corner of the selection. Click on the icon, select TOTALS and various quick calculations appear. You can use the arrows on the left and right side of the icons to scroll through the list. Once you find the calculation you want, click on it and the calculated values will be placed at the bottom of each column in your range.

 TIP This tool will not calculate across the row. If you try, it will overwrite any information in the row beneath your selection.

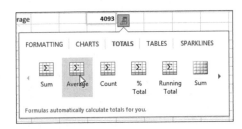

FIGURE 6.7

The Quick Analysis tool can be used to calculate a column, but not a row.

Using Lookup Functions to Match a Value and Return Another

This section reviews some of the methods available for returning a value by looking up another. There are functions that can return a value dependent on its position in a list or return a value in the same row as a match. You can even combine multiple functions to return a value by looking up and matching multiple variables.

In the function's syntax, an argument in square brackets is an optional argument.

CHOOSE

The CHOOSE function returns a value from the list based on an index number. For example, if the values in the list are 10 through 20 and the index number is 5, the fifth value in the list, 14, is returned.

The syntax of the CHOOSE function is as follows:

CHOOSE(index_num, value1, [value2],...)

- If the index_num is a decimal, it will be rounded to the next lowest integer. For example, if it is 4.8, the formula will use 4.

- If the index_num is less than 1 or greater than the number of available values, the function will return a #VALUE! error.

- You can enter 1 to 254 argument values.

- Arguments can be numbers, cell references, names, formulas, functions, or text.

Figure 6.8 shows a list of students, their grades on three tests, and the average of those grades. In the Result column, CHOOSE is used to provide a letter grade for the average, as shown in the formula bar.

F2	▼	:	×	✓	fx	=CHOOSE(E2,"F","D","C","B","A")

▲	A	B	C	D	E	F
1	Name	Test 1	Test 2	Test 3	Average	Result
2	Norah Jones	1	5	2	3	C
3	Paul Mccartney	4	5	5	5	A
4	Bill Jelen	4	3	1	3	C
5	Jon Tessmer	1	5	5	4	B
6	Susan Halloran	3	4	2	3	C

FIGURE 6.8

CHOOSE works for simple choices where you want to change a numerical value to something else, such as a text equivalent.

VLOOKUP

The VLOOKUP function matches your lookup value to a value in a table and returns data from a specified column in the matching row. This has many uses, such as returning customer information based on the customer ID or finding out if a value in list A is also in list B.

The syntax of the VLOOKUP function is as follows:

VLOOKUP(lookup_value, table_array, col_index_num, [range_lookup])

- **lookup_value**—The value to match in the leftmost column of the table_array.

- **table_array**—The entire range from which you want to look up and return a value.

- **col_index_num**—The column from the table_array from which to return the value. This is not equivalent to the column heading but instead is the location of the column in the table. For example, if the table begins in column G and the col_index_num is 2, a value from column H is returned.

- **range_lookup**—If TRUE or omitted, the table must be in ascending order by the first column for the function to match correctly. The function attempts to do an exact match. If this isn't possible, it finds the first closest match from the top of the table, without exceeding the lookup value. If FALSE, the function only looks for an exact match. If not found, a #N/A error is returned.

Figure 6.9 shows how VLOOKUP can be used to return customer information to an invoice. The customer's name is entered in cell B3. Functions in cells B4:B5 match the customer's name in the table on the sheet Customer Data and return address and phone information. Note the use of IFERROR with VLOOKUP. If an exact match is not found, "Not Available" is entered in the cells, instead of the #N/A error.

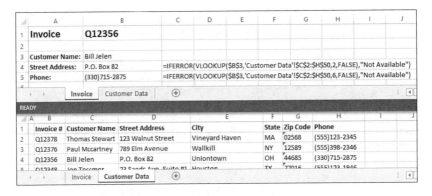

FIGURE 6.9

Use VLOOKUP formulas to return customer information from a table on another sheet.

TIP Even though range_lookup is optional it's a good habit to include. Most of the time, FALSE is used—if you leave it blank, another user might not know that you mean TRUE, as that option is used a lot less.

VLOOKUP Troubleshooting

If VLOOKUP returns an error or incorrect value but you can manually verify that the lookup value is present in the table, the exact issue may be one of the following:

- If using FALSE for the range_lookup, the entire cell contents must match 100%. If you're looking up "Bracelet" and the term in the table is "Bracelets," Excel does not return a match.

- Be careful of extra spaces before and after a word. "Bracelet " and "Bracelet" are not matches—the first occurrence has a space at the end.

- If matching numbers, make sure both the lookup value and the matching value are formatted the same type—for example, both as General or one as General and the other as Currency, allowing Excel to still see them as numbers. Sometimes when importing data, numbers get formatted as Text. If you have a lookup value formatted as General and the matching value is formatted as Text, Excel does not see this as a match. See the section "When Cell Formatting Doesn't Seem to Be Working Right" in Chapter 4, "Formatting Sheets and Cells," for instructions on how to force the numbers stored as text to become true numbers.

- Make sure the table_array encompasses the entire table.

MATCH and INDEX

VLOOKUP works only when returning data from columns to the right of the lookup column. If your data is also to the left of the lookup column, use MATCH and INDEX together. For example, if you have a customer phone number, but not the name, and the table is set up like the one in Figure 6.9, you can use MATCH to return the row the phone number is in, then use that result in INDEX with the column you do want (column C).

The syntax of the MATCH function is as follows:

MATCH(lookup_value, lookup_array, [match_type])

The syntax of the INDEX function is as follows:

INDEX(array, row_num, [column_num])

 NOTE There are two syntaxes for the INDEX function, array or reference, but this section only uses the array version.

The MATCH function looks up a value and returns its position (row or column) in an array:

- **lookup_value**—The value to match and return the location of

- **lookup_array**—The range from which to return the location

- **match_type**—A 1, 0, or -1 telling the function how to match the lookup_value

  - If 1, the function returns the largest value that is less than or equal to the lookup_value. The lookup_array must be sorted in ascending order.

  - If 0, the function returns the first value that is an exact match to the lookup_value.

  - If -1, the function returns the smallest value that is greater than or equal to the lookup_value. The lookup_array must be sorted in descending order.

The INDEX function returns a value based on a row and column number:

- **array**—A range of cells from which to return a value

- **row_num**—The number of the row within the range to return a value from

- **column_num**—The number of the column within the range to return a value from

Figure 6.10 shows how the two functions are used to return information to the left of the customer name column. First, the MATCH function is used to locate which row in the customer list matches the name. That information is used in the INDEX function to tell it from which row to return the value.

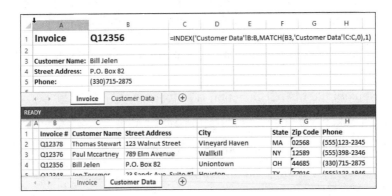

FIGURE 6.10

Use MATCH and INDEX to return information located to the left of the customer name.

TIP It's not always easy to type in a formula that uses multiple functions. You might find it easier to place each function in a different cell, referencing the results of a previous function as needed. When you've verified that each piece works, cut the function (without the equal sign) out of its cell and paste it over the cell address in the parent function.

OFFSET and MATCH

The INDEX function requires an array to be preselected to extract values from it. But if the size of the range increases and you don't have a dynamic range formula setup, the function could fail. An alternative is the similar OFFSET function, which allows you to specify a cell a specific number of rows and columns from another cell.

 NOTE A dynamic range formula is a formula that always returns the size of of a range, even if the range increases or decreases in size. This is very useful if you're importing a different amount of records every day.

The MATCH function is laid out in the previous section. The syntax of the OFFSET function is as follows:

OFFSET(reference, rows, cols, [height], [width])

- **reference**—The range from which you want to base the offset from.
- **rows**—The number of rows, either up (negative) or down (positive) you want to move from the reference.
- **cols**—The number of columns, either left (negative) or right (positive) you want to move from the reference.
- **[height]**—An optional value. It's the number of rows by which you want to expand the selection. For example, if the reference is a single row and a height of 2 is used, then the selection will be two rows high.
- **[width]**—An optional value. It's the number of columns by which you want to expand the selection. For example, if the reference is a single column and a width of 2 is used, then the selection will be two columns wide.

For example, you need to calculate the commission for your salespeople. You can place the sales values and commission rates in a table. Use a combination of the OFFSET and MATCH functions to look up and return the commission rate. The commission table may look like this:

9,999 or less: 1%

10,000 to 14,999: 1.2%

15,000 to 24,999: 1.3%

25,000 or higher: 1.5%

Create a table as shown at the top of Figure 6.11. Notice that the minimum and maximum sales values are placed in increasing order and that each value has its own column.

	A	B	C	D	E	F	G
1	**Min**	**Max**	**Rate**				
2	0	9999	1.0%				
3	10000	14999	1.2%				
4	15000	24999	1.3%				
5	25000		1.5%				
6							
7	**Employee**	**Sales $**	**Commission**				
8	Scott	5000	1.0%	=OFFSET($A$1,MATCH(B8,$A$2:$A$5,1),2)			
9	Jason	12000	1.2%				
10	Karen	32000	1.5%				
11	Wilma	15000	1.3%				

FIGURE 6.11

Instead of embedded IF statements, consider using a lookup table using lookup functions to return commission rates or other values based on comparisons.

NOTE The Max column is not required but might make it easier for some to read and interpret the rates.

The second table is the calculation table for the commission rate. First, MATCH is used to look up the Sales $ value in the above rate table. A match_type argument of 1 is used to return the row of the largest value that is less than or equal to the lookup value. With that information, we can now calculate the position of the correct rate. The reference is A1, the upper-left corner of the rate table. I could just as easily use C1, but for consistency in my formulas, I prefer to use the upper-left corner of the lookup table. Next is the MATCH function, returning the number of rows away from the reference and finally the number of columns away from the reference. All this together tells Excel exactly what cell and value I want returned.

INDIRECT

When you place a cell address in a formula, you aren't just putting in some letters and numbers. That cell address has certain properties you can't see or access, but Excel knows they are there. If you were to try to build a cell address by joining text, for example ="B" & "1", all you would get in the cell is B1. But if you wrap that formula in INDIRECT, you turn that formula into a true cell address.

The INDIRECT function returns a reference specified by a string, allowing for dynamic cell references. Another way you can use INDIRECT is if you have sheet names that are also salespeople's names; you can use INDIRECT to build a sheet name reference in a formula based on the salesperson's name, as shown in Figure 6.12. You can change the name in the cell referenced by the function and instantly refer to another sheet.

The syntax of the INDIRECT function is as follows:

INDIRECT(ref_text, [a1])

- **ref_text**—Specifies a cell or string reference.

- **a1**—Specifies the type of reference in the cell ref-text. If TRUE or omitted, ref_text is treated as an A1-style reference. If FALSE, the ref-text is treated as an R1C1-style reference.

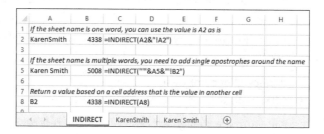

FIGURE 6.12

INDIRECT provides flexibility in creating dynamic cell references. There are a few rules to keep in mind if you're going to use the function to create sheet name references.

SUMIFS

 CAUTION   The SUMIFS function works only in Excel 2007, 2010, and 2013. If sharing the workbook with legacy Excel users, check out the SUMPRODUCT function for summing cells based on multiple criteria.

SUMIFS allows you to sum a single column based on multiple criteria. For example, you can sum revenue between two dates or sum the quantity of a specific product in a specific region.

The syntax of the function is (optional arguments are in square brackets) as follows:

SUMIFS(sum_range, criteria_range1, criteria1, [criteria_range2, criteria2],...)

- **sum_range**—The range containing the cells to sum

- **criteria_range1**—The range of cells to evaluate for the first criteria

- **criteria1**—A number, expression, or text to match in criteria_range1

 NOTE If you have only a single criteria, you can also use SUMIF, which has similar syntax to SUMIFS and is compatible with legacy Excel.

The sum_range and criteria_range must be the same number of rows. Key items to keep in mind when entering the criteria arguments in the function (cell references refer to Figure 6.13):

- An argument can be a direct cell reference, for example $H5 in the formula shown in cell I8.

- Words must be entered in quotation marks, for example "East" in the formula shown in cell I9.

- Equality and inequality symbols (<, >, >=, <=,=, <>) must be placed in quotation marks with the value in the comparison, as shown in cell I14.

- If using equality and inequality symbols with a cell reference, the cell reference should be outside the quotation marks around the symbol. Also, build the statement using the ampersand (&), as shown in cell I14.

	A	B	C	D	F	G	H	I	J	K	L	M	N	O
1	Region	Product	Date	Quantity	Revenue									
2	East	Multi-Func	1/1	1000	22810									
3	Central	Laser Print	1/2	200	4514		*Fill in the table below based on the row and column headers*							
4	East	Basic Color	1/2	500	10245			**Multi-Func**	**Laser Printe**	**Basic ColorJet Printers**				
5	Central	Multi-Func	1/3	500	11240		**East**	76843	76347	120012				
6	Central	Multi-Func	1/4	400	9204		**Central**	73814	4514	80003				
7	East	Laser Print	1/4	800	18552		**West**	22950	15809	62711				
8	East	Multi-Func	1/4	400	9152		I5=SUMIFS($F$2:$F$1000,$A$2:$A$1000,$H5,$B$2:$B$1000,I$4)							
9	Central	Basic Color	1/5	400	6860		J5=SUMIFS($F$2:$F$1000,$A$2:$A$1000,"East",$B$2:$B$1000,J$4)							
10	East	Basic Color	1/7	400	8456									
11	East	Laser Print	1/7	1000	21730		*Sum the Revenue between the date range and Quantity less than 600*							
12	West	Multi-Func	1/7	600	13806		1/3/2012	1/5/2012						
13	Central	Basic Color	1/9	800	16416		25216							
14	East	Multi-Func	1/9	900	21015		=SUMIFS(F2:F1000,C2:C1000,">" & I12,C2:C1000,"<=" & J12,D2:D1000,"<600")							

FIGURE 6.13

SUMIFS sums a column based on one or more criteria.

SUMPRODUCT

The SUMPRODUCT function multiplies corresponding components in argument arrays of the same size and returns the sum of the products. For example, if array1 is A1:A10 and array2 is B1:B10, the function is actually doing this: ((A1*B1)+(A2*B2)+(A3*B3)...(A10*B10)).

NOTE Although the arrays do not have to be the same rows, as in the preceding example, they must be the same size. So if array1 has 10 rows, array2 must also have 10 rows.

The syntax of the function is (optional arguments are in square brackets) as follows:

SUMPRODUCT(array1, [array2], [array3], ...)

SUMPRODUCT can also be used as a multiple criteria lookup, returning the sum of the values matching the criteria. This was a common use for the function before SUMIFS was introduced in Excel 2007 and is still useful if you're sending a workbook to legacy Excel users.

The function can deal only with numbers. If the lookup values are strings, Excel has to be tricked into treating them like numbers. You can do this by placing a "--" (two unary minuses) in front of the comparison argument, like this: --(C1:C5="Karen").

When the function does the comparison (C1=Karen), it returns TRUE or FALSE. The first unary minus changes a TRUE to a -1 and a FALSE to -0 (there is no such thing as -0, so you would see 0 only if you looked into it). The second unary minus negates the first, changing TRUE to 1 and FALSE to 0. Now we have 1s and 0s, numbers that can be multiplied together with the value to sum.

Figure 6.14 shows a detailed breakdown of how the function works to do a sum with multiple criteria that include text values. Column A lists the number of printers and scanners sold by Karen and Joe. G1 uses SUMPRODUCT to calculate the number of printers sold by Karen.

	A	B	C	D	E	F	G	H	I	J	K	L	M
1	10	Printer	Joe		**Printers sold by Karen**		7						
2	6	Scanner	Karen										
3	9	Scanner	Joe		=SUMPRODUCT(--(C1:C5="Karen"),--(B1:B5="Printer"),A1:A5)								
4	5	Printer	Karen		=SUMPRODUCT(--(FALSE,TRUE,FALSE,TRUE,TRUE),--(TRUE,FALSE,FALSE,TRUE,TRUE),(10,6,9,5,2))								
5	2	Printer	Karen		=SUMPRODUCT((0,-1,0,-1,-1),(-1,0,0,-1,-1),(10,6,9,5,2))								
6					=SUMPRODUCT((0,1,0,1,1),(1,0,0,1,1),(10,6,9,5,2))								
7													
8					Karen	Printer	Value	Karen*Printer*Value					
9					0	1	10	0					
10					1	0	6	0					
11					0	0	9	0					
12					1	1	5	5					
13					1	1	2	2					
14								0+0+0+5+2 = 7					
15													

FIGURE 6.14

SUMPRODUCT can be used to do a multiple criteria lookup of text values.

Starting in E3, you can see the steps SUMPRODUCT takes to calculate the value. E3 shows the original formula in G1. E4 shows the first step into the calculation where Excel "opens" up the array and does the logic comparison (does C1 = Karen?) or lookup (A1=10, A2=6, etc.).

E5 uses the first unary minus to convert the TRUE and FALSE results to their numerical values of 0 and -1. E6 uses the second unary minus to convert any -1 values to 1.

The table starting at E8 shows the numerical values in a table layout so you can see the actual calculation. As you read across a row, multiply each value. For example, in row 9, it's 0*1*10=0. Once each row value is calculated (column H), the values from each row are added together, as shown in H14, giving us the final result, 7.

Logical Functions

Logical functions allow decision making to be used on spreadsheets, either on their own, such as the IF function, or combined with other functions, such as the AND function.

The logical functions are (optional arguments are in square brackets) as follows:

- **IF**—Specifies a logical test to perform, returning one value if the formula evaluates to TRUE and another if it evaluates to FALSE. The function syntax is

  IF(logical_test, [value_if_true], [value_if_false])

- **IFERROR**—Returns the value specified if the formula evaluates to an error; otherwise, returns the result of the formula. The function syntax is

  IFERROR(value, value_if_error)

- **AND**—Returns TRUE if all its arguments are TRUE. Returns FALSE if any of the arguments evaluate to FALSE. The function syntax is

  AND(logical1, [logical2], ...)

- **OR**—Returns TRUE if any of its arguments are TRUE. Returns FALSE if all the arguments evaluate to FALSE. The function syntax is

  OR(logical1, [logical2, ...])

- **NOT**—Reverses the logic of its arguments. The function syntax is

  NOT(logical)

- **TRUE**—Returns TRUE. TRUE can be entered directly into cells and formulas; it is provided as a function for compatibility with other spreadsheet applications.

- **FALSE**—Returns FALSE. FALSE can be entered directly into cells and formulas; it is provided as a function for compatibility with other spreadsheet applications.

IF/AND/OR/NOT

If you were to read an IF statement aloud, it would sound like this: "If this is true, then do this, else do this." The first argument of an IF statement is a logic test usually using at least one of the comparison operators in Table 6.1. If the comparison resolves to TRUE, the second argument is returned to the cell. If the comparison resolves to FALSE, the third argument is returned.

TABLE 6.1 Comparison Operators

Comparison Operator	Definition	Example
>	Greater than	A1>B1
<	Less than	A1<B1
=	Equal to	A1=100
>=	Greater than or equal to	A1>=0
<=	Less than or equal to	A1<=B1
<>	Not equal to	A1<>"Karen"

The second and third arguments can be numbers, text, formulas, or functions. If text, the words must be enclosed in quotations marks, unless returning TRUE or FALSE, because these are functions in their own right.

AND, OR, and NOT can be used to expand the first argument, allowing multiple comparisons or reversing a comparison. Figure 6.15 shows four examples of combining these functions to compare the data in columns A, B, and C in multiple ways. Below the title of each example is an example of the formula being used. All three calculated rows in each example use the same formula. The following sections review these examples.

Basic IF

Cells D1:D5 show an example of a basic IF statement "If the value under Q2 is greater than the value under Q1, then put Gain in the cell, else, put Loss."

IF/NOT

Cells E1:E5 show an example of an IF statement using NOT to reverse the results of the logical test. The logical test is B4+C4<5000 and the result is FALSE (6346<5000). The use of NOT reverses the result, changing the FALSE to TRUE. So now, the IF statement would be read "If the sum of Q1 and Q2 is not less than 5000, then put Above 5000 in the cell, else, put Below 5000."

IF/AND

Cells D7:D11 show an example of an IF statement using AND to do multiple logical tests. If both logical tests return TRUE, then the overall result is TRUE. But if just one of the tests returns FALSE, then the result is FALSE. The IF statement would be read "If Q1 and Q2 are both greater than 2000, then put TRUE in the cell, else, put FALSE."

IF/OR

Cells E7:E11 show an example of an IF statement using OR to do multiple logical tests. If either of the logical tests returns TRUE, then the overall result is TRUE. The only way to have FALSE returned is if both logical tests return FALSE. The IF statement would be read "If either Q1 or Q2 is greater than 2000, then put TRUE in the cell, else, put FALSE."

	A	B	C	D	E
1	**Sales**			**Basic IF**	**IF / NOT**
2		**Q1**	**Q2**	D3=IF(C3>B3,"Gain","Loss")	E4 = IF(NOT(B4+C4<5000),"Above 5000", "Below 5000")
3	John	1396	3239	Gain	Below 5000
4	Karen	4338	2008	Loss	Above 5000
5	Sara	1500	1980	Gain	Below 5000
6					
7				**IF / AND**	**IF / OR**
8				D9 = IF(AND(B3>2000,C3>2000),TRUE,FALSE)	E11 = IF(OR(B5>2000,C5>2000),TRUE,FALSE)
9				FALSE	TRUE
10				TRUE	TRUE
11				FALSE	FALSE

FIGURE 6.15

Use AND, OR, or NOT with IF statements to expand on the type of comparison the function can do.

Nested IF Statements

A nested IF statement is when an IF statement is used as an argument within an IF statement, like this:

=IF(A1>B1, IF(B1>C1,0,IF(D1=C1,D1*B1,A1)),FALSE)

The above could be read "If A1 is greater than B1, then check if B1 is greater than C1. If it is, put 0 in the cell. Else, check if D1=C1 and if it is calculate D1*B1, else, put the value from A1 in the cell. But if A1 is not greater than B1, then put FALSE in the cell." The second and third IF statements only get checked if the first IF statement is TRUE and the third statement only gets checked if the second one is FALSE.

Excel 2007, 2010, and 2013 allow 64 nested IF statements, but if you're sharing the workbook with legacy Excel users, you're limited to seven nested IF statements. Also, too many nested IF statements can be difficult to read, though you can use Alt+Enter to force line breaks in a formula. An alternative is to create a user-defined function using Select Case statements. For more information on this, refer to Chapter 15, "An Introduction to Using Macros and UDFs."

Another alternative may be to rethink your formula and consider a different setup and function. Let's say you need to calculate the commission for your salespeople. You may be tempted to do nested IF statements, but there are other solutions, some of which might be easier to read and update. Instead of putting all those values into the formula, place them in a table, and use a combination of the OFFSET and MATCH functions. See the section "OFFSET and MATCH" for a more detailed example.

IFERROR

CAUTION   The IFERROR function works only in Excel 2007, 2010, and 2013. If you're sharing the workbook with legacy Excel users, you will not be able to use this function.

If there's a chance a formula may return an error, use the IFERROR function to prevent the error from appearing in the cell. Instead of an error, a text message or other value may appear.

In Figure 6.16, the top table uses a straightforward division formula (see formula in cell G5) to calculate the unit price. In cell F9, the column is summed, but returns an error because of the error in cell F5.

The bottom table in Figure 6.16 uses IFERROR to return the text "No Sales" if an error occurs in the calculation, as shown in cell F12. In cell F17, the SUM function is used again, but this time there isn't an error in the range to throw Excel off, and so the sum is calculated.

▲	A	B	C	D	E	F	G	H	I
1	Region	Product	Date	Quantity	Revenue	Unit Price			
2	East	Multi-Func	1/1/2012	1000	22810	22.81			
3	Central	Laser Print	1/2/2012	200	2257	11.285			
4	East	Basic Color	1/2/2012	500	10245	20.49			
5	Central	Multi-Func	1/3/2012	0	0	#DIV/0!	=E5/D5		
6	Central	Multi-Func	1/4/2012	400	9204	23.01			
7	East	Laser Print	1/4/2012	800	18552	23.19			
8	East	Multi-Func	1/4/2012	400	11240	28.1			
9						#DIV/0!	=SUM(F2:F8)		
10									
11	Central	Basic Color	1/5/2012	400	8456	21.14			
12	East	Basic Color	1/7/2012	0	0	No Sales	=IFERROR(E12/D12,"No Sales")		
13	East	Laser Print	1/7/2012	1000	21730	21.73			
14	West	Multi-Func	1/7/2012	600	13806	23.01			
15	Central	Basic Color	1/9/2012	800	16416	20.52			
16	East	Multi-Func	1/9/2012	900	21015	23.35			
17						109.75	=SUM(F11:F16)		

FIGURE 6.16

Use IFERROR to resolve potential problems in calculations before they arise.

Date and Time Functions

Dates and times in Excel are not stored the same way we're used to seeing them. For example, you may type 9/8/12 into a cell, but Excel actually sees 41160. That number, 41160, is called a date serial number. The formatted value, 9/8/12, is called a date value. Storing dates and times as serial numbers allows Excel to do date and time calculations.

Time serial numbers are stored as decimals, starting at 0.0 for 12:00 a.m. and ending at 0.999988425925926 for 11:59:59 p.m. The rest of the day's decimal values are equivalent to their calculated percentage, based on the number of hours in a day, 24. For example, 1:00 a.m. is 1/24 or .04166. 6:00 p.m. would be the 18th hour of the day, 18/24 = 0.75.

Understanding how Excel stores dates and times is important so that you can successfully use formulas and functions when calculating with dates and times.

You might already be familiar with the functions that return the system date and time. DATE() returns the system date. NOW() returns the system date and time. The next few sections review additional functions in Excel for dealing with dates and times.

Functions to Convert and Break Down Dates

Table 6.2 lists the functions that can convert a date value to its serial value, or vice versa. It also lists the functions that can return part of a date, such as the month. The date used in the examples is September 8, 2012.

NOTE When there are multiple codes or return types that can be used, an in-cell tip appears to show you the choices. Not all choices may be listed in Table 6.2.

Table 6.2 Date Conversion Functions

Function	Description	Example
DATE (year, month, day)	Returns the serial number of a date. Note: Because Excel automatically reformats date cells, you may have to format the cell to General yourself.	=DATE(2012,9,8) returns 41160
DATEVALUE (date_text)	Converts a text date to a serial number. If you try to use a date value, the function will return an error.	=DATEVALUE("9/8/12") returns 41160
DAY (serial_number)	Returns the day from a serial number.	=DAY(41160) returns 8
MONTH (serial_number)	Returns the month from a serial number.	=MONTH(DATEVALUE("9/8/12")) returns 9
YEAR (serial_number)	Returns the year from a serial number.	=YEAR(41160) returns 2012
EDATE[1] (start_date, months)	Returns the serial number of the date indicated by the months before or after the start date. The start_date must be the serial number of the date. The returned date will be the same day as the start date. Use a negative months value to return a previous month.	=EDATE(DATEVALUE("9/8/12"),3) returns 41251, which is 12/8/12
EOMONTH[1] (start_date, months)	Returns the serial number of the last day of the month indicated by the months before or after the start date. The start_date must be the serial number of the date. Use a negative months value to return a previous month.	=EOMONTH(41160, -3) returns 41090, which is 6/30/2012
WEEKDAY (serial_number, [return_type])	Converts a serial number to a day of the week. Return_type is a value expressing what Excel should consider the first and last day of the week. The default is 1, meaning 1 is Sunday and 7 is Saturday.	=WEEKDAY(41160) returns 7, which is Saturday. =WEEKDAY(41160,3) returns 5 because the value 3 code tells the function to count Monday as the beginning of the week starting with 0 and ending with 6 for Sunday.

Function	Description	Example
WEEKNUM[1] (serial_number, [return_type])	Converts a serial number to a week number representing what week of the year the date falls on. There are two systems used by this function, with the return type determining which system is used. System 1 counts the week with January 1 as the first week of the year. System 2 counts the week with the first Thursday of the year as the first week. Return_type is a value expressing what day of the week is the beginning of the week. The default is 1 – the week begins on Sunday. Use 2 if the week needs to begin on Monday. Both of these are System 1 values. If you need to use a System 2 calendar, use 21, which also starts the week on a Monday.	=WEEKNUM(41160) returns 36, with the week starting on Sunday. =WEEKNUM(41160, 2) returns 37 because the week doesn't begin until Monday.

[1]Function was originally part of the Analysis Toolpak. If you send the workbook to a legacy Excel user who does not have the toolpak installed or active, the function will return an error.

Function to Convert and Break Down Times

Table 6.3 lists the functions that can convert a time value to its serial value or vice versa. It also lists the functions that can return a part of a time, such as the hour. The time used in the examples is 4:53 p.m.

 NOTE When there are multiple codes or return types that can be used, an in-cell tip appears to show you the choices. Not all choices may be listed in Table 6.3.

TABLE 6.3 Time Conversion Functions

Function	Description	Example
TIME PM(hour, minute, second)	Returns the time value of the specified time based on a 24-hour clock	=TIME(16,53,0) returns 4:53
TIMEVALUE time_text)	Converts a time in the form of text to a serial number	=TIMEVALUE("4:53 PM") returns 0.70347

Function	Description	Example
HOUR (serial_number)	Returns the hour as a serial number, based on a 24-hour clock	=HOUR(0.70347) returns 16, which is 4 PM
MINUTE (serial_number)	Returns the minutes as a serial number	=MINUTE(TIMEVALUE("4:53 PM")) returns 53
SECOND (serial_number)	Returns the seconds as a serial number	=SECOND(0.70347) returns 0

Using Date Calculation Functions

 CAUTION   The following functions were originally part of the Analysis Toolpak add-in. If you send the workbook to a legacy Excel user who does not have the add-in installed or active, the function will return an error.

Table 6.4 lists functions that return calculated information, such as the end date based on a starting date, or the number of days between two dates. The date used in the examples is September 8, 2012. Square brackets denote optional arguments.

 NOTE   When there are multiple codes or return types that can be used, an in-cell tip appears to show you the choices. Not all choices may be listed in Table 6.4.

TABLE 6.4 Date Calculation Functions

Function	Description	Example
WORKDAY (start_date, days, [holidays])	Returns the serial number of the date before or after a specified number of workdays. Holidays can be a range of dates, or an array constant list of serial dates.	=WORKDAY(DATEVALUE("9/8/2012"),3) returns 41164, which is 9/12/2012 =WORKDAY(DATEVALUE("9/8/2012"), 60,{41060, 41094}) 41060 is the serial value of May 31, 2012. 41094 is the serial value of July 4, 2012. DATEVALUE cannot be used within the array constant. Also the curly brackets are entered manually; this is not an array formula. If you have a lot of holidays, it would be easier to select a range.

WORKDAY.INTL (start_date, days, [weekend], [holidays])	Returns the serial number of the date before or after a specified number of workdays, taking into account which days during the week are considered weekends and what dates are holidays. Weekend is a code value. Holidays can be a range of dates, or an array constant list of serial dates.	=WORKDAY.INTL(41160,10,3) returns 41174, which is 9/22/12. The code value of 3 tells Excel Monday, Tuesday are to be considered weekends.
NETWORKDAYS (start_date, end_date, [holidays])	Returns the number of workdays between two dates. Holidays can be a range of dates, or an array constant list of serial dates.	=NETWORKDAYS(41160,DATEVALUE("9/30/12")) returns 15.
NETWORKDAYS.INTL (start_date, end_date, [weekend], [holidays])	Returns the number of workdays between two days, taking into account which days during the week are considered weekends and what dates are holidays. Weekend is a code value. Holidays can be a range of dates, or an array constant list of serial dates.	=NETWORKDAYS.INTL(41160,DATEVALUE("9/30/12"),3) returns 17. The code value of 3 tells Excel Monday, Tuesday are to be considered weekends.
YEARFRAC (start_date, end_date, [basis])	Returns a decimal year value of the number of whole days between dates. Basis is a code value of the type of date count basis to use.	=YEARFRAC(DATE(2012,1,1),DATE(2013,1,1)) returns 1. The basis count of 0, the default, instructs Excel to count the days based on 30/360 American plan. =YEARFRAC(DATE(2012,1,1),DATE(2013,1,1),3) returns 1.002739. The basis code of 3 instructs Excel to count the actual days between the dates divided by 365.

Calculating Days Between Dates

If you need to find the number of days between two dates on a sheet, you can enter a direct formula, such as =F21-F20. After pressing Enter, you may get an odd answer, such as 1/25/1900. You didn't have the formula cell formatted as date, but because the arguments are dates, Excel feels the answer should also be formatted as one. There's nothing you can do about this—you will have to manually format the cell as General to get the actual number of days between the dates.

If you get a ###### error, the formula is trying to subtract a new date from an older date.

Calculating Overtime

You have a sheet similar to the one in Figure 6.17 where start and end times are entered; then the number of hours worked each day are calculated by subtracting the start time from the end time. At the end of the week, all the times are added together—and you get a number that is most definitely not correct, as shown in cell D7.

⊿	A	B	C	D	E	F	G
1		Start	End	Time Elapsed			
2	Monday	9:00 AM	5:00 PM	8:00	=C2-B2		
3	Tuesday	9:00 AM	5:00 PM	8:00			
4	Wednesday	8:30 AM	5:00 PM	8:30			
5	Thursday	9:00 AM	5:00 PM	8:00			
6	Friday	9:00 AM	6:00 PM	9:00			
7	Total			17:30	=SUM(D2:D6) formatted h:mm		
8				41:30	=SUM(D2:D6) formatted [h]:mm		
9				1:30	=MAX(0,D8-(40/24))		

FIGURE 6.17

Use the proper time format to see the calculated time.

The problem isn't the method of summing the column, but instead, the format applied to the cell. The standard format of h:mm can't handle more than 24 hours. To get Excel to show more than 24 hours, change the format of the calculated cell to [h]:mm, as shown in cell D8.

 NOTE See the section on date and time formatting in Chapter 4 for more details on time formats.

If you have a sheet with daily work times, and you need to calculate the total number of hours worked and also the overtime, follow these steps:

1. For each workday, calculate the time elapsed, as shown in cell E2 of Figure 6.17.

2. Select the range of elapsed time.

3. Go to Home, Editing, and click the AutoSum button.

4. Right-click the cell containing the totaled time and select Format Cells.

5. On the Number tab, select the Custom category.

6. In the Type field, enter `[h]:mm`. Click OK to return to the sheet.

7. In the overtime cell, enter a MAX function that returns the greater of 0 or the calculated overtime. To calculate the overtime, divide the number at which overtime begins (example 40) by 24. Take that calculation and subtract it from the calculated time, as shown in cell D9.

8. Right-click the cell containing the overtime and select Format Cells.

9. On the Number tab, select the Custom category.

10. In the Type field, enter `[h]:mm`. Click OK to return to the sheet. This is a precaution in case the amount of overtime exceeds 24 hours.

Troubleshooting Dates and Times Stored as Strings

As long as the dates on a sheet are serial dates, you can perform a variety of calculations with them. If you receive a sheet where the dates are stored as strings (you may see '4/19/12 in a cell and your formulas don't work), there are two ways to convert the dates: either using Paste Special to add a blank cell onto the range or using text to columns to convert the column.

Using Paste Special to Convert Text to Dates and Times

To convert text dates to real dates using paste special, follow these steps:

1. Copy a blank cell.

2. Select the range of text dates to convert.

3. Go to Home, Clipboard, Paste, Paste Special, and select Add.

4. Click OK and the text dates will convert to dates that can be formatted and that Excel can do calculations with.

Using Text to Columns to Convert Text to Dates and Times

To convert a column of text dates to real dates using text to columns, follow these steps:

1. Select the range of text dates.

2. Go to Data, Data Tools, Text to Columns.

3. From the wizard dialog box that appears, make sure Delimited is selected and click Next.

4. In step 2, make sure the Space delimiter is *not* selected. Any other delimiter not being used in your cell can be selected. Click Next.

5. In step 3, select the Date option then the desired format.

6. Click Finish and the text dates/times will convert to dates/times that can be formatted and that Excel can do calculations with.

Goal Seek

Goal Seek, found under Data, Data Tools, What-If Analysis, adjusts the value of a cell to get a specific result from another cell. For example, if you have the price, term, and rate of a loan, you can use the PMT function to calculate the payment. But what if the calculated payment wasn't satisfactory and you wanted to recalculate with additional prices? You could take the time to enter a variety of prices, recalculating the payment. Or use Goal Seek to tell Excel what you want the payment to be and let it calculate the price for you. A couple of things to keep in mind when using Goal Seek:

*   You must have the formula in the Set Cell. Goal Seek works by plugging in values into your existing formula.

*   A clear mathematical relationship between the starting and ending cells must exist.

Figure 6.18 calculates the monthly payment in cell B4 based on the price, term, and rate. I've decided I can make a larger monthly payment, but instead of entering prices, I'll use Goal Seek to tell Excel my desired payment and have it figure out what value in the price cell will bring me closest to my payment. To do so, follow these steps:

1. Select cell B4, which is the cell whose value you want to be a specific value.

2. Go to Data, Data Tools, What-If Analysis, Goal Seek.

3. In the Set Cell field should be the address of the cell selected in step 1. If not, select the cell whose value you want sought.

4. In the To Value field, enter the value you want the Set Cell to be, such as **630**.

5. In the By Changing Cell field, select the cell whose value you want Excel to change so the Set Cell field calculates to the desired value, in this case, cell B1.

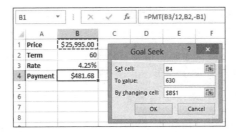

FIGURE 6.18

Use Goal Seek to find one value by changing one in another cell.

6. Click OK. Excel attempts to return a solution as close to the desired value as possible. If it succeeds, a message box appears showing the target value and the actual value it attained.

Using the Function Arguments Dialog Box to Troubleshoot Formulas

 NOTE Refer to the "Error Messages" section in Chapter 5, "Using Formulas," for more information on actual error messages.

If you have one function using other functions as arguments and the formula returns an error, you can use the Function Arguments dialog box to track down which function is generating the error. To do this, place your cursor in the function name in the formula bar and click the fx button to the left of the formula. The dialog box opens, with the selected function filled in. You can review the arguments to make sure they are correct and falling into the correct fields. To check the next function, click the function name in the formula bar—you do not need to close the dialog box and start from the beginning.

Figure 6.19 shows a commission table returning incorrect values in the range C8:C11. The formula uses two functions, so it's difficult to say exactly which one is the problem. To use the Function Arguments dialog box to inspect the formula and find the problem, follow these steps:

1. Select the cell with the formula to troubleshoot.

2. Place your cursor in the first function OFFSET in the formula bar.

3. Click the fx button to the left of the formula bar. The Function Arguments dialog box opens for the selected function, with its arguments filled in.

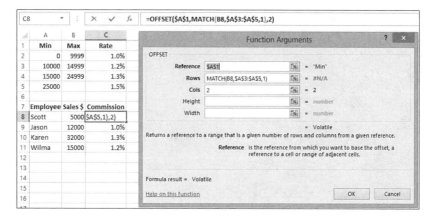

FIGURE 6.19

Use the Function Arguments dialog box to narrow down which function is causing a problem.

4. If you see the error in the selected function, you can fix it and click OK to recalculate the formula. Otherwise, continue to the next step.

5. In this case, the #N/A being returned for the Rows field shows that the error is somewhere in the MATCH function. It could be the MATCH function itself, or if that function used another function, you may have to dig deeper. To inspect another function, click it in the formula bar and it will load in the dialog box. In the case of the example, the Lookup_array of the MATCH function is not looking at all the data it needed to—the correct range is $A$2:$A$5.

THE ABSOLUTE MINIMUM

There are over 400 functions available in Excel, but now you know several ways of looking for one you can use. If a single function doesn't exist, you can use multiple functions together to create the desired formula. Be careful, though, if you're sharing a workbook with legacy Excel users—they won't always have the newer functions, such as SUMIFS, available.

IN THIS CHAPTER

- Sort data with one click.
- Sort using a custom, nonalphabetical order.
- Sort by color or icon.
- Rearrange columns with a few clicks of the mouse and keyboard.

7

SORTING DATA

This chapter shows you the various ways you can sort your data, even by color. Sorting data is a significant capability in Excel, allowing you to view data from least to greatest, greatest to least, by color, or even by your own customized sort listing.

Preparing Data

Your data should adhere to a few basic formatting guidelines to make the most of Excel's sorting capabilities:

- There should be no blank rows or columns. The occasional blank cell is acceptable.

- Every column should have a header.

- Headers should be in only one row.

If these guidelines aren't followed, Excel can get confused and is unable to find the entire table or header row on its own. Also, Excel can only work with one header row—any rows after the first header row get treated like data.

Opening the Sort Dialog Box

The Sort dialog box allows up to 64 sort levels. Through the dialog box, you can sort multiple columns by values, cell color, font color, or by conditional formatting cell icons. The sort order can be ascending, descending, or by a custom list (see the section "Sorting with a Custom Sequence"). If your data has headers, they will be listed in the Sort By drop-down; otherwise, the column headings (A, B, C, etc.) will be used.

There are four ways to access the Sort dialog box:

- On the Home tab, select Editing, Sort & Filter, Custom Sort.

- On the Data tab, select Sort & Filter, Sort.

- Right-click any cell and select Sort, Custom Sort.

- From a filter or Table drop-down, select Sort by Color, Custom Sort.

Sorting by Values

When you use the Sort dialog box, Excel applies each sort in the order it appears in the list. In Figure 7.1, the Region column will be sorted first. The Customer column will be sorted second, as outlined in the following steps:

1. Ensure that the data has no blank rows or columns and that each column has a one-row header.

2. Select a cell in the data. Excel will use this cell to determine the location and size of the data table.

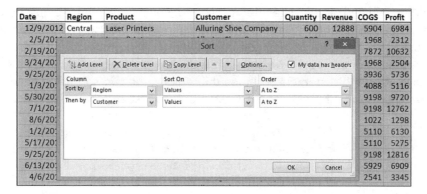

Date	Region	Product	Customer	Quantity	Revenue	COGS	Profit
12/9/2012	Central	Laser Printers	Alluring Shoe Company	600	12888	5904	6984
2/5/20						1968	2312
2/19/20						7872	10632
3/24/20						1968	2504
9/25/20						3936	5736
1/3/20						4088	5116
5/30/20						9198	9720
7/1/20						9198	12762
8/6/20						1022	1298
1/2/20						5110	6130
5/17/20						5110	5275
9/25/20						9198	12816
6/13/20						5929	6909
4/6/20						2541	3345

FIGURE 7.1

Use the Sort dialog box to sort data by multiple levels.

3. Go to Home, Editing, Sort & Filter, Custom Sort to open the Sort dialog box.

4. Make sure the My Data Has Headers check box is selected. Excel will not select the headers themselves, only the data.

5. Make sure all the data's columns and rows are selected. If they are not all selected, a blank column or row exists, confusing Excel as to the size of your table. Exit from the Sort dialog box, delete the blank columns and rows, and start the process again.

 NOTE If for some reason you can't delete the blank columns or rows, then preselect the entire table before opening the Sort dialog box.

6. From the Sort By drop-down, select the first column header, Region, to sort by.

7. From the Sort On drop-down, select Values.

8. From the Order drop-down, select the order by which the column's data should be sorted, A to Z.

9. To add another sort column, this time for Customer, click Add Level and repeat steps 6 to 8. Repeat these steps until all the columns to sort by are configured, as shown in Figure 7.1.

10. If you realize that a field is in the wrong position, use the up or down arrows at the top of the dialog box to move the field to the correct location.

11. Click OK to sort the data.

When you look at the data after it is sorted, you'll notice the regions are grouped together; for example, Central will be at the top of the list. Within Central, the customer names will be alphabetized. If you scroll down to the next region, East, the customer names will be alphabetized within that region. If the data should have listed the customers and then the regions, the two sort fields need to be switched so that Excel sorts the Customer field first and the Region field second.

 TIP Normally, Excel doesn't pay attention to case when sorting text: ABC is the same as abc. If case is important in the sort, you need to direct Excel to include case as a parameter. This is done by clicking the Options button in the Sort dialog box. If Case Sensitive is selected, Excel will sort lowercase values before uppercase values in an ascending sort.

Sorting by Color or Icon

Although sorting by values is the most typical use of sorting, Excel can also sort data by fill color, font color, or an icon set from conditional formatting. You can apply fill and font colors through conditional formatting or the cell format icons.

In addition to sorting colors and icons through the Sort dialog box, the following options are also available when you right-click a cell and select Sort from the context menu:

- Put Selected Cell Color on Top

- Put Selected Font Color on Top

- Put Selected Cell Icon on Top

If you use one of the preceding options to sort more than one color or icon, the most recent selection is placed above the previous selection. So, if yellow rows should be placed before the red rows, sort the red rows first, and then sort the yellow rows.

In Figure 7.2, conditional formatting was used to highlight in red the top 10 profit record, and yellow was used to highlight the ones in the bottom 10%. The data was then sorted using the following steps so that the red cells are at the top and the yellow directly beneath:

Region	Product	Date	Customer	Quantity	Revenue	COGS	Profit
Central	Laser Pri	1/2/2012	Alluring Shoe Company	500	11240	5110	6130
Central	Multi-Fu	1/26/2012	Alluring Shoe Company	500	10445	4235	6210
Central	Basic Col	2/19/2012	Alluring Shoe Company	800	18504	7872	10632
Central	Multi-Fu	8/21/2012	Alluring Shoe Company	800	15544	6776	8768
Central	Laser Pri	9/25/2012	Alluring Shoe Company	900	22014	9198	12816
Central	Laser Pri	5/30/2012	Alluring Shoe Company	900	18918	9198	9720
Central	Multi-Fu	6/13/2012	Alluring Shoe Company	700	12838	5929	6909
Central	Laser Pri	7/1/2012	Alluring Shoe Company	900	21960	9198	12762
Central	Multi-Fu	9/26/2012	Alluring Shoe Company	900	17712	7623	10089
Central	Basic Col	12/9/2012	Alluring Shoe Company	600	12888	5904	6984
Central	Laser Pri	8/6/2012	Alluring Shoe Company	100	2320	1022	1298
Central	Multi-Fu	12/26/2012	Alluring Shoe Company	100	1861	847	1014
Central	Laser Pri	1/3/2012	Alluring Shoe Company	400	9204	4088	5116

FIGURE 7.2

You can use the Sort dialog box to sort cells by more than just their values, such as the cell color.

1. Ensure that the data has no blank rows or columns and that each column has a one-row header.

2. Select a cell in the data. Excel will use this cell to determine the location and size of the data and highlight what it sees as the data table.

3. Right-click the cell and select Sort, Custom Sort.

4. Make sure the My Data Has Headers check box in the upper-right corner is selected. Excel will not select the headers themselves.

5. Make sure all the data's columns are selected. If they are not all selected, a blank column exists, confusing Excel as to the size of your table.

6. From the Sort By drop-down, select the first column header to sort by, Profit.

7. From the Sort On drop-down, select Cell Color.

8. From the first Order drop-down, select the color by which the column's data should be sorted.

9. From the second Order drop-down, select whether the color should be sorted to the top or bottom of the data. If you select multiple colors to sort at the top of the data, the colors will still appear in the order chosen.

10. Click Add Level to include the yellow Profit cells in the sort and repeat steps 6 to 9. Repeat these steps until all the columns to sort by are configured.

11. If you realize a field is in the wrong order, use the up or down arrows to move it to the correct location.

12. Click OK to sort the data.

 TIP If your data is formatted as a Table (Insert, Tables, Table) you don't have to go through the Custom Sort dialog box. Instead, click the arrow in the header, go to Sort by Color, and select the color you want sorted to the top of the table.

Using the Quick Sort Buttons

CAUTION Sort options are retained for a sheet during a session. So if you set up a custom sort with the Case Sensitive option turned on and then do a quick sort, the quick sort will be case sensitive.

The quick sort buttons offer one-click access to sorting cell values. They do not work with colors or icons. There are four ways to get to the quick sort buttons:

- On the Home tab, select Editing, Sort & Filter, Sort A to Z[1] or Sort Z to A[1].

- On the Data tab, select Sort & Filter, AZ or ZA.

- Right-click any cell and select Sort, Sort A to Z[1], or Sort Z to A[1].

- From a filter drop-down, select Sort A to Z[1] or Sort Z to A[1].

The quick sort buttons are very useful when sorting a single column. When sorting just one column, make sure you select just one cell in the column. If you select more than one cell, Excel sorts the selection, not the column. It prompts to verify that this is the action you want taken before doing it. Also ensure there are no adjacent columns or Excel will want to include them in the sort. If there are adjacent columns, select the entire column before sorting.

If you use the quick sort buttons to sort a table of more than one column, Excel sorts the entire table automatically. Because there is no dialog box, it's very important that every column have a header. If just one header is missing, Excel will not treat the header row as such and will include it in the sorted data.

TIP If you have filters turned on for the table, Excel automatically treats the row where the filter arrows are as the header row.

Quick Sorting Multiple Columns

If you keep in mind that Excel keeps previously organized columns in order as new columns are sorted, you can use this to sort multiple columns. For example, if the Customer column is organized, Excel doesn't randomize the data in that column when the Region column is sorted. Instead, Customer retains its order to the

---

[1]The actual button text may change depending on the type of data in the cell. For example, if the column contains values, the text will be Sort Smallest to Largest. If the column contains text, it will be Sort A to Z.

degree it falls within the Region sort. The trick is to apply the sorts in reverse to how they would be set up in the Sort dialog box.

To manually perform the "Sort by Values" example shown in Figure 7.2, follow these steps:

1. Make sure all columns have headers. If even one column header is missing, Excel will not sort the data properly.

2. Select a cell in the column that should be sorted last, the Customer column.

3. Click the desired quick sort button on Data, Sort & Filter.

4. Select a cell in the next column, Region, to be sorted.

5. Click the desired quick sort button on Data, Sort & Filter.

6. The table is now sorted by Region and then Customers within each region.

Randomly Sorting Data

Excel doesn't have a built-in tool to do a random sort, but by using the RAND function in a column by the data and then sorting, you can create your own randomizer. For example, you have your alphabetical list of students ready to give their project presentations. Instead of going in alphabetical order, you can randomize the list by following these steps:

1. Add a new column to the right of the data. Give the column a header, such as Random.

2. In the first cell of the new column, type **=RAND()** and press Ctrl+Enter (this keeps the formula cell as the active cell). The formula will calculate a value between 0 and 1.

3. Double-click the fill handle in the lower-right corner of the cell to copy the formula to the rest of the rows in the column.

4. Select one cell in the new column.

5. Go to Home, Editing, Sort & Filter, AZ. The list will be sorted in a random sequence, as shown in Figure 7.3.

6. Delete the data in the temporary column that you added in step 1.

B2	▾	:	✕ ✓	fx	=RAND()

	A	B
1	**Student Name**	**Random**
2	Thomas Stewart	0.516564
3	Susan Halloran	0.252405
4	Anja Kennedy	0.106298
5	Clara Hill	0.091251
6	Stephanie Lennon	0.944626

FIGURE 7.3

Randomly sort the list of students with the RAND function instead of using the expected alphabetical order.

 NOTE Right after Excel performs the sort, it recalculates the formula in the temporary column, so it may appear that the numbers are out of sequence.

Sorting with a Custom Sequence

At times, data might need to be sorted in a custom sequence that is neither alphabetical nor numerical. For example, you might want to sort by month, by weekday, or by some custom sequence of your own. You can do this by sorting by a custom list.

Within the Sort dialog box, you can select Custom List from the Order field for each level of sort configured. When this option is selected, the Custom Lists dialog box opens, from which you can select the custom list to sort the selected column by.

The data table in Figure 7.4 has three types of printers: Basic ColorJet, Laser, and Multi-Function. You need to sort the data by Laser, ColorJet, then Multi-Function, but that isn't alphabetical or reverse alphabetical. To do this sort, first create a custom list with the exact text used in the table. Then, you can sort the table by your custom list. To create a custom list and sort your data by it, follow these steps:

1. Ensure that the data has no blank rows or columns and that each column has a one-row header.

2. Select a cell in the data. Excel will use this cell to determine the location and size of the data.

3. Go to Home, Editing, Sort & Filter, Custom Sort to open the Sort dialog box.

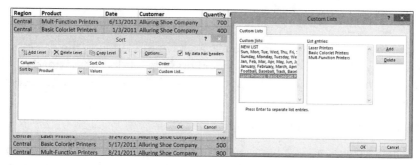

FIGURE 7.4

Data can be sorted by a custom list, such as a specific order of products.

4. Make sure the My Data Has Headers check box in the upper-right corner is selected. Excel will not select the headers themselves.

5. Make sure all the columns and rows are selected. If they are not all selected, a blank column or row exists, confusing Excel as to the size of your data. Exit from the Sort dialog box, remove the blank column or rows, and then return to the Sort dialog box.

6. From the Sort By drop-down, select the column header, Product, to sort by.

7. From the Sort On drop-down, select Values.

8. From the Order drop-down, select Custom List. The Custom Lists dialog box, shown in Figure 7.4, appears.

9. The list box on the left provides a list of available custom lists. Selecting one will display all the entries in the right list box. Select the desired list and click OK.

 NOTE Refer to the "Creating Your Own Series" section in Chapter 3, "Getting Data onto a Sheet," for instructions on creating your own custom list.

10. If you need to sort by other columns, click Add Level. Otherwise, skip to step 13.

11. Repeat steps 6 to 8. If you don't need to use another custom list, select the desired order from the drop-down instead of Custom List.

12. If you realize that a field is in the wrong order, use the up or down arrows to move it to the correct location.

13. Click OK to sort the data.

Rearranging Columns Using the Sort Dialog Box

If you receive a report where you always have to rearrange the columns to suit yourself, you can use the option of sorting from left to right instead of from top to bottom. To create a custom sort order and then sort your data according to it, follow these steps:

1. Insert a new blank row above the headers.

2. In the new row, type numbers corresponding to the new sequence of the columns, with 1 being the leftmost column, then 2, 3, and so on, until each column has a number denoting its new location.

3. Select a cell in the data range.

4. Press Ctrl+* (or Ctrl+Shift+8) to select the current region, including the two header rows.

5. Go to Home, Editing, Sort & Filter, Custom Sort to open the Sort dialog box.

6. Click the Options button to open the Sort Options dialog box.

7. Select Sort Left to Right.

8. Click OK to return to the Sort dialog box.

9. In the Sort By drop-down, select the row in which the numbers you added in step 2 are located.

10. In the Order drop-down, make sure Smallest to Largest is selected.

11. Click OK and Excel will rearrange the columns.

12. Delete the temporary row added in step 1.

Rearranging Columns Using the Mouse

If you have just a few columns to rearrange, you can use a combination of keyboard shortcuts and the mouse to rearrange them quickly. To quickly move a column to a new position, follow these steps:

1. Select a cell in the column to move.

2. Press Ctrl+Spacebar to select the entire column.

3. Place the cursor on the dark border surrounding the selection, hold down the right mouse button, and drag the column to the new location.

4. When you release the mouse button, a context menu appears, as shown in Figure 7.5. Select Shift Right and Move.

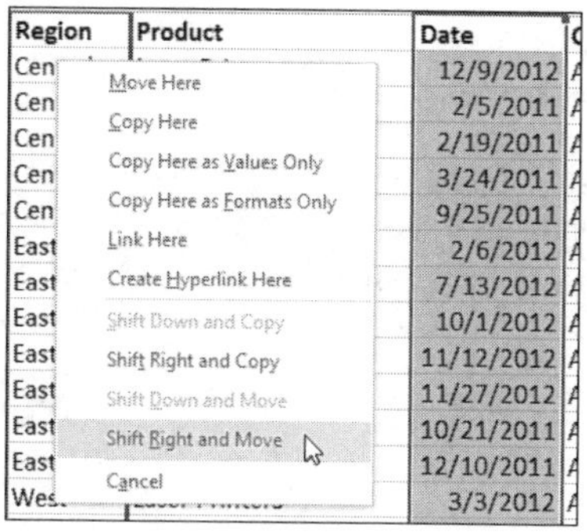

FIGURE 7.5

Use Shift Right and Move to quickly move a column to a new location.

5. The data will rearrange itself, inserting the column in the new location and moving other columns over to the right to make room.

Fixing Sort Problems

If it looks like the data did not sort properly, refer to the following list of possibilities:

*   Make sure no hidden rows or columns exist.

*   Use a single row for headers. If you need a multiline header, either wrap the text in the cell or use Alt+Enter to force line breaks in the cell.

*   If the headers were sorted into the data, there was probably at least one column without a header.

*   Column data should be of the same type. This might not be obvious in a column of ZIP Codes where some, such as 57057 are numbers, but others that start with 0s are actually text. To solve this problem, convert the entire column to text.

*   If sorting by a column containing a formula, Excel will recalculate the column after the sort. If the values change after the recalculation, such as with RAND, it may appear that the sort did not work properly, but it did.

THE ABSOLUTE MINIMUM

Data can be sorted by more than just values. It can be sorted by color, icons, and even custom lists. Sorting can even be used to rearrange column order. Sorting is easily done when data is laid out properly, with no blank columns or rows and with column headers at the top of each column.

IN THIS CHAPTER

- Remove duplicate rows.
- Create a unique list of items.
- Combine information from multiple workbooks.
- Focus on specific data by filtering by values, color, or icon.

8

FILTERING AND CONSOLIDATING DATA

This chapter shows you how to use Excel's filtering functionality to look at just the desired records. It also shows you how to create a list of unique items, delete duplicates, and consolidate data.

Filtering and consolidating data are important tools in Excel, especially when you are dealing with large amounts of data. The filtering tools can quickly reduce the data to the specific records you need to concentrate on. The consolidation tool can bring together information spread between multiple sheets or workbooks.

Preparing Data

To make the most out of Excel's filtering capabilities, your data should adhere to a few basic formatting guidelines:

- There should be no blank rows or columns. The occasional blank cell is acceptable.

- There should be a header above every column.

- Headers should be in only one row.

If these guidelines aren't followed, Excel can get confused and is unable to find the entire table or header row on its own. Also, Excel can only work with one header row—any rows after the first header row get treated like data.

Applying a Filter to a Data Set

Filtering allows you to view only the data you want to see by hiding the other data. You can apply a filter to multiple columns, narrowing down the data. As you filter the data and rows are hidden, the row headers (1, 2, 3, etc.) become blue. Anytime you see blue row headers, you know the data has been filtered. An icon that looks like a funnel will replace the arrow on the column headings that have a filter applied, as shown in the Customer heading in Figure 8.1.

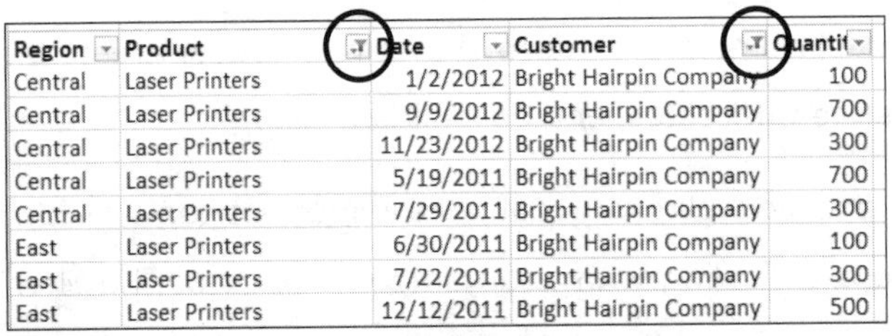

Region ▾	Product	☑ Date ▾	Customer	☑ Quantit ▾
Central	Laser Printers	1/2/2012	Bright Hairpin Company	100
Central	Laser Printers	9/9/2012	Bright Hairpin Company	700
Central	Laser Printers	11/23/2012	Bright Hairpin Company	300
Central	Laser Printers	5/19/2011	Bright Hairpin Company	700
Central	Laser Printers	7/29/2011	Bright Hairpin Company	300
East	Laser Printers	6/30/2011	Bright Hairpin Company	100
East	Laser Printers	7/22/2011	Bright Hairpin Company	300
East	Laser Printers	12/12/2011	Bright Hairpin Company	500

FIGURE 8.1

You can tell which column(s) are filtered by the filter icon where the drop-down arrow used to be.

The Filter button is a toggle button. Click it once to turn filtering on and click it again to turn filtering off. To activate the filtering option, select a single cell in the data set and use one of the following:

- On the Home tab, select Editing, Sort & Filter, Filter.

- On the Data tab, select Sort & Filter, Filter.

- When a data set is turned into a Table (Insert, Tables, Table), the headers automatically become filter headers.

CAUTION It is very important to select only a single cell because it is possible to turn on filtering in the middle of a data set if you have more than one cell selected.

When a filter is applied to a data set, drop-down arrows appear in the column headers. Click on an arrow to open up the Filter dialog box, which remains open until you click OK, Cancel, or click outside the dialog box. One or more selections can be made from each drop-down, filtering the data below the headers. Filters are additive, which means that each time a filter selection is made, it works with the previous selection to further filter the data.

TIP If you have a long list of items or need to widen the dialog box to see the full text of a line, place your cursor over the three dots in the lower-right corner of the dialog box, and click and drag to resize. The change in size will not be saved—you'll need to do it again next time you open the dialog box.

Clearing a Filter

A filter can be cleared from a specific column or for the entire data set. To clear all the filters applied to a data set, use one of the following methods:

- On the Home tab, select Editing, Sort & Filter, Clear.
- On the Data tab, select Sort & Filter, Clear.
- Turn off the filter entirely using one of the following methods:
  - On the Home tab, select Editing, Sort & Filter, Filter.
  - On the Data tab, select Sort & Filter, Filter.

To clear all the filters applied to a specific column, use one of the following methods:

- Click the filter drop-down arrow and select Clear Filter from Column Header.
- Click the filter drop-down arrow and select Select All from the filtering list.
- Right-click a cell in the column to clear and select Filter, Clear Filter from Column Header.

Reapplying a Filter

If data is added to a filtered range, Excel does not automatically update the view to hide any new rows that don't fit the filter settings. You can refresh the filter's settings so they include the new rows through one of the following methods:

- On the Home tab, select Editing, Sort & Filter, Reapply.
- On the Data tab, select Sort & Filter, Reapply.
- Right-click a cell in the filtered data set and select Filter, Reapply.

Turning Filtering On for One Column

Filtering can be turned on for a single column or for two or more adjacent columns. Even though you can only select a filter item in select columns, the filter is applied to the entire table. This can be useful if you want to limit the filtering users can apply. If the sheet is then protected, users cannot turn on filtering for the other columns (see "Allowing Filtering on a Protected Sheet" for more information).

To control what column has filtering, select the header and the first cell directly beneath the header. Then do one of the following:

- On the Home tab, select Editing, Sort & Filter, Filter.
- On the Data tab, select Sort & Filter, Filter.

Filtering for Listed Items

The filter listing, shown in Figure 8.2, is probably the most obvious filter tool when you open the drop-down. For text, numbers, and ungrouped dates, a listing of all unique items in the column appears (see the "Filtering the Grouped Dates Listing" section if dates appear grouped by year and month). All items will be checked because they are all visible the first time you open the drop-down, but you can select just the items that should appear in the data. Any item that no longer bears a check mark will be hidden.

We have a table of the sales of various printers in 2011 and 2012. We want to narrow the table down to Laser Printers sold to Bright Hairpin Company. To filter columns for specific items, follow these steps (if filtering a Table [Insert, Tables, Table], skip to step 3):

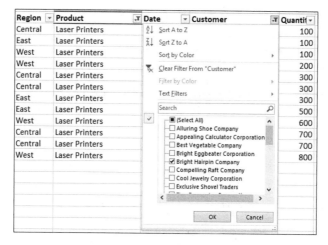

FIGURE 8.2

Filter a column by selecting the item(s) you want to see from the dialog box.

1. Select a single cell in the data set to apply filtering to.

2. Go to Data, Sort & Filter, Filter.

3. Open the drop-down of the Product column.

4. Unselect the Select All item to clear all the check marks in the list.

5. Select Laser Printers and click OK. Now only Laser Printers are shown in the table.

6. Repeat steps 3–5 for the Customer column and Bright Hairpin Company.

7. Click OK. The sheet will update, showing only the items selected.

Filtering the Grouped Dates Listing

NOTE This section applies to dates that are grouped, as shown in Figure 8.3. The grouping is controlled by a setting found under File, Options, Advanced, Display Options for This Workbook, Group Dates in the AutoFilter Menu. By default, this option is selected. If unselected, the dates will appear in a list like the filter for number and text items. You can refer to the section "Filtering for Listed Items" for more information on that type of filter listing.

Dates in the filter listing are grouped by year, month, and day. All items will be checked because they are all visible the first time you open the drop-down, but you can select just the items that should appear in the data. Any item that no longer bears a check mark will be hidden.

If you click the + icon by a year, it opens up, showing the months. Click the + icon by a month and it opens up to show the days of the month. An entire year or month can be selected or unselected by clicking the desired year or month. For example, to deselect 2011 and January 2012 in Figure 8.3, deselect the 2011 group, and then deselect the January group under 2012. The data filters to show only February through December 2012.

FIGURE 8.3

By default, dates are grouped by year and month in the Filter dialog box.

To filter for only June 12–14, 2012, follow these steps (if filtering an existing Table, skip to step 3):

1. Select a single cell in the data set to apply filtering to.

2. Go to Data, Sort & Filter, Filter. Click OK to continue.

3. Open the drop-down of the Date column to filter.

4. Deselect the Select All item to clear all the check marks in the list.

5. Click the + icon to the left of 2012.

6.   Click the + icon to the left of June.

7.   Select 12, 13, and 14.

8.   Click OK. The sheet updates, showing only the dates selected.

Using the Search Function to Filter for or Exclude Items

If you have a long list of items in the filter listing, you can do a search for items to include or exclude from the filter. Searches are done on the entire data list, not just the items currently filtered on. Use an asterisk (*) as a wildcard for one or more characters before, after, or in between any of the search terms.

When a search term is entered in the Search field, the filter listing below the field updates with all matches selected. You can deselect the items you want to exclude from the filter, check Add Current Selection to Filter if you do not want to lose any items you previously filtered for, and click OK.

You should keep the following in mind when using the Search function:

- The search looks through the entire column, including items you may have already filtered out.

- The Search function is additive when the Add Current Selection to Filter is selected. If not selected, each search's results are treated as a new filter.

- To exclude items from the listing, deselect them from the result.

Column A of Figure 8.4 is a list of various television models. I want to narrow the list to just Samsung, non-LED models. To perform the two filters, follow these steps:

1.   Open the filter drop-down.

2.   In the Search field, type **Samsung**.

3.   Click OK. The list on the sheet filters to just the Samsung models.

4.   Open the filter drop-down again.

5.   In the Search field, type **LED**.

6.   Because I actually want all types except LEDs, deselect Select All Search Results.

7. Because I want to retain my previous Samsung results, select Add Current Selection to Filter.

8. Click OK. The list filters to all non-LED Samsung TVs, as shown in Figure 8.4.

Original List		Filtered for Samsung		Samsung Except for LED
Televisions		Samsung UN55C8000 LED - 55"		Samsung LN32B360 LCD - 32"
Vizio VF552XVT LED - 55"		Samsung LN32B360 LCD - 32"		Samsung LN46B650 LCD - 46"
Vizio VF552XVT LED - 55"		Samsung UNB558500 LED - 55"		Samsung LN52B750 LCD - 52"
Samsung UN55C8000 LED - 55"	Search for	Samsung UN46B8000 LED - 46"	Search for LED	Samsung LN46A550 LCD - 46"
LG 47LE8500 LED - 47"	Samsung	Samsung LN46B650 LCD - 46"	Deselect All Results	Samsung LN46A750 LCD - 46"
Sony KDL-46EX700 LED - 46"		Samsung LN52B750 LCD - 52"	Select Add Current	Samsung LN52A650 LCD - 52"
Sony KDL-52NX800 LED - 52"		Samsung UN46B6000 LED - 46"	Selection to Filter	Samsung LN32A450 LCD - 32"
LG 47SL80 LCD - 47"		Samsung UN46B7000 LED - 46"		Samsung PN50B850 plasma - 50"
Mitsubishi LT-46249 LCD - 46"		Samsung LN46A950 LED - 46"		Samsung PN50B650 plasma - 50"
Westinghouse SK-32H640G LCD - 32"		Samsung LN46A550 LCD - 46"		Samsung PN63A760 plasma - 63"
Sharp LC-32D47UT LCD - 32"		Samsung LN46A750 LCD - 46"		Samsung PN50A650 plasma - 50"
LG 32LH20 LCD - 32"		Samsung LN52A650 LCD - 52"		Samsung PN50A550 plasma - 50"
Samsung LN32B360 LCD - 32"		Samsung LN32A450 LCD - 32"		Samsung HL61A750 RPTV - 61"

FIGURE 8.4

The Search function can be used to narrow down items to include in or exclude from the filter.

Using the Search Function on Grouped Dates

If you have a lot of dates in the filter listing, you can search for specific years, months, or dates to include or exclude from the filter. Searches are done on the entire data list, not just the items currently filtered on.

The Search function for grouped dates includes a drop-down, shown in Figure 8.5, allowing you to search by year, month, or date. The Search drop-down has the following options:

- **Year**—Search results are grouped by year.

- **Month**—Search results are grouped by year and then month. The search term must be the long version of the month, such as January.

- **Date**—Search results are grouped by year, then month, then day. Because the search will return partial matches, you should use the two-digit variation for dates. For example, to search for the 1st of a month, enter 01 instead of 1. If you enter 1, every date with a 1, such as 10, 11, 12, will be returned.

- **All**—Search results are grouped by year, then month, then day. This option looks for a match anywhere in the date. For example, if your data set includes dates from 2009 and the search term is 09, all dates from 2009 will be returned, such as September 9 (09/09). If you want only the 9th day returned, use the Date option.

TIP The Search field does not allow you to search for an entire date, such as 04/19/2010 when the dates are grouped. To search for a specific date, turn off the date grouping by going to File, Options, Advanced, Display Options for This Workbook and unselecting Group Dates in the AutoFilter Menu.

Because searches are additive, proper application of the Add Current Selection to Filter in the search results allows you to include or exclude the results from the filter. For more information, see the section "Using the Search Function to Filter for or Exclude Items."

You need to create a report with all the records from the first of every month available in 2011 and the 15th of every month in 2012. Using the additive search property, you can quickly filter to those specific records. To do so, follow these steps:

1. Open the drop-down of the Date column to filter.

2. Select Date from the Search drop-down.

3. Type in the two-digit date, 01.

4. Because the results are open to show everything, scroll to the top of the list and click the + by the years to minimize the list.

5. Deselect 2012 and click OK. The results now show all the first of the month records from 2011.

6. Open the drop-down of the Date column to filter again.

7. Select Date from the Search drop-down.

8. Type in the two-digit date, 15.

9. Scroll to the top and deselect Select All Search Results.

10. Select 2012 to select all 2012 results.

11. Select Add Current Selection to Filter, as shown in Figure 8.5.

12. Click OK.

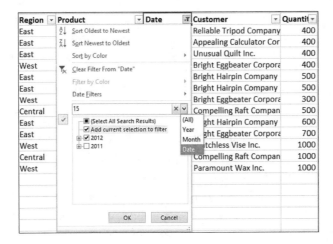

FIGURE 8.5

With proper use of the additive search property, you can easily create a report of specific dates.

Using Text, Number, and Date Special Filters

With careful planning or additional columns, you can filter for all types of reports such as top 10, quarterly reports, and ranges of values. But not all filtering is easy or quick. The filter listing has options to make it easier. Special filters are available in the filter drop-down depending on which data type (text, numbers, or dates) appears most often in a column. All the special filters, except for ones that take action immediately, open the Custom AutoFilter dialog box, allowing two conditions to be combined using AND or OR.

If the column contains mostly text, Text Filters is available from the filter listing. Choosing Text Filters opens a list with the following options: Equals, Does Not Equal, Begins With, Ends With, Contains, and Does Not Contain. Selecting one of these options opens a Custom AutoFilter dialog box, in which you can enter text to filter by.

 TIP When entering the text you want to filter by, you can use wildcards. Use an asterisk (*) to replace multiple characters or a question mark (?) to replace a single character.

If the column contains mostly numbers, Number Filters is available with the following options: Equals, Does Not Equal, Greater Than, Greater Than Or

Equal To, Less Than, Less Than or Equal To, Between Top 10, Above Average, and Below Average. Selecting Top 10, Above Average, or Below Average automatically updates the filter to reflect the selection.

If Top 10 is selected, you can specify the top or bottom items or percent to view. For example, you could choose to view the bottom 15% or the top seven items.

For columns with dates, the special filter, Date Filters, offers a wide selection of options, including additional options under All Dates in the Period. The options dealing with quarters refer to the traditional quarter of a year, January through March being the first quarter, April through June being the second quarter, and so on. When using the Custom AutoFilter option, the dialog box for dates includes calendars to aid in data entry.

To create the bottom 25% report for the previous quarter shown in Figure 8.6, follow these steps:

1. Open the drop-down of the Date column.

2. Select Date Filters, All Dates in the Period, Quarter 2. The data automatically filters to the 2nd quarter, April–June.

3. Open the drop-down of the numeric column, Quantity, to filter.

4. Select Number Filters, Top 10. The Top 10 AutoFilter appears.

5. Select Bottom from the leftmost drop-down.

6. Enter **25** in the middle field.

7. Select Percent from the rightmost drop-down.

8. Click OK; the table filters show the bottom 25%.

FIGURE 8.6

The special filters make it easier to create quarterly reports reflecting records that fall within specific parameters.

Filtering by Color or Icon

Data can be filtered by font color, color (set by cell fill or conditional formatting), or icon by going to the Filter by Color option in the filter listing. There, colors and/or icons used in the column are listed, as shown in Figure 8.7.

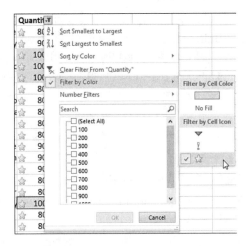

FIGURE 8.7

You can filter by the colors and icons in the table.

The data table in Figure 8.7 uses conditional formatting icons to denote which record quantities are below average (arrow), average (exclamation mark), or above average (star). Also, quantities greater than or equal to 1,000 have a green cell fill. To filter to show only the above average items, open the drop-down filter for the Quantity column. Select Filter by Color and then from the icons listed, select the star. The list automatically updates to show only the star records.

 NOTE   Refer to the section "Dynamic Cell Formatting with Conditional Formatting" in Chapter 4, "Formatting Sheets and Cells," for steps on how to apply your own custom icon formatting.

Filtering by Selection

Even without the filter turned on, you can right-click any cell in a column, go to Filter, and choose to filter by the cell's value, color, font color, or icon. Doing so turns on the AutoFilter and configures the filter for the selected cell's property.

This filtering is additive. If you filter a cell by one value and then go to a cell in another column and filter by its value, the result will be those rows that satisfy both filter criteria. You cannot filter by a property more than once within the same column, but you can filter a column by multiple properties—for example, filter by icon and then value.

To use filter selection to filter records meeting a specific value and icon, such as the below average East records in Figure 8.8, follow these steps:

1. Right-click a cell in the Region column containing the value (East) to filter by.

2. Go to Filter, Filter by Selected Cell's Value. The AutoFilter drop-downs appear in the column header and the table updates to show only East records.

3. Right-click a cell in the Quantity column containing the icon (a down arrow) to filter by.

4. Go to Filter, Filter by Selected Cell's Icon. The table now shows all below average records from the East region.

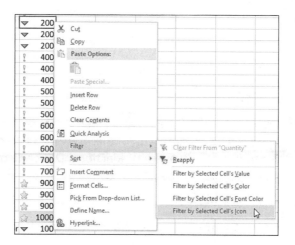

FIGURE 8.8

Right-clicking on a specific cell allows you to quickly filter by that cell's value, cell color, font color, or icon.

Allowing Filtering on a Protected Sheet

Normally, if you set up filters on a sheet, protect the sheet, and then send it out to other users, the recipients won't be able to filter the data. If you want others to be able to filter your protected sheet, follow these steps:

1. Select a single cell in the data set to apply filtering to.

2. Go to Home, Sort & Filter, Filter. The filter will be turned on for the data set.

3. Go to Review, Changes, Protect Sheet.

4. In the listing for Allow All Users of This Worksheet To, scroll down and select Use AutoFilter.

5. If applying a password to the sheet, enter it in the Password to Unprotect Sheet field. Otherwise, skip to step 6.

6. Click OK.

7. If you entered a password in step 5, Excel prompts you to reenter the password. Do so and click OK.

Users won't be able to modify the data you've protected, but they'll be able to use Excel's various AutoFilter tools to filter the data as needed.

 NOTE For more information on protecting your data, see "Protecting the Data on a Sheet" in Chapter 9, "Distributing and Printing a Workbook."

Using the Advanced Filter Option

Advanced Filter, found under Data, Sort & Filter, Advanced, may be a bit of a misnomer. Despite the visual simplicity of the Advanced Filter dialog box, shown in Figure 8.9, it can perform a variety of functions. Depending on the options selected and the setup on the sheet, the Advanced Filter can do the following:

- Filter records in place

- Filter records to a new location on the same or different sheet

- Reorganize columns

- Use formulas as criteria

- Filter for unique records

Under Action, you can choose either Filter the List, In-Place or Copy to Another Location to tell the function where to put the resulting data set. If copying the results to a new location, specify the location in the Copy To field. When specifying this range, consider the following:

- If the results include all columns of the data set in the original order, only the location of the first header needs to be specified.

- If the results consist of any change to the headers, whether it's a new order or fewer headers, copy the headers to use in the desired order to a new location. The Copy To range must include the entire new range of headers.

- If results need to be on another sheet, the Advanced Filter must be called from the sheet where the results will be placed.

FIGURE 8.9

With proper use of the Advanced Filter dialog box, you can do more than filter your data.

List Range is the data set, including required headers. Most Advanced Filter functions require each column to have a header.

Criteria Range is where rules are configured for the filter. See "Filtering by Criteria Range" for details.

Select Unique Records Only if duplicates should not be included in the results. See "Creating a List of Unique Items" for an example of how the option is useful for removing duplicates from a single column.

Filtering by Criteria Range

Criteria are the rules you want to execute the filter by. It's an optional field. Criteria can consist of exact values, values with operators, wildcards, or formulas. You should keep the following things in mind when setting up the criteria range:

- Except for when the criterion is a formula, the first row must consist of the column header used by the filter.

- Starting in the second row, enter the criterion to filter for in the column.

- Criteria entered on the same row are read as joined by AND. In the top table of Figure 8.10, the criteria in the first row are read West AND Laser Printers.

- Criteria entered on different rows are read as joined by OR. In the top table of Figure 8.10, the criteria are read West AND Laser Printers OR East AND Laser Printers.

Revenue	COGS	Profit		Region	Product		Date	Customer	Profit	Region	Product
12888	5904	6984		West	Laser Printers		1/16/2011	Compelling Raft Compan	3009	East	Laser Printers
4280	1968	2312		East	Laser Printers		1/20/2011	Compelling Raft Compan	4080	West	Laser Printers
18504	7872	10632					1/21/2011	Compelling Raft Compan	3783	West	Laser Printers
4472	1968	2504					1/24/2011	Compelling Raft Compan	3288	East	Laser Printers
9672	3936	5736					1/31/2011	Compelling Raft Compan	2772	East	Laser Printers

F	G	H	I	J	K	L	M	N	O	P	Q	R
Revenue	COGS	Profit		Region	Product		Date	Customer	Profit	Region	Product	
12888	5904	6984		West	Laser Printers		1/1/2011	Bright Hairpin Company	6010	East	Mult-Function Printers	
4280	1968	2312		East			1/8/2011	Safe Treadmill Partners	11817	East	Basic ColorJet Printers	
18504	7872	10632					1/9/2011	Alluring Shoe Company	12267	East	Basic ColorJet Printers	
4472	1968	2504					1/16/2011	Compelling Raft Compan	3009	East	Laser Printers	
9672	3936	5736					1/20/2011	Compelling Raft Compan	4080	West	Laser Printers	
21800	9840	11960					1/21/2011	Compelling Raft Compan	3783	West	Laser Printers	

FIGURE 8.10

The top table shows the criteria properly configured to return all Laser Printers for West and East regions. The configuration of the bottom table's criteria will return Laser Printers for West, but all products for East.

- If a cell in the criteria range is blank and has a column header, this is read as returning all records that match the column header. In the bottom table in Figure 8.10, the data returned will be West and Laser Printers or all data in East.

- Operators (<, >, <=, >=, <>) can be combined with numeric values for a more general filter.

- Wildcards can be used with text values. An asterisk (*) replaces any number of characters. A question mark (?) replaces a single character. The tilde (~) allows the use of wildcard characters in case the text being filtered uses such a character as part of its value.

- If the criterion is a formula, do not use a column header as it is applied to the entire data set. The formula should be one that returns TRUE or FALSE.

You can combine the header criteria with formulas to create your report. For example, you need to create a report of region west customers from whom you generated more than $4,000 in profit by selling Laser Printers. Your data spans a couple of years, so you want to narrow those results down to February and March of the current year. You also want to return any non-west region profits from January of the current year. Finally, you want the report generated on a new sheet.

First, you'll need to set up the header criteria:

1. Starting in G1, enter the headers you want to filter by: **Region**, **Product**, **Profit**. The text must match exactly, so if in doubt of the spelling, copy and paste the titles.

2. Under each column header, in row 2, enter the filter values: **West**, `Laser Printers`, `>4000`.

Next, create the criteria formulas. The one to be applied with the West column criteria needs to be entered in the same row and in an adjacent column (J). The second formula should be entered directly beneath the first.

3. In J2, place the following formula:

`=AND(YEAR(C2)=YEAR(TODAY()),OR(MONTH(C2)=2,MONTH(C2)=3))`

4. In J3, place the following formula:

`=AND(A2<>"West",YEAR(C2)=YEAR(TODAY()),MONTH(C2)=1)`

Notice that both formulas were written referring to the first row of data and used relative referencing. Finally, set up the Report sheet and configure the Advanced Filter dialog box, as shown in Figure 8.11.

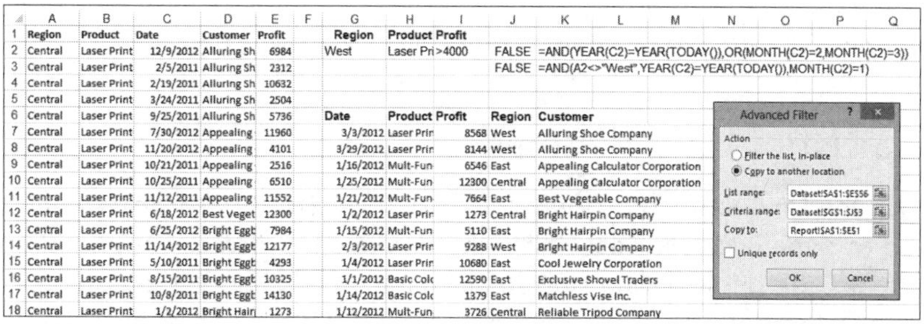

FIGURE 8.11

The Advanced Filter can use a combination of criteria to filter a data set. Note: Results in G6:K18 are a representation of the actual results on the Report sheet.

5. On the Report sheet, enter the column headings to include in the report: **Date**, **Product, Profit, Region, Customer**.

6. Because the results are on a sheet other than the data sheet, we need to start the Filter dialog box from the report sheet. Select a blank cell on the report sheet that is not directly beneath the headings.

7. Go to Data, Sort & Filter, Advanced.

8. Select Copy to Another Location.

9. Place the cursor in the List Range field and select the data set sheet. Select the entire data table.

TIP   A quick way of selecting a contiguous range of data is to select the first row, then press Ctrl+Shift+Down Arrow.

10. Place the cursor in the Criteria Range field. You will be brought back to the report sheet, so return to the data set sheet.

11. Select the criteria range, including the headers. Do not include any blank rows.

NOTE   If the criteria range was just a formula, you would need to include a blank cell above the formula. That blank cell would need to be included in the selection.

12. Place the cursor in the Copy To field. You are brought back to the report sheet.

13. Select the column headers on the report sheet.

14. Click OK. The report sheet updates with the results.

Creating a List of Unique Items

When the Unique Records Only option is selected, the Advanced Filter can be used to remove duplicates. Unlike the Remove Duplicates command on the Data tab, the original data set remains intact if you choose to copy the results to a new location. But also unlike the Remove Duplicates command, you cannot specify multiple columns to filter by. The Advanced Filter automatically looks at all columns in the List Range field.

TIP   The List Range field works only with a single range. So if you want to create a unique list based on multiple columns, the columns must be adjacent. Then select only those columns when setting up the List Range.

If Filter the List, In-Place is selected, the duplicate rows will be hidden. Go to Data, Sort & Filter, Clear to clear the filter and unhide the rows.

The table in Figure 8.12 shows two years of sales. You need to generate a list of companies products were sold to in that time. To quickly filter out duplicates in the Customer column and copy the results to a new location, follow these steps:

1. Select a cell outside the data table.

2. Go to Data, Sort & Filter, Advanced Filter.

3. Place the cursor in the List Range field.

4. Select the column to create the unique listing from, column D. As long as you don't have another table beneath this one, you can select the entire column by clicking on the header.

5. Select Copy to Another Location.

6. Place your cursor in the Copy To field.

7. Select a cell on the sheet where you want the first cell of the filtered range copied to, for example, J1.

8. Select Unique Records Only.

9. Click OK. A list of all unique customers is generated, as shown in Figure 8.12.

Customer	Quantity	Revenue	COGS	Profit		Customer	
Alluring Shoe Company	600	12888	5904	6984		Alluring Shoe Company	
Alluring Shoe Company	200					Appealing Calculator Corporation	
Alluring Shoe Company	800					Best Vegetable Company	
Alluring Shoe Company	200					Bright Eggbeater Corporation	
Alluring Shoe Company	400					Bright Hairpin Company	
Appealing Calculator Cor	1000					Compelling Raft Company	
Appealing Calculator Cor	300					Exclusive Shovel Traders	
Appealing Calculator Cor	200					Matchless Vise Inc.	
Appealing Calculator Cor	500					Reliable Tripod Company	
Appealing Calculator Cor	800					Remarkable Meter Corporation	
Best Vegetable Company	1000					Safe Flagpole Supply	
Bright Eggbeater Corpora	800					Safe Treadmill Partners	
Bright Eggbeater Corpora	900	21033	8856	12177		Succulent Jewelry Inc.	
Bright Eggbeater Corpora	300	7245	2952	4293		Superior Vegetable Corporation	

Advanced Filter dialog box overlay:

Action
- Filter the list, in-place
- Copy to another location

List range: $D:$D
Criteria range:
Copy to: $J$1
☑ Unique records only

OK   Cancel

FIGURE 8.12

Use the Advanced Filter to create a unique list of items from your data set.

Removing Duplicates from a Data Set

You've received a report where a user duplicated data by importing twice. You could try sorting the data and creating a formula in another column that compares rows, but with over 700,000 rows, it could take a while for the formula to calculate and you aren't even sure if the process is foolproof. Instead, use the Remove Duplicates option to ensure the process. Remove Duplicates can be found under Data, Data Tools, Remove Duplicates, or if the data set is a Table, under Table Tools, Design, Tools, Remove Duplicates.

 CAUTION The tool permanently deletes data from a table based on the selected columns in the Remove Duplicates dialog box. Unlike other filters, it does not just hide the rows. Because of this, you may want to copy the data before deleting the duplicates.

To remove duplicates based on the Region, Product, Date, and Customer, follow these steps:

1. Select a cell in the data set.

2. Go to Data, Data Tools, Remove Duplicates.

3. Excel highlights the data set. If columns are missing in the selection, go back and make sure there are no blank separating columns.

4. From the Remove Duplicates dialog box, make sure My Data Has Headers is selected if the data set has headers.

5. By default, all the columns are selected. A selected column means the tool will use the columns when looking for duplicates. Duplicates in an unselected column will be ignored. In the Columns list box, select the columns to use in the search for duplicates, as shown in Figure 8.13.

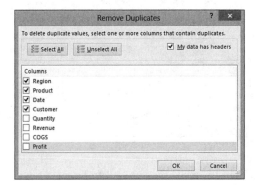

FIGURE 8.13

Remove Duplicates allows you to specify which columns you want to use to verify duplicate records.

6. Click OK. The data set updates, deleting any duplicate rows. A message box appears informing you of the number of rows deleted and the number remaining in the data set.

Consolidating Data

The Remove Duplicates tool is great for completely removing duplicates, but what if you wanted to remove duplicates based on some fields and, at the same time, combine the data of other fields? For example, you have a sheet with 2011 data and a sheet with 2012 data. You need to create a quantity sold report combining the data based on the company name but separating the different years. You could create a pivot table or use the Consolidate tool. The Consolidate tool, found under Data, Data Tools, helps you create a report of unique records with combined data. It even combines data from different sheets and workbooks. You can do this in one of three ways:

- **By Position**—Sum[1] data found on different sheets or in different workbooks based on their positions in the data sets. For example, if the ranges are A1:A10 and C220:C230, the results will be A1+C220, A2+C221, A3+C222, and so on. Do not select either of the options under Use Labels In.

- **By Category**—Sum[1] data found on different sheets or in different workbooks based on matching row and column labels, similar to a pivot table report. The references must include the labels in the leftmost column of the ranges. Select either or both of the options under Use Labels In to have the labels appear in the final data.

- **By Column**—Combine the data to a new sheet, with each data set in its own column. Select the Top Row option under Use Labels In.

The Reference field is where the data sets are entered. Click Add to add the selection to the All References list. If the data set is in a closed workbook, you can reference it only by using a range name. Click the Browse button to find and select the workbook. After the exclamation point (!) at the end of the path, enter the range name assigned to the data set.

 NOTE See "Using Names to Simplify References" in Chapter 5, "Using Formulas," for details on how to create a range name.

If Create Links to Source Data is selected, the consolidated data updates automatically when the source is changed. Also, the consolidated data is grouped, as shown in Figure 8.14. Click the + icon to the left of the data to open the group and see the data used in the summary. Column B of the report shows the name of the workbook in the first instance of its data.

---

[1] The function applied to the data can be any listed in the drop-down in the Consolidate dialog box. These include Sum, Count, Average, and more.

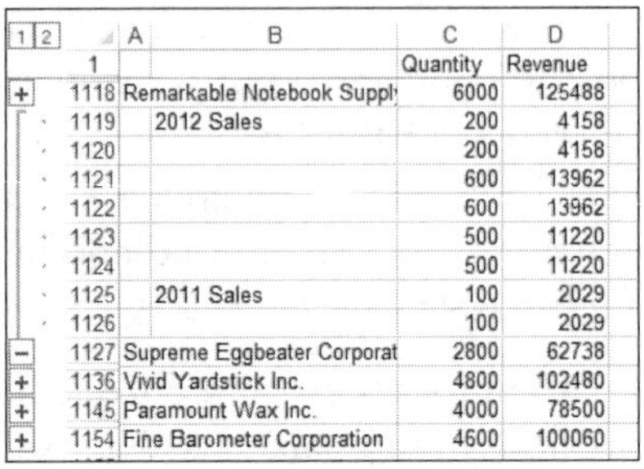

1 2	A	B	C	D
1			Quantity	Revenue
	1118	Remarkable Notebook Suppl	6000	125488
	1119	2012 Sales	200	4158
	1120		200	4158
	1121		600	13962
	1122		600	13962
	1123		500	11220
	1124		500	11220
	1125	2011 Sales	100	2029
	1126		100	2029
	1127	Supreme Eggbeater Corporat	2800	62738
	1136	Vivid Yardstick Inc.	4800	102480
	1145	Paramount Wax Inc.	4000	78500
	1154	Fine Barometer Corporation	4600	100060

FIGURE 8.14

When Create Links to Source Data is selected, the final report includes the individual values of the selected references.

A few things to keep in mind when using this tool:

- The range selected must be adjacent columns.

- If your reference field consists of multiple sheets, as you go from sheet to sheet, Excel automatically selects the same range as the previous sheet.

- If you select Left column, data is combined based on the leftmost column of the selection and the selected function is used on all other columns in the range.

- If doing a consolidatation by position or by column, you have to select a specific range, versus clicking the column headers to select the entire column.

- The range on which the function is applied must be numerical.

You have two reports, sales from 2011 and sales from 2012 on separate sheets. To combine the customers and the quantity sold onto a single report, follow these steps:

1. Select the top leftmost cell where the consolidated report should be placed, such as cell A1. If other data is on the sheet, make sure there is enough room for the new data.

2. Go to Data, Data Tools, Consolidate.

3. Select the desired function, SUM, from the Function drop-down.

4. Place the cursor in the Reference field.

5. Go to the sheet with the desired data set.

6. Select the data set, making sure the labels to be combined are in the leftmost column and that the column headers are included in the selection.

7. Click the Add button.

8. Repeat steps 4 to 7 for each additional data set, as shown in Figure 8.15.

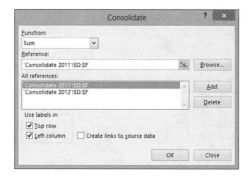

FIGURE 8.15

Use Consolidate to combine records from multiple sheets into a single report.

9. To include the top and/or left column labels, select the corresponding option. If combining text fields, as we are here, Left Column must be selected.

10. Click OK.

THE ABSOLUTE MINIMUM

The AutoFilter tool provides many options for filtering your data, making it easier to focus on just the data that's important at the moment. And you aren't limited to just filtering values. The tool includes options for filtering by icon, font color, or cell color. With the Advanced Filter tool, you can do even more complex filtering, but you can also hide duplicates and create unique lists. If you need to completely remove duplicates, then the Remove Duplicates tool may be the one you need, especially with its ability to choose which columns you want to base the duplicates on. For combining data into a single report, even between workbooks, use the Consolidate tool and select Create Links to Source Data to ensure your report updates automatically.

IN THIS CHAPTER

- Insert cell comments to guide users on entering data on a sheet.

- Allow multiple users access to your workbook.

- Hide sheets from other users.

- Customize your header by adding a logo.

- Print one sheet or the entire workbook.

- Protect formulas or text from accidental overwrite.

- Verify your workbook will work with different versions of Excel.

- Recover lost data from a backup file.

9

DISTRIBUTING AND PRINTING A WORKBOOK

Once you're done designing your workbook, you probably want to share it with others. But first, you may want to do a little cleanup, such as adding comments so users can understand what goes in specific fields, hiding sheets you don't want users to see, or protecting certain cells so users cannot accidently erase your formulas. You can also protect the file so the wrong eyes can't pry into it.

Once all that's done, you have to decide how you want to share it. For example, will you print it out, put it on the network and allow multiple users access to it at the same time, or email it? And if you have users with different versions of Excel, such as Excel 2003, you need to ensure those users can access the workbook without a problem. This chapter shows you how to do this and more.

Using Cell Comments to Add Notes to Cells

Cell comments are comments or images you can attach to a cell that appear when a cursor is placed over the cell. By default, the cell comment looks like a yellow sticky note. You can tell if a cell has a comment by the red triangle in the upper-right corner of the cell, as shown in cell A2 of Figure 9.1. Use cell comments to explain to the user what type of data to enter into the cell, explain what the data in the cell is used for, show the user an image of the product being referenced, or any other information you want to convey.

FIGURE 9.1

Use cell comments to convey additional information to a user without using valuable sheet space.

Inserting and Editing a Cell Comment

To insert a comment, select a cell and go to Review, Comments, New Comment or right-click the cell where the comment should be placed and select Insert Comment. A yellow comment box appears, with the Excel user-defined name already entered to indicate who is entering the comment. If you want, you can delete this text. Otherwise, type the text you want into the comment box. When you're done, click any cell on the sheet to exit from the comment.

To edit a hidden comment, select the cell and go to Review, Comments, Edit Comment or right-click the comment's cell and select Edit Comment to make it visible. Your cursor will automatically be placed within the comment box. If the comment is already visible, you can click in the comment box and make changes to the text.

Formatting a Cell Comment

Once you've inserted a cell comment, you can format the text and the box or insert an image as the background fill. There are two dialog boxes available when you right-click on a comment and select Format Comment. The first, which you open by right-clicking on the *inside* of the comment box, only allows you to format the text in the comment. The other opens when you right-click on the comment box while your cursor is a four-headed arrow, as shown in Figure 9.2. It allows you to format the text or box.

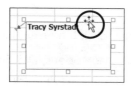

FIGURE 9.2

Once your cursor changes to a four-headed arrow (shown here), right-click and select Format Comment to format the text or box.

Inserting an Image into a Cell Comment

You can insert an image into a cell comment as a background fill, as shown in Figure 9.3. The image will take up the entire box and resize as you resize the box. You can still type text in the comment and it will appear on top of the image.

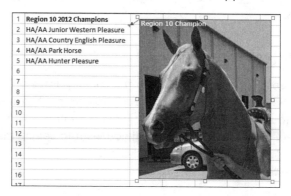

FIGURE 9.3

Insert an image into a cell comment to give the users a visual reference to a label.

To insert an image in a cell comment and change the color of the text so that it shows up over the image, follow these steps:

1. Right-click the cell where you want the comment and select Insert Comment. A cell comment appears with the cursor inside.

2. Place your cursor along any edge of the comment until it turns into a four-headed arrow, then right-click and choose Format Comment. If the Format Comment dialog box that opens only has one tab—Font—close the dialog box and try again. The dialog box that appears should have multiple tabs.

3. Go to the Colors and Lines tab of the Format Comment dialog box.

4. From the Color drop-down in the Fill section, select Fill Effects to open the Fill Effects dialog box.

5. Go to the Picture tab and click the Select Picture button.

6. The Insert Pictures dialog box opens, allowing you to browse for a picture on the computer, at Office.com, anywhere online, or from your SkyDrive. Once you find the image, click Insert and you'll be returned to the Fill Effects dialog box.

7. Select Lock Picture Aspect Ratio to lock the image ratio. Click OK twice to return to Excel.

8. Resize the comment box if necessary to see the entire image.

9. Highlight the text in the comment box.

10. Right-click within the comment box and select Format Comment.

11. From the Color drop-down of the Font tab, select a new color for the font. Click OK.

Showing and Hiding Cell Comments

A cell comment becomes visible when the cursor passes over the cell then hides again once the cursor is past. If you need the comment to stay open, select the cell and go to Review, Comments, Show/Hide Comment or right-click over the cell and select Show/Hide Comment. If you want to see all the comments on the sheet, go to Review, Comments and click Show All Comments. Select the option again to hide the comment(s).

Deleting a Cell Comment

To delete a comment, select the cell and go to Review, Comments, Delete or right-click over the cell's comment and select Delete Comment.

Allowing Multiple Users to Edit a Workbook at the Same Time

Excel workbooks are not designed to be accessed by multiple users at the same time. But Microsoft understands that sometimes there is a need for more than one person to edit a workbook at the same time and has provided a limited option. Go to Review, Changes, Share Workbook and the Share Workbook dialog box opens. Select Allow Changes by More Than One User at the Same Time. Go to the Advanced tab to configure how long the change history should be kept, how copies are updated, and how conflicts should be handled. Click OK. Excel prompts you to save the workbook. Click OK to share the workbook.

Sharing a workbook is a double-edged sword. Although it allows for multiple user access, what users can do is severely limited. A shared workbook cannot have Tables, conditional formatting, validation, charts, hyperlinks, subtotals, or scenarios. Users cannot insert or delete rows and columns. Cells cannot be merged and pivot tables cannot be changed. Nor can users write macros or edit array formulas. Basically, only the simplest workbook, such as for data entry, is shareable.

 TIP   If you need to share a workbook with more advanced options available, such as pivot tables, consider uploading the workbook to your SkyDrive. Although not as powerful as the desktop version of Excel, the Excel Web App offers a lot of options. See Chapter 16, "Introducing the Excel Web App," for more information.

Hiding and Unhiding Sheets

There may be sheets in your workbook that you do not want others to see, such as calculation sheets, data sheets, or sheets with lookup tables. You can hide sheets from users by navigating to the sheet you want to hide and then selecting Home, Format, Hide & Unhide, Hide Sheet. This hides the active sheet—the one you were looking at. You can also hide a sheet by right-clicking on the sheet's tab and selecting Hide.

 CAUTION   A workbook must have at least one sheet visible.

To unhide a sheet, go to Home, Format, Hide & Unhide, Unhide Sheet. A dialog box listing all hidden sheets opens. Select the sheet you want to unhide and click Unhide. If you have multiple sheets to unhide, you must repeat these steps for each sheet.

Of course, it's also possible for a user to open the Unhide dialog box and unhide sheets. To prevent this, you need to protect the workbook. See the "Setting Workbook-Level Protection" section later in this chapter for more information.

Locking Rows or Columns in Place

If you've set up your data in a Table, Excel places the Table headings into the column headers when you scroll down the sheet, as shown in Figure 9.4. But normally, when you scroll through a sheet and your data isn't formatted as a Table, your row and column headings disappear. This can be inconvenient when you have a lot of data and need the identifying headings. With the Freeze Panes options, you can force the top rows, leftmost columns, or both to remain visible as you scroll around the sheet.

TIP If you have your data formatted as a Table and the headings do not appear in the column headers when scrolling, ensure that you don't have the Freeze Panes option turned on and ensure that you do have a cell in the Table selected.

Region ⯆	Product ⯆	Date ⯆	Customer ⯆	Quantity ⯆	Revenue ⯆	COGS ⯆	Profit ⯆	
East	Laser Printe	1/9/2011	Alluring Shoe Company	900	21465	9198	12267	
West	Laser Printe	1/11/2011	Alluring Shoe Company	400	9144	4088	5056	
Central	Multi-Funct	1/26/2011	Alluring Shoe Company	500	10445	4235	6210	
Central	Basic Color)	2/5/2011	Alluring Shoe Company	200	4280	1968	2312	

FIGURE 9.4

Table column headings become part of the column headers so that they are always visible when you scroll down the sheet.

Three options are available under View, Window, Freeze Panes:

- **Freeze Panes**—Freezes rows and/or columns depending on the cell you have selected at the time. This option changes to Unfreeze Panes if any rows or columns are already frozen.

- **Freeze Top Row**—Freezes the first visible row of the sheet.

- **Freeze First Column**—Freezes the first visible column of the sheet.

CAUTION When using the Freeze Top Row or Freeze First Column options, the selection of one automatically undoes the selection of the other. So, if you want to freeze both the top row and first column, you must use the Freeze Panes option.

Freezing Multiple Rows and Columns

The Freeze Top Row and Freeze First Column options allow you to freeze the first row or first column on the sheet; however, if you need to freeze multiple rows and/or columns, you need to use the Freeze Panes option. This option freezes the sheet based on the cell selected when the option is selected. It freezes any rows above and any columns to the left of the selected cell. For example, to freeze row 1 and columns A and B at the same time, select cell C2, then select View, Window, Freeze Panes, Freeze Panes. Now, when you scroll around the sheet, you will always see row 1 and columns A and B.

Clearing Freeze Panes

To turn off the Freeze Panes option, go to View, Window, Freeze Panes, Unfreeze Panes. If you have rows and columns frozen, you can't choose to unfreeze one or the other. You must unfreeze it all and then refreeze the part you want to keep frozen.

Creating Custom Views of Your Data

View, Workbook View, Custom Views allows you to save the way you have a workbook set up. The hidden rows and columns, filter settings, print settings, and which sheets are hidden are all saved, making it easy to switch between a data entry mode, which shows all your data, and a presentation mode, which hides your calculation sheets.

 CAUTION Custom views will not work if there's a Table in the workbook.

You have a workbook with a data sheet, a calculation sheet, and a formatted report that needs to be distributed every week after you update it. You want to hide the data and calculation sheets from your viewers. You've hidden the sheets, but when it comes time to update them, you have to go through the unhide process twice to unhide both sheets. Instead, create a custom view called Distribution and one called All Data that you can easily switch between as needed, like this:

1. With all sheets unhidden, go to View, Workbook View, Custom Views. The Custom Views dialog box opens.

2. Click Add.

3. Enter a name for the view, such as `All Data`, in the Name field. If you want the print settings, hidden rows, hidden columns, and filter settings also saved in the view, select the corresponding check box. Click OK.

4. Hide the calculation and data sheets. If you want to hide any rows or columns or set up any filters on the report, do it now.

5. Go to View, Workbook View, Custom Views and click Add.

6. Enter a name for this new view, such as `Distribution`. If you had any rows or columns hidden, or filter settings, ensure the check box is selected. Click OK.

7. Next time you have to distribute the report, click Distribution before saving. When it's time to update the workbook, select All Data to show all your sheets.

Configuring the Page Setup

Page setup refers to settings that control how a sheet will look when it is printing. These settings not only include standard print settings, such as the page orientation (portrait or landscape), paper size, and page margins, but they also include settings for the following:

- Repeating specific rows or columns on each printed page

- Printing in black and white

- Printing the gridlines

- Printing 1-2-3 row and A-B-C column headings

- Printing comments

- How cell errors should be displayed

- The order multiple pages should print in (down then over or over then down)

Some of these options are available directly on the Page Layout tab. To access all of these sheet options, go to Page Layout, Page Setup, Print Titles. The Page Setup dialog box opens directly to the Sheet tab, shown in Figure 9.5.

Repeating Rows or Columns on Each Printed Page

When you have a report that spans several pages, you probably want to repeat your row or column headings on all the pages. Follow these steps to have your heading row repeat at the top of each printed page:

1. Go to Page Layout, Page Setup, Print Titles. The Page Setup dialog box opens to the Sheet tab, as shown in Figure 9.5.

2. Click the Collapse Dialog button on the far-right side of the Rows to Repeat at Top field. This minimizes the dialog box and allows you to more easily interact with the sheet.

3. Select the row(s) you want to repeat by clicking the numbered row header(s). You can only select the entire row, not just a few columns of it.

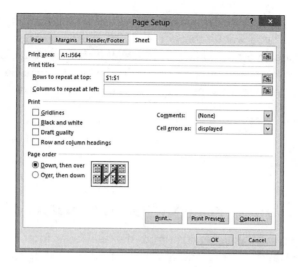

FIGURE 9.5

Instead of breaking up your table and repeating the heading so that it prints on each page, use the Print Titles option to have Excel automatically copy the row onto each page.

4. Click the button on the far-right side of the Rows to Repeat at Top field to return to the dialog box.

5. Click OK. The selected row(s) will now repeat at the top of each printed page.

Scaling Your Data to Fit a Printed Page

You may find your data is a few rows too long or a few columns too wide to print on a single page. From Page Layout, Scale to Fit, you can adjust the scaling options available to get your data to print as you see fit. These options are also available in the Page Setup dialog box on the Page tab, though the labels are slightly different.

The Width drop-down is useful if you have a few columns going to the next page. From the drop-down, you can choose how many pages you want to force the table to print to. For example, if your report is printing on two pages because you have a column going to the second page, choose 1 page from the drop-down to have Excel adjust the settings, forcing that last column to stay with the others. Similarly, the Height drop-down is used when you have a few too many rows going to another page.

NOTE When you customize the Width and Height, you cannot adjust the Scale. To adjust the Scale, the Width and Height must be set to Automatic.

Scale allows you to configure how a sheet will print by setting the percentage of the normal size you want it to print at. 100% is the normal size of the table. Set the percentage to 50% and Excel reduces the size of the table by 50%, allowing for more of it to appear on a sheet, and shrinking the text. Set the percentage to 150% and Excel increases the size of the table and the text.

 TIP Sometimes you need to increase the font size of a printed report. Instead of increasing the font on the sheet, adjust the scale when printing.

Creating a Custom Header or Footer

There are two ways you can customize the header or footer. One method is through the Header/Footer tab of the Page Setup dialog box, which you can open using the Page Setup shortcut. Once you're on the tab, click Custom Header or Custom Footer to design the header or footer. The other method is available when you are viewing your sheet in Page Layout view and you click in the header or footer area, opening the Header & Footer Tools, Design tab. Both provide the same design options, just in a different manner.

 NOTE See the "Taking a Closer Look at the Excel Window" section in Chapter 1, "Understanding the Microsoft Excel Interface," for more information on Page Layout view.

The header and footer are unique to each sheet. Each header and footer is broken into three sections: left section, center section, and right section. You can customize each of these three sections in the following ways:

- Add page numbering.
- Add the current date and time.
- Add the file path of the workbook.
- Add the workbook name.
- Add the sheet name.
- Insert text.
- Format any text, including the above options.
- Insert and format an image.

To add one of the options to a section of a header or footer, first select the section, and then click the corresponding button. You can then select the text or image and apply formatting to it.

Adding an Image to the Header and Footer

You can add a company logo to a header so that it appears when printed, instead of taking up space on the computer screen. It's an easy way to give a report a more professional look. To insert a logo in the header's left section, as shown in Figure 9.6, follow these steps:

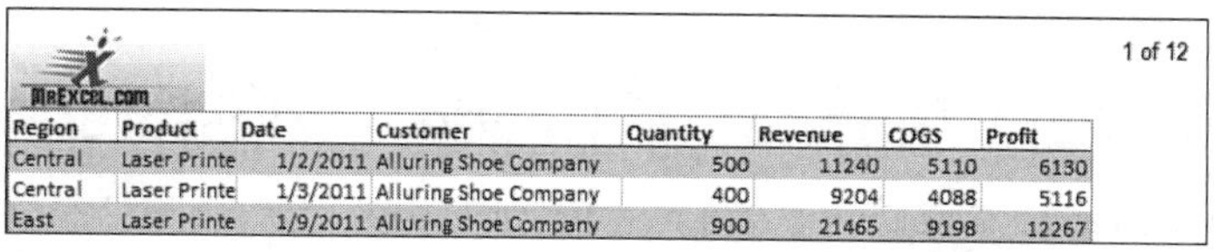

Region	Product	Date	Customer	Quantity	Revenue	COGS	Profit
Central	Laser Printe	1/2/2011	Alluring Shoe Company	500	11240	5110	6130
Central	Laser Printe	1/3/2011	Alluring Shoe Company	400	9204	4088	5116
East	Laser Printe	1/9/2011	Alluring Shoe Company	900	21465	9198	12267

1 of 12

FIGURE 9.6

Use the header to add a company logo to a printed sheet.

CAUTION You can only insert one image per section of a header or footer.

1. Go to View, Workbook View and select Page Layout.

2. As you move your cursor over the area that says "Click to Add Header," the three sections of the header appear highlighted. Click on the leftmost section. This places your cursor in that section.

3. Go to Header & Footer Tools, Design, Header & Footer Elements, and then click Picture.

4. From the Insert Pictures dialog box, browse or search for the image to import. You can look for images on your local drive, online at Office.com, on the web (you can search through Bing), or on your SkyDrive.

5. When you find the desired image, select it and click Insert.

NOTE At this time, you won't see the image in the header. Instead, you will see the code for the image: &[Picture]. Anytime you're in Edit mode—your cursor is in a section—you will see the code. Once you are no longer editing the header or footer, the image will appear.

6. Select Format Picture from the Header & Footer Elements group of the Design tab. Adjust the size on the Size tab. Go to the Picture tab if you need to change the color of the image or crop it. Click OK.

 TIP If you know the needed height for the image to fit in the header but not the width, make sure Lock Aspect Ratio is selected before you adjust the height. The width will automatically adjust, preserving the ratio of the image.

7. Click anywhere outside the header, and the image appears. If you need to modify the image even more, click in the section and repeat step 6.

Adding Page Numbering to the Header and Footer

Page numbering is set up in the header or footer of a sheet. You can show just the page number (1, 2, 3, etc.) or you can show the page number out of the total number of pages, as shown in the right header section in Figure 9.6. If you select multiple sheets when printing, the page numbering will be consecutive for all the sheets in the order they appear in the workbook. (See the "Printing Sheets" section for more information.)

To insert page numbering based on the total number of pages, follow these steps:

1. Go to View, Workbook View and select Page Layout.

2. As you move your cursor over the area that says "Click to Add Header," the three sections of the header appear highlighted. Click on the rightmost section. This places your cursor in that section.

3. Go to Header & Footer Tools, Design, Header & Footer Elements, and then click Page Number. This places the code for page numbering, &[Page], in the section.

4. You may not see it, but after placing the code, your cursor was placed at the end of the text. So begin typing the following right away: Type a space then the word **of** followed by another space. Note that you may not see the second space appear.

5. Click Number of Pages. You should now see the following in the section: &[Page] of &[Pages]. Click anywhere outside the footer and you will see the current page number and the total number of pages.

Using Page Break Preview to Set Page Breaks

When in the Page Break Preview viewing mode, you can see where columns and rows will break to print onto other pages. Blue dashed lines signify automatic breaks that Excel places based on settings, such as margins. Blue solid lines are manually set breaks. You can move these lines to set the page breaks where you want by clicking and dragging them to a new location. Follow these steps to change the location of a column break:

1. Select Page Break Preview from the View tab.

2. Place your cursor over the blue column line you want to move until it becomes a double-headed arrow, as shown in Figure 9.7. The line can be solid or dashed.

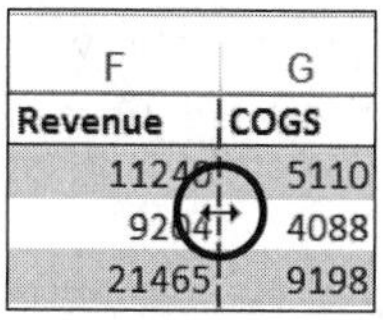

F	G
Revenue	COGS
11240	5110
9204	4088
21465	9198

FIGURE 9.7

Place your cursor over the blue line so the cursor becomes a double-headed arrow.

3. Hold down the mouse button and drag the blue line to where you want the column break to be.

4. Release the mouse button. The dashed blue line becomes a solid blue line, as shown in Figure 9.8.

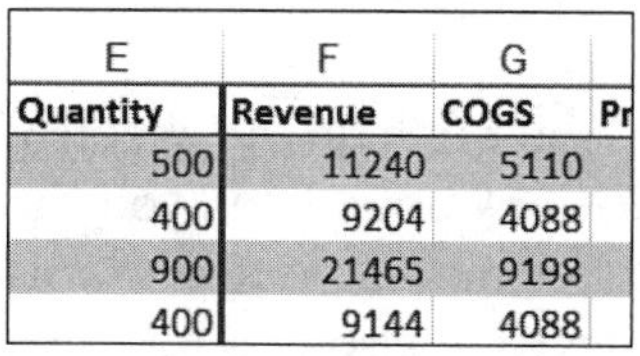

E	F	G	Pr
Quantity	Revenue	COGS	
500	11240	5110	
400	9204	4088	
900	21465	9198	
400	9144	4088	

FIGURE 9.8

After you've moved an automatically set column break, it changes from a dashed line to the solid line of a manually set break.

You can also insert additional (row) page breaks by selecting a cell in the row you want to be first on the next printed page, then selecting Page Layout, Page Setup, Breaks, Insert Page Break. A solid blue line appears above the selected cell. To remove a manually inserted page break, select a cell directly beneath the solid blue line and then select Page Layout, Page Setup, Remove Page Break.

Printing Sheets

To print the active sheet, go to File, Print. The Print screen is split in two parts. On the left side are the print settings, such as the number of copies and the printer to print to. On the right side of the screen is a print preview of the sheet. You can move through the pages using the scroll wheel of the mouse, using Page Up and Page Down keys on the keyboard, or using the arrows at the lower left of the Print Preview window. When you're ready to print, click the Print button on the left side.

If you need to print the entire workbook, open the Print Active Sheets drop-down underneath Settings, shown in Figure 9.9, and select Print Entire Workbook. This prints all visible (unhidden) sheets in the workbook. If you have page numbering setup on the sheets, the numbers will update to show the page's position in the workbook.

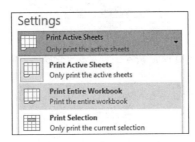

FIGURE 9.9

Choose to print all visible sheets by selecting Print Entire Workbook.

To print specific sheets, you can hide the sheets you don't want to print and then use the Print Entire Workbook option. Or, you can use the Ctrl key to select the desired sheets to print. This method doesn't require you to select a different print option or hide the sheets, yet it also updates the page numbering. For more information on selecting multiple sheets, see the "Selecting Multiple Sheets" section in Chapter 2, "Working with Workbooks, Sheets, Rows, Columns, and Cells."

 TIP If you don't want consecutive page numbering across sheets, you need to force the first page number of each sheet. To do this, go to Page Layout, Page Setup and click the dialog box launcher in the corner of the group. At the bottom of the

Page tab of the Page Setup dialog box is the field for First Page Number. By default, it is set to Auto, but if you want each page numbering to start at 1 (or another number), you can set the page number here. If you do want the page numbering to be consecutive but it is not, make sure the field is set to Auto.

Protecting Your Workbook from Unwanted Changes

After spending time setting up a workbook exactly right, you don't want another user to mess up your hard work. Or, perhaps your workbook contains sensitive data that should only be seen by certain people. Either way, Excel offers various methods of protection you may find useful.

Setting File-Level Protection

Set a password at the file level to prevent an unauthorized user from opening a workbook. You can also allow a user to open the workbook but not save any changes, except as a new file. The permission level is set when the workbook is saved by selecting General Options from the Tools drop-down in the Save As dialog box. From the General Options dialog box, enter a password in the Password to Open field if you want only specific people to be able to open the workbook. If you want anyone to be able to open the workbook but only certain people to make changes, enter a password in the Password to Modify field. Selecting Read-Only Recommended prompts users to open the file as read-only. After clicking OK, Excel prompts you to reenter the password. Once you have completed the save function, the file will be password protected.

To remove the protection, go to the General Options dialog box, clear the fields, and save the workbook.

Setting Workbook-Level Protection

Protection at the workbook level prevents a user from adding, deleting, or moving sheets. To protect the workbook structure, go to Review, Protect Workbook. The Protect Structure and Windows dialog box opens. At the time of writing, there are two options in the dialog box: Structure and Windows. Windows is grayed out. If you deselect Structure, the OK button grays out because without Structure selected, there is nothing to protect. If you want, you can also enter a password. You will have to enter it twice.

NOTE In previous versions of Excel, selecting the Windows option would prevent users from resizing the workbook, though they could still resize the Excel window.

Protecting the Data on a Sheet

Protecting a sheet prevents users from changing the content of locked cells. By default, all cells have the locked option selected and you purposefully unlock them (see the following section "Unlocking Cells"). Sheet protection must be applied to each sheet individually.

To protect a sheet, go to Review, Protect Sheet. The Protect Sheet dialog box opens, from which you can select what actions a user can do to the sheet. You can also enter a password. You will have to enter it twice.

Unlocking Cells

While a sheet is still unprotected, you can unlock specific cells so that when the sheet is protected, users can still enter information in the cells you want. To change the protection of selected cells, go to Home, Cells, Format, Format Cells, or right-click on the selection and choose Format Cells. In the Format Cells dialog box, go to the Protection tab and unselect the Locked option. Once you've unlocked the desired cells, protect the sheet to protect the other cells.

Allowing Users to Edit Specific Ranges

Unlocking cells and protecting the sheet is an all-or-none solution. That is, none of your users will be able to modify the protected cells unless they can unprotect the sheet first. Suppose you have a form where traveling employees fill in the top half and accounting fills in the bottom half. You want to protect the sheet, so that travelers can't accidentally fill in the bottom half, but you don't want to provide the sheet password to accounting so they can fill in the bottom half. Review, Changes, Allow Users to Edit Ranges lets you assign a password to specific ranges, allowing authorized users to edit those ranges.

Figure 9.10 is a travel log. The employee fills out the top table while a member of the accounting department signs off at the bottom. The top table is unlocked for all users but the bottom half, below the "To be filled out by Accounting only" line, is password protected. To apply a password to a selective range while the entire sheet is protected, follow these steps:

Date	Expense Description	Airfare	Lodging	Ground Transport	Meals & Tips	Conferences / Seminars	Miles	Mileage Reimbursement	Miscellaneous	Exchange Rate	Expense Currency	Total
Total		$0.00	$0.00	$0.00	$0.00	$0.00	0	$0.00	$0.00			$0.00
To be filled out by Accounting only:												
Name					Authorized by			Per Mile Reimbursement				
Department					Date Submitted			Total Reimbursement Due				
Period												

FIGURE 9.10

Create and protect a sheet that can be used with users of varying permission levels.

1. Ensure the sheet is unprotected.

2. Select the specific accounting only cells: in this example, C11, C13, C15, H11, H13, L11, L13. To select multiple cells, hold down the Ctrl key while you select the cells.

3. Go to Review, Changes, Allow Users to Edit Ranges. The dialog box shown in Figure 9.11 opens.

FIGURE 9.11

Configure Allow Users to Edit Ranges with cells that can be unprotected with a password.

4. Click New. The New Range dialog box opens. Enter a title, such as **Accounting**. The Refers to Cells already reflects the cells you want to configure. In the Range Password field, enter the password members of the accounting department will use to unprotect those cells.

5. Click OK. Reenter the password to confirm it.

6. If you want to create a log of what you've done, check the Paste Permissions Information into a New Workbook check box. When you click OK, the configuration will be logged in a new workbook.

7. If you're ready to protect the sheet, click the Protect Sheet button.

8. Click OK.

The first time a user tries to enter data in an accounting cell, a password prompt will appear. If the user enters the correct password, the prompt won't appear again until the workbook is closed and reopened.

Preventing Changes by Marking a File as Final

You can set a workbook as read-only by going to File, Info, Protect Workbook, Mark as Final. This prevents users from accidentally making any changes to the file. When open, a status message appears above the formula bar stating that the workbook is MARKED AS FINAL, but it gives users the option to Edit Anyway. If users click the Edit button, the final status will be lost and they will be able to make changes and save the workbook.

Restricting Access Using IRM

If your organization has configured a Digital Rights Management Server, you can limit your workbook to predefined groups configured by your organization. To enable this option, go to File, Info, Protect Workbook, Restrict Access.

Certifying a Workbook with a Digital Signature

Digital signatures are often used at websites, such as banking sites, to verify their authenticity. You can also add a digital signature to a workbook to authenticate it and prevent others from making changes.

Digital signatures are purchased from third-party certifying authorities. Once you have installed the certificate, go to File, Info, Protect Workbook, Add a Digital Signature. From the Sign dialog box, select the type of signature—created, approved, or both—and enter a reason for signing the workbook. By clicking the Details button, you can provide more information, such as an address. At the bottom of the dialog box is the digital signature Excel found. If it isn't the correct one, click the Change button to select another.

Once you have your settings entered, click Sign. When users open the workbook, they are notified of the signature. If the user makes changes and saves them, the signature will be removed.

CAUTION Excel allows you to sign with a local, token certificate, but because such a certificate does not have an online presence, it is considered invalid and will appear as such to users.

Sharing Files Between Excel Versions

Excel has made many changes over the years. If you plan to send your workbook to users with versions other than Excel 2013, you should ensure that the workbook is compatible with their version(s) of Excel. To do this, go to File, Info, Check for Issues, Check Compatibility. From the dialog box, shown in Figure 9.12, you can select the version(s) to test from the Select Versions to Show drop-down. If there are any compatibility issues, they appear in the box below the drop-down, with a brief explanation and the versions affected. You can decide if it's an issue you need to resolve, such as a function not available in previous versions of Excel, or one you can safely ignore, such as a new color in Excel. Excel also gives its opinion on whether the issue is significant or minor. If a Find link appears next to the issue, Excel takes you directly to the issue when you click the link.

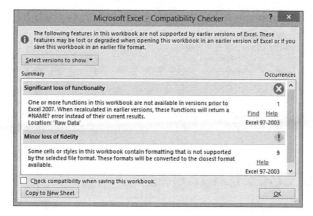

FIGURE 9.12

Use the Compatibility Checker to verify your workbook will open properly in earlier versions of Excel.

Removing Hidden or Confidential Information

An Excel workbook can hide data in various places such as document properties, cell comments, and hidden rows. The Document Inspector can find much of this information and help you remove it. To run the inspector, go to File, Info,

Check for Issues, Inspect Document. After Excel warns you that it could remove important data and that it's important to save first, the Document Inspector dialog box opens. You can choose the type of content you want the inspector to look for. When you click Inspect, a report of what Excel has found appears by the selected content, as shown in Figure 9.13. You can then choose whether to let Excel remove the content.

FIGURE 9.13

Use the Document Inspector to remove information you don't want to share, such as your name.

Recovering Lost Changes

If you've ever closed a file without saving it or had a power failure—this option might be the lifesaver you're looking for. Excel automatically creates backups of your workbook as you work on it. Depending on its configuration, it also saves a copy of your workbook if you close it without saving.

To check your settings, go to File, Options. From the Excel Options dialog box, go to the Save tab. Under Save Workbooks, ensure that Save AutoRecover Information Every 10 Minutes is selected. This tells Excel to create backups of your workbooks. Set the number of minutes to a time frame that will work best for all of your workbooks.

When Save AutoRecover is selected, the Keep the Last Autosaved Version If I Close Without Saving option becomes available. Select this option and Excel saves the last backup copy it made if you close the workbook without saving. To recover this backup, open the original workbook. Then go to File, Info and by the Manage Versions drop-down, if Excel has a copy saved, it informs you, as shown in Figure 9.14. Click the icon below Versions and Excel opens the file. Review the file, and if you want to keep the work, click the Restore button in the status message above the formula bar. Excel then overwrites the original workbook with this restored version.

FIGURE 9.14

Closing without saving doesn't have to be the end of the world. Excel has settings to automatically back up and recover your work.

Excel won't keep the autorecover files forever. The backed-up copies of the workbook will be deleted under the following circumstances:

- When the file is manually saved

- When the file is saved with a new filename

- If you turn off autorecover for the workbook (refer to the following Tip)

- If you deselect Save AutoRecover in Excel Options

- When you close the file

- When you quit Excel

 TIP   You can turn off autorecover for a specific workbook by going to File, Options, Save and under AutoRecover Exceptions For: *Current Workbook*, select Disable AutoRecover for This Workbook Only.

Sending an Excel File as an Attachment

You can email your workbook right from Excel by going to File, Share, Email and selecting the format you want to send it in. Once you select an option, Excel generates an email message with the file attached. You just need to fill in the rest of the information and send the message with the file.

Keep in mind that the Outlook window you see isn't a normal one. It's the Excel version, and while it's open, you won't be able to access the real Outlook window. If you need to get into Outlook, click the Save icon in the message's Quick Access Toolbar and close the message by clicking the X in the upper-right corner of the window. It will be saved to the Drafts folder in Outlook. You can do what's needed in Outlook then go to the Drafts folder, open the saved message, and continue emailing your file.

CAUTION Outlook gives you the option to open workbooks from within emails. When you do this, a temporary copy of the workbook is created, like a virtual file. Because some functionality in Excel requires a properly saved file, you may get errors when you try to do something. A safe practice is to always save a workbook to your desktop or another location on your hard drive before opening it.

Sharing a File Online

You don't need to email a file or save it to a network to share it with others. Microsoft offers space on SkyDrive, a place online where you can save your file and give others access to it. You can save your file to your SkyDrive account by going to File, Save As and choosing your SkyDrive from the Places list. For more information on creating a workbook to share on SkyDrive, see Chapter 16.

THE ABSOLUTE MINIMUM

Cell comments, freeze panes, and hidden sheets are just a few of the finishing touches you can make to your workbook before presenting it to other users. You may also want to protect your work, especially at the sheet level, so that users don't accidentally overwrite your formulas.

If you're going to print out your sheet for distribution through your company or as an invoice to a client, a logo in the header can give the sheet a nice but subtle touch of professionalism. If, instead, you're going to distribute the workbook electronically, you may want to remove any personal information.

SUBTOTALS AND GROUPING

This chapter shows you how data can be summarized and grouped together using Excel's Subtotal and grouping tools. The ability to group and subtotal data allows you to summarize a long sheet of data to fewer rows. The individual records are still there, so that you can unhide them if you need to investigate a subtotal in detail.

Using the SUBTOTAL Function

The SUBTOTAL function calculates a column of numbers based on the code used in the function. With the correct code, SUBTOTAL can calculate averages, counts, sums, and eight other functions listed in Table 10.1. It can also ignore hidden rows when the 100 version (101, 102, etc.) of the code is used.

TABLE 10.1 SUBTOTAL Function Numbers

Function_num (Includes Hidden Values)	Function_num (Ignores Hidden Values)	Function	Function Description
1	101	AVERAGE	Averages the numbers in the range
2	102	COUNT	Counts the number of cells containing numbers in the range
3	103	COUNTA	Counts the number of cells that are not empty in the range
4	104	MAX	Returns the largest value in the range
5	105	MIN	Returns the smallest value in the range
6	106	PRODUCT	Multiplies together all the numbers in the range
7	107	STDEV	Calculates the standard deviation of the range based on a sample
8	108	STDEVP	Calculates the standard deviation based on the entire range
9	109	SUM	Adds up all the numbers in the range
10	110	VAR	Estimates the variance based on a sample
11	111	VARP	Calculates the variance based on the entire range

The syntax of the SUBTOTAL function is as follows:

SUBTOTAL(function_num, ref1,[ref2],...)

Figure 10.1 shows the SUBTOTAL function in action versus the SUM function. The SUBTOTAL function with a code of 109 ignores any cells in the range that include SUBTOTAL functions themselves, as shown in the Grand Total. Column E uses the SUM function instead of SUBTOTAL and does not ignore the hidden rows or previous SUM formulas in the Grand Total.

	A	B	C	D	E
			Quantity with		Quantity with
1	Region	Product	SUBTOT		SUM
2	Central	Laser Printers	500		500
3	Central	Laser Printers	400		400
4	Central	Multi-Function	400		400
5	Central	Multi-Function	100		100
6	Central	Laser Printers	900		900
7	Central	Multi-Function	900		900
8	Central	Multi-Function	500		500
9	Central	Laser Printers	400		400
10	Central Total		4100	=SUBTOTAL(109,C2:C9)	4100
11					
12	East	Multi-Function	500		500
13	East	Laser Printers	900		900
14	East	Laser Printers	900		900
15	East	Basic ColorJet F	300		300
16	East	Multi-Function	400		400
17	East	Basic ColorJet F	300		300
18	East	Multi-Function	800		800
19	East	Basic ColorJet F	200		200
20	East	Basic ColorJet F	600		600
21	East Total		4900	=SUBTOTAL(109,C12:C20)	4900
22					
23	West	Laser Printers	600		600
24	West	Laser Printers	400		400
25	West	Multi-Function	1000		1000
26	West	Basic ColorJet F	300		300
27	West	Basic ColorJet F	300		300
28	West	Multi-Function	300		300
29	West	Multi-Function	1000		1000
30	West Total		3900	=SUBTOTAL(109,C23:C29)	3900
31					
32	Grand Total		12900	=SUBTOTAL(109,C2:C29)	25800

FIGURE 10.1

SUBTOTAL can ignore hidden rows and other SUBTOTAL calculations, as shown in the Grand Total. The SUM function adds up all data in its range.

Summarizing Data Using the Subtotal Tool

The SUBTOTAL function is very useful, but if you have a large data set, it can be time consuming to insert all the Total rows. When your data set is large, use the Subtotal tool from the Data tab in the Outline group. This tool groups the sorted data, applying the selected function.

CAUTION You cannot use the Subtotal tool on a data set that has been converted to a Table (Insert, Tables, Table).

From the Subtotal dialog box, shown in Figure 10.2, you can select the column to group the data by, the function to subtotal by, and which columns to apply the subtotal to.

FIGURE 10.2

Use the Subtotal tool to group data and apply subtotals to specific columns.

Figure 10.3 shows a report where the quantity sold was summarized by region. When data is subtotaled with this method, group/ungroup buttons are added along the row headers. You can use the (-) buttons to group the data rows together, showing only the Total, as was done for the Central region. Click a (+) button to expand the data. To create the report shown in Figure 10.3, follow these steps:

1. Sort the data by the column the summary should be based on, the Region column.

 NOTE See Chapter 7, "Sorting Data," for more information about sorting by columns.

2. Select a cell in the data set.

3. Go to Data, Outline, Subtotal. The Subtotal dialog box, shown in Figure 10.2, opens.

4. From the At Each Change In field, select the column by which to summarize the data, Region.

5. From the Use Function field, select the function to calculate the totals by. Because we want to sum the quantities, choose SUM, but there are many functions to choose from.

6. From the Add Subtotal To field, select the column(s) the totals should be added to, Quantity. Notice that, by default, the last column is already selected.

7. Click OK. The data is grouped and subtotaled, with a grand total at the very bottom.

		A	B	C	D
	1	Region	Product	Customer	Quantity
+	10	Central Total			4100
·	11	East	Multi-Function Printers	Bright Hairpin Company	500
·	12	East	Laser Printers	Safe Treadmill Partners	900
·	13	East	Laser Printers	Alluring Shoe Company	900
·	14	East	Basic ColorJet Printers	Compelling Raft Compan	300
·	15	East	Multi-Function Printers	Compelling Raft Compan	400
·	16	East	Basic ColorJet Printers	Compelling Raft Compan	300
·	17	East	Multi-Function Printers	Safe Flagpole Supply	800
·	18	East	Basic ColorJet Printers	Compelling Raft Compan	200
·	19	East	Basic ColorJet Printers	Remarkable Meter Corpc	600
−	20	East Total			4900
·	21	West	Laser Printers	Tasty Kettle Inc.	600
·	22	West	Laser Printers	Alluring Shoe Company	400
·	23	West	Multi-Function Printers	Safe Flagpole Supply	1000
·	24	West	Basic ColorJet Printers	Compelling Raft Compan	300
·	25	West	Basic ColorJet Printers	Compelling Raft Compan	300
·	26	West	Multi-Function Printers	Safe Flagpole Supply	300
·	27	West	Multi-Function Printers	Appealing Calculator Cor	1000
−	28	West Total			3900
−	29	Grand Total			12900

FIGURE 10.3

Use the Subtotal tool to quickly summarize the quantity by region. You can then group the data, showing only the Total rows, like the Central Total.

Placing Subtotals Above the Data

By default, subtotals appear below the data being summarized. If the subtotals need to appear above the data instead, deselect Summary Below Data in the Subtotal dialog box. This also places the Grand Total row at the top of the data, directly below the headings.

Expanding and Collapsing Subtotals

When data is grouped and subtotaled, outline symbols appear to the left of the row headings, as shown in Figure 10.3. Click the numbered icons at the top (1,2,3 in Figure 10.3) to hide and unhide the data in the sheet. For example, clicking the 2 hides the data rows, showing only the Total and Grand Total rows. Clicking the

1 hides the Total rows, showing only the Grand Total. Clicking the 3 unhides all the rows.

Below the numbered icons, next to each Total and Grand Total, are the expand (+) and collapse (-) icons. These expand or collapse the selected group.

Removing Subtotals or Groups

To remove all the subtotals and groups, click the Remove All button in the Subtotal dialog box. To remove only the group and outline buttons, leaving the subtotal row intact, select Data, Outline, Ungroup, Clear Outline. You can also use Ctrl+8 to toggle the visibility of the outline buttons.

 CAUTION You cannot undo Clear Outline. If you accidentally select the option, click a cell in the table, bring up the Subtotal dialog box and click OK. The symbols will be replaced.

Copying the Subtotals to a New Location

If you hide the data rows, copy all the Subtotal rows and paste them to another sheet. All the data, including the hidden data rows, will appear in the new sheet. To copy and paste only the subtotals, follow these steps to select only the visible cells:

1. Click the Outline icon so that only the rows to copy are visible.

2. Select the entire data set. If the headers are to be included, this can be quickly done by selecting a single cell in the data set and pressing Ctrl+A.

3. Go to Home, Editing, Find & Select, Go to Special, and select Visible Cells Only, as shown in Figure 10.4. Note: The dashed lines in the figure are shown for emphasis only. They will appear in the next step.

4. Select Home, Clipboard, Copy.

5. Select the cell where the data is to be pasted.

6. Select Home, Clipboard, Paste. The SUBTOTAL formulas are converted to values automatically.

 TIP A shortcut for step 3 is to press Alt+; (semicolon).

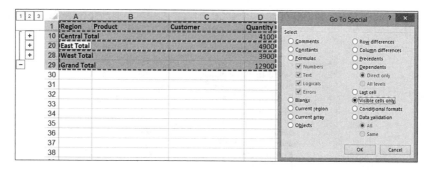

FIGURE 10.4

Select Visible Cells Only to copy and paste only the Total rows.

Formatting the Subtotals

If you hide the data rows, select the subtotal rows, and apply formatting to them, all the data, including the hidden data rows, will reflect the new formatting. To format just the subtotals, follow these steps to select only the visible cells:

1. Click the Outline icon so that only the rows to copy are visible.

2. Select the entire data set. If the headers are to be included, this can be quickly done by selecting a single cell in the data set and pressing Ctrl+A.

3. Go to Home, Editing, Find & Select, Go to Special, and select Visible Cells Only, as shown in Figure 10.4.

4. Apply the desired formatting.

 TIP A shortcut for step 3 is to press Alt+; (semicolon).

Applying Different Subtotal Function Types

A data set can have more than one type of subtotal applied to it—for example, a sum subtotal of one column and a count subtotal of another. Because you can only select one function at a time, you will have to use the Subtotal dialog box multiple times. Make sure the Replace Current Subtotals option in the dialog box is deselected so that each subtotal will be applied; otherwise, the previous subtotal(s) will be cleared before the new function is applied. Each subtotal will be calculated and placed on its own row, pushing any existing subtotal rows down, as shown in Figure 10.5 where the Quantity total was added before the Revenue average.

Region	Product	Quantity	Revenue
East	Basic ColorJet Printers	300	5961
West	Basic ColorJet Printers	300	7032
West	Basic ColorJet Printers	300	6735
East	Basic ColorJet Printers	300	6240
East	Basic ColorJet Printers	200	4740
East	Basic ColorJet Printers	600	12672
	Basic ColorJet Printers Average		7230
	Basic ColorJet Printers Total	2000	
	Laser Printers Average		14726
	Laser Printers Total	5000	
	Multi-Function Printers Average		11375
	Multi-Function Printers Total	5900	
	Grand Average		11456
	Grand Total	12900	

FIGURE 10.5

You can subtotal multiple columns, mixing different Subtotal function types.

To create the report in Figure 10.5 where, for each change in product, the Quantity column is summed and the Revenue column is averaged, follow these steps:

1. Sort the data by the column the summary should be based on, column B.

2. Select a cell in the data set.

3. Go to Data, Outline, Subtotal.

4. From the At Each Change In field, select the column, Product, by which to summarize the data.

5. From the Use Function field, select the function, SUM, to calculate the totals by.

6. From the Add Subtotal To field, select the Quantity column the total should be added to. Notice that, by default, the last column is already selected and you may have to deselect it.

7. Click OK.

8. Go to Data, Outline, Subtotal.

9. Deselect Replace Current Subtotals.

10. Repeat steps 4 to 6, selecting a new function, AVERAGE, from the Use Function field and a new column, Revenue, to apply the subtotal to. Be sure to deselect the previously selected column, Quantity.

11. Click OK. The data set reflects two subtotals.

Combining Multiple Subtotal Results to One Row

When applying multiple function types, Excel places each subtotal on its own row, as shown in Figure 10.5. There is no built-in option to have the subtotals appear on the same row. But you can manipulate Excel to make this happen by including the column when you apply subtotals to other columns and then manually changing the formula to use the subtotal code actually needed.

 NOTE   See the "Using the SUBTOTAL function" section for a list of subtotal codes.

The report in Figure 10.6 sums the Quantity, Revenue, COGS, and Profit columns, but has a count of the Customer column.

Region	Product	Customer	Quantity	Revenue	COGS	Profit
West	Laser Printers	Tasty Kettle Inc.	600	13806	6132	7674
West	Laser Printers	Alluring Shoe Company	400	9144	4088	5056
West	Multi-Function Print(	Safe Flagpole Supply	1000	19110	8470	10640
West	Basic ColorJet Printe(	Compelling Raft Compan	300	7032	2952	4080
West	Basic ColorJet Printe(	Compelling Raft Compan	300	6735	2952	3783
West	Multi-Function Print(	Safe Flagpole Supply	300	6207	2541	3666
West	Multi-Function Print(	Appealing Calculator Cor	1000	19250	8470	10780
West Total			7	3900	81284	35605	45679
Central Total			8	4100	88926	38577	50349
East Total			9	4900	104726	46571	58155
Grand Total			24	12900	274936	120753	154183

FIGURE 10.6

Columns D:G are sums of the grouped data, but column C is a count of the data.

To have multiple function types appear on a single row, follow these steps:

1. Sort the data by the column the summary should be based on, the Region column.

2. Select a cell in the data set.

3. Go to Data, Outline, Subtotal.

4. From the At Each Change In field, select the column you want to summarize data by, Region.

5. From the Use Function field, select the function to calculate the majority of totals by, SUM.

6. From the Add Subtotal To field, select the columns the totals should be added to. Include the column where you want to apply the second function type, like the Customer column selected in Figure 10.7.

FIGURE 10.7

The Customer column is selected as a temporary holder for the actual subtotal formula that will be used.

7. Click OK. The Total rows are inserted.

8. Collapse the data set to show only the Total rows by clicking the "2" outline symbol.

9. Select the data in the column where the second function type should be, the Customer column.

10. Go to Home, Editing, Find & Select, Go to Special, and select Visible Cells Only.

 TIP A shortcut for step 10 is to press Alt+; (semicolon).

11. Go to Home, Editing, Find & Select, Replace.

12. In the Find What field, type (9. 9 is the code for the SUM function that was applied in step 5.

13. In the Replace With field, type the SUBTOTAL function using the desired function number. For example, in Figure 10.8, (3 will replace the SUM function with the COUNTA function.

14. Click Replace All.

15. Click OK to close the Excel notification of the number of replacements made.

16. Click Close. If needed, apply any required formatting to the selected cells.

FIGURE 10.8

Use Find and Replace to replace the automated subtotals with the desired function code.

Subtotaling by Multiple Columns

Figure 10.9 shows a report where the Revenue, COGS, and Profit columns are summed by Region and Product. To subtotal by multiple columns, sort the data set by the desired columns and then apply the subtotals, making sure Replace Current Subtotals is not selected. The subtotals should be applied in order of greatest to least. For example, if the data is sorted by Region, with the products within each region sorted, apply the subtotal to the Region column and then the Product column, like this:

1. Sort the data by the columns the summary should be based on. Because the report is to be by Region then Product, sort by Region first, then Product.

2. Select a cell in the data set.

3. Go to Data, Outline, Subtotal.

4. From the At Each Change In field, select the major column, Region, by which to summarize the data.

5. From the Use Function field, select the function, SUM, to calculate the totals by.

6. From the Add Subtotal To field, select the columns the totals should be added to—Revenue, COGS, Profit.

7. Click OK.

8. Repeat steps 3 to 7 for the secondary column, selecting the minor column, Product, and unselecting Replace Current Subtotals.

1	Region	Product	Quantity	Revenue	COGS	Profit
2	Central	Laser Printers	500	11240	5110	6130
3	Central	Laser Printers	400	9204	4088	5116
4	Central	Laser Printers	900	21888	9198	12690
5	Central	Laser Printers	400	10044	4088	5956
6		**Laser Printers Total**		52376	22484	29892
7	Central	Multi-Function Printers	400	6860	3388	3472
8	Central	Multi-Function Printers	100	1740	847	893
9	Central	Multi-Function Printers	900	17505	7623	9882
10	Central	Multi-Function Printers	500	10445	4235	6210
11		**Multi-Function Printers Total**		36550	16093	20457
12	**Central Total**			88926	38577	50349

FIGURE 10.9

Apply subtotals to both Region (the major column) and then Product (the minor column) to get subtotals of both.

Sorting Subtotals

If you try to sort a subtotaled data set while viewing all the data, Excel informs you that to do so will remove all the subtotals. Although the data itself cannot be sorted, the subtotal rows can be, and the grouped data will remain intact. To do this, collapse the data so that only the subtotals are being viewed, and then apply the desired sort.

Adding Space Between Subtotaled Groups

When subtotals are inserted into a data set, only subtotal rows are added between the groups. The report may appear crunched together for some reviewers (see Figure 10.10), and they may request that rows be inserted, separating the subtotaled groups from each other. You can insert extra space into a subtotaled report in two ways.

Separating Subtotaled Groups for Print

If the report is going to be printed, blank rows probably don't need to be inserted. Just the illusion needs to be created because the actual need is for more space between the subtotal and the next group. This can be done by adjusting the row height of the subtotal rows. To increase the amount of space when the subtotal is placed below the data, follow these steps:

1. Collapse the data set so that only the subtotals are in view.

2. Select the entire data set, except for the header row.

3. Press Alt+; (semicolon) to select the visible cells only.

4. Go to Home, Cells, Format, and select Row Height.

5. Enter a new value in the Row Height dialog box.

6. Click OK.

7. Go to Home, Alignment, and select the Top Align button.

8. Spacing now appears between each group, as shown in Figure 10.11.

Region	Product	Customer	Quantity	Revenue	COGS	Profit
Central	Laser Printers	Alluring Shoe Company	500	11240	5110	6130
Central	Laser Printers	Alluring Shoe Company	400	9204	4088	5116
East	Laser Printers	Alluring Shoe Company	900	21465	9198	12267
West	Laser Printers	Alluring Shoe Company	400	9144	4088	5056
Central	Multi-Function Printers	Alluring Shoe Company	500	10445	4235	6210
		Alluring Shoe Company Total		61498	26719	34779
Central	Multi-Function Printers	Appealing Calculator Corporation	900	17505	7623	9882
West	Multi-Function Printers	Appealing Calculator Corporation	1000	19250	8470	10780
		Appealing Calculator Corporation Total		36755	16093	20662
East	Multi-Function Printers	Bright Hairpin Company	500	10245	4235	6010
		Bright Hairpin Company Total		10245	4235	6010
East	Basic ColorJet Printers	Compelling Raft Company	300	5961	2952	3009
West	Basic ColorJet Printers	Compelling Raft Company	300	7032	2952	4080
West	Basic ColorJet Printers	Compelling Raft Company	300	6735	2952	3783
East	Multi-Function Printers	Compelling Raft Company	400	8164	3388	4776
East	Basic ColorJet Printers	Compelling Raft Company	300	6240	2952	3288
East	Basic ColorJet Printers	Compelling Raft Company	200	4740	1968	2772
		Compelling Raft Company Total		38872	17164	21708

FIGURE 10.10

The close rows in this report can make it difficult to see the different groups.

Region	Product	Customer	Quantity	Revenue	COGS	Profit
Central	Laser Printers	Alluring Shoe Company	500	11240	5110	6130
Central	Laser Printers	Alluring Shoe Company	400	9204	4088	5116
East	Laser Printers	Alluring Shoe Company	900	21465	9198	12267
West	Laser Printers	Alluring Shoe Company	400	9144	4088	5056
Central	Multi-Function Printers	Alluring Shoe Company	500	10445	4235	6210
		Alluring Shoe Company Total		61498	26719	34779
Central	Multi-Function Printers	Appealing Calculator Corporation	900	17505	7623	9882
West	Multi-Function Printers	Appealing Calculator Corporation	1000	19250	8470	10780
		Appealing Calculator Corporation Total		36755	16093	20662
East	Multi-Function Printers	Bright Hairpin Company	500	10245	4235	6010
		Bright Hairpin Company Total		10245	4235	6010
East	Basic ColorJet Printers	Compelling Raft Company	300	5961	2952	3009
West	Basic ColorJet Printers	Compelling Raft Company	300	7032	2952	4080
West	Basic ColorJet Printers	Compelling Raft Company	300	6735	2952	3783
East	Multi-Function Printers	Compelling Raft Company	400	8164	3388	4776
East	Basic ColorJet Printers	Compelling Raft Company	300	6240	2952	3288
East	Basic ColorJet Printers	Compelling Raft Company	200	4740	1968	2772
		Compelling Raft Company Total		38872	17164	21708

FIGURE 10.11

Adjust the row height and text alignment of the subtotal rows to separate the groups.

TIP If the subtotal row is above the data, then skip step 7 as, by default, alignment is set to Bottom Align.

Separating Subtotaled Groups for Distributed Files

It's a bit involved, but a blank row can be inserted between groups in a file that you're going to distribute. The method involves using a temporary column to hold the space below where a blank row is needed.

 CAUTION This method will disable Excel's capability to manipulate the subtotals in the data set. The Total rows will remain, but the outline icons no longer work properly, and future subtotal changes will require the groupings and subtotals to be manually removed first.

To insert blank rows when subtotals are placed below the data, follow these steps:

1. Collapse the data set so only the subtotals are in view.

2. In a blank column to the right of the data set, select a range as long as the data set.

3. Press Alt+; (semicolon) to select the visible cells only.

4. Type a **1** and press Ctrl+Enter to enter the value in all visible cells.

5. Expand the data set by clicking the outline icon with the largest number.

6. Select the cell above the first cell with a 1 in it.

7. Go to Home, Cells, Insert, Insert Cells.

8. From the Insert dialog box, select Shift Cells Down and click OK, as shown in Figure 10.12. This shifts the 1 one row down.

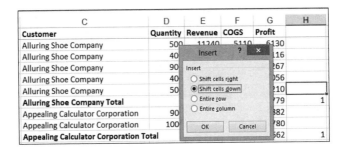

FIGURE 10.12

Select the cell above the first cell with a 1 in it then insert a new cell to shift all the values in the column down one row.

9. Highlight the column with the 1s in it.

10. Go to Home, Editing, Find & Select, Go to Special.

11. From the Go to Special dialog box, select Constants and click OK.

12. Go to Home, Cells, Insert, Insert Sheet Rows. A blank row is inserted above the row containing a 1.

13. Delete the temporary column.

Region	Product	Customer	Quantity	Revenue	COGS	Profit
Central	Laser Printers	Alluring Shoe Company	500	11240	5110	6130
Central	Laser Printers	Alluring Shoe Company	400	9204	4088	5116
East	Laser Printers	Alluring Shoe Company	900	21465	9198	12267
West	Laser Printers	Alluring Shoe Company	400	9144	4088	5056
Central	Multi-Function Printers	Alluring Shoe Company	500	10445	4235	6210
		Alluring Shoe Company Total		61498	26719	34779
Central	Multi-Function Printers	Appealing Calculator Corporation	900	17505	7623	9882
West	Multi-Function Printers	Appealing Calculator Corporation	1000	19250	8470	10780
		Appealing Calculator Corporation Total		36755	16093	20662
East	Multi-Function Printers	Bright Hairpin Company	500	10245	4235	6010
		Bright Hairpin Company Total		10245	4235	6010

FIGURE 10.13

Use a temporary column to insert blank rows between groups.

Grouping and Outlining Rows and Columns

Selected rows and columns can be grouped together manually using the options in Data, Outline, Group. This is helpful if you have a sheet designed for multiple users and you want to only show them rows and/or columns specific to the user. Once the data is grouped, an Expand/Collapse button will be placed below the last row in the selection or to the right of the last column in the selection.

 CAUTION An outline can only have up to eight levels.

If the data to be grouped includes a calculated Total row or column between the groups, you can use the Auto Outline option found in the Group drop-down. This option creates groups based on the location of the rows or columns containing formulas. If the data set contains formulas in both rows and columns, though, the option will create groups for both rows and columns. This tool works best if there are no formulas within the data set itself, unless you do want the groups to be created based off those calculations.

Use the Group option for absolute control of how the rows or columns are grouped. For example, if you have a catalog with products grouped together, users can expand or collapse each group to view the products, as shown in Figure 10.14. By default, the Expand/Collapse buttons will appear below the data. To get them to appear above the grouped data, first apply a subtotal to the data set with Summary Below Data deselected. Then undo the change and apply the desired groupings.

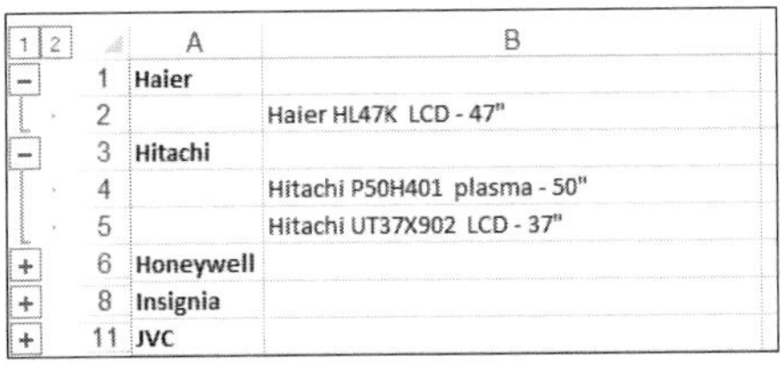

FIGURE 10.14

Group items together to make it easier for users to view only the desired items.

To manually group rows with the Expand/Collapse button above the grouped data set, follow these steps:

1. Select a cell in the data set.

2. Go to Data, Outline, Subtotal.

3. A message may appear that Excel cannot determine which row has column labels. Click OK.

4. In the Subtotal dialog box, deselect Summary Below Data and click OK.

5. Excel inserts subtotal rows in the data. Click the Undo button in the Quick Access toolbar to remove the rows. While it may appear that you've just undone all the previous steps, these steps were required to configure where the outline icon would appear.

6. Select the first set of rows to group together. Do not include the header. For example, to create the Hitachi grouping in Figure 10.14, select rows 4 and 5 to group. To create the Haier group, select only row 2.

7. Go to Data, Outline, Group, Group, or just select the Group button itself.

8. Repeat steps 6 and 7 for each group of rows.

TIP   Press the F4 key to repeat the last command performed in Excel. So, after grouping one set of rows, select the next group and press F4, then another group, press F4, and so on. As long as you don't perform another command, pressing F4 will group the selected rows.

Groups can be cleared one of two ways from the Data, Outline, Ungroup drop-down:

- **Ungroup**—Ungroups the selected data. Will ungroup a single row from a larger group if that is all that is selected.

- **Clear Outline**—Clears all groups on a sheet unless more than one cell is selected, in which case the selected item will be ungrouped. If used on data that was subtotaled using the Subtotal button, the subtotals will remain; only the groupings will be removed.

THE ABSOLUTE MINIMUM

SUBTOTAL is a special function that ignores other SUBTOTAL functions in the same row or column, preventing the duplication of calculations. Although you can enter the formula manually, if you use the Subtotal tool to enter it automatically, you can take advantage of Excel's grouping ability. You can also group items without subtotaling using the grouping tool.

IN THIS CHAPTER

- Quickly add a chart to a sheet.
- Create a chart mixing bars and lines.
- Make a pie chart easier to read.
- Insert sparklines into a report.

11

CREATING CHARTS AND SPARKLINES

Charts are a great way to graphically portray data. They're a quick and simple way to emphasize trends in data. Some people prefer to look at them instead of trying to make sense of rows and columns of numbers. Excel offers two methods of charting data—charts and sparklines. Charts, which you are most likely familiar with, are large graphics with a title and numbers and/or text along the left and bottom. Sparklines are miniature charts in cells with only markers to represent the data. This chapter provides you with the tools to create simple, but useful, charts. For further information, refer to *Charts & Graphs: Microsoft Excel 2013* (ISBN 978-0-7897-4862-1) by Bill Jelen.

Preparing Data

The first step in creating a chart is ensuring that the data is set up properly. Although the following rules aren't going to prevent a chart from being created, heeding these rules allows Excel to help you create a chart by identifying the chart components:

- Ensure that there are no blank rows or columns.

- Ensure that headers along the left column and top row identify each series.

- If your row or column headers include numbers, leave the upper-left corner of the chart blank (see cell A1 in Figure 11.1). If the cell isn't blank, Excel may be confused when it tries to help you create the chart and it may assume there are no category labels and chart the header as data.

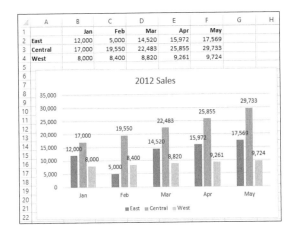

FIGURE 11.1

A basic chart and its source data. A chart consists of many components that you can configure.

Elements of a Chart

A chart is a graphical representation of numerical data. Behind every chart is a data range on a sheet, like the table shown in A1:F4 in Figure 11.1. This range is called the *source data*.

A *series* is a row or column from the source data represented on the chart as a line, a bar, or other marker used to portray the data. A typical series consists of the following:

- **Series name**—The cell with the name of the series that will appear in the legend

- **Series values**—The row or column containing the data to be charted

- **Category labels**—The range containing the label that will appear along the axis, identifying the series value

In Figure 11.1, the series names are East, Central, and West. The series values are presented by the thick-shaded vertical columns. The category labels are the months, Jan through May, along the horizontal axis, also known as the x-axis.

 NOTE If using the Quick Analysis tool or Recommended Charts options, Excel will help you create a chart by trying to ascertain whether the rows or columns in the source data are to be used as a series. Normally, the row or column set consisting of fewer items will default to the series, but Excel may switch this depending on the chart type. If the number of rows and columns are equal, Excel may offer a chart of each type. In Figure 11.1, Excel correctly determined that East, Central, and West were the series for the chart because the source data had fewer rows (three) than columns (five).

 CAUTION The following chart elements are the most common. Not all may appear depending on the selected chart's type.

Gridlines are horizontal or vertical lines in the chart that help make it easier to read the values of the markers.

The *axes* consist of major and minor gridlines that usually go below and to the left of the charted data (except for pie charts), labeling or marking intervals of the data. An axis may also have an Axis Title or Display Units Label. The horizontal axis, the one that goes left to right, is also known as the x-axis. The vertical axis, the one that goes up and down, is also known as the y-axis.

The *legend* is the color code for the chart series, identifying each series by the name assigned to it. In Figure 11.1, the legend is placed along the bottom of the chart.

Data labels are text that appears in the chart by the series marker, identifying the value of the points being charted, as shown in Figure 11.1.

The *chart title* is located at the top of the chart. By default, it isn't linked to a cell on the sheet—you must manually type it in.

TIP   See the section "Editing and Formatting a Chart Title" for a tip on linking a chart title to a cell.

Error bars are markers on a chart that look like the capital letter I. They're used to see margins of error in the data.

A *trendline* is a line on a chart that shows data trends, including future values. Trendlines can only be added to the following nonstacked, 2D charts: bar, column, line, area, stock, and scatter.

Put together, a chart has two areas:

- **Plot area**—Consists of the series and inner gridlines
- **Chart area**—Consists of the area surrounding the plot area, including the frame of the chart

Types of Charts

There are ten chart groups, each with several types you can select from, in Excel. Further manual changes, such as mixing chart types, provide even more variations. The ten charts groups are:

TIP   In the Charts group on the Insert tab, there are eight buttons, with the Radar drop-down button listing Stock, Surface, and Radar.

- **Column**—Includes 2D Column and 3D Column chart types that feature markers relating the vertical height to size. They are useful for showing data changes over a period of time or comparing items. 3D Cylinder, 3D Cone, and 3D Pyramid charts can be created by modifying a 3D Column chart.
- **Line**—Includes 2D Line and 3D Line chart types. They are useful for displaying continuous data over time against a common scale.
- **Pie**—Includes 2D Pie, 3D Pie, and Doughnut chart types. Pie charts are most suitable for single-series data sets. They are useful for showing how an item is proportional to the sum of all items. A doughnut chart is similar to a pie chart in that it shows how an item is proportional to the whole, but unlike a pie chart, it can include more than one series.
- **Bar**—Includes 2D Bar and 3D Bar chart types that feature markers relating the horizontal width to size. They are useful for comparing items. 3D Cylinder, 3D Cone, and 3D Pyramid charts can be created by modifying a 3D Column chart.

- **Area**—Includes 2D Area and 3D Area chart types. They are similar to line charts except that the area underneath the line is filled with color. Area charts emphasize the magnitude of change over time.

- **Scatter (XY)**—Includes Scatter chart types of just markers, just lines, or combined markers and lines. They show the relationships among numeric values in several data series or can be used to plot two groups of numbers as one series of x,y coordinate. Also includes 2D Bubble and 3D Bubble chart types used to plot data points with the size of a bubble suggesting its relationship to the other bubbles.

- **Stock**—Illustrates the fluctuation of the data, such as stocks or temperatures.

- **Surface**—Finds the optimum combinations between two sets of data.

- **Radar**—Compares the total values of several data series.

- **Combo**—Helps you combine multiple chart types. See the section "Creating a Chart with Multiple Chart Types" for more information.

Column, Line, Bar, and Area chart types have three basic patterns available:

- **Clustered**—In a clustered chart, the markers are plotted side by side, making it easier to compare markers. The downside is that it is more difficult to tell if the data is increasing or decreasing in comparison with the next cluster. When viewing the chart types, clustered chart types show a light marker next to a dark marker.

- **Stacked**—In a stacked chart, the markers are plotted on top of each other, making it easier to see how the sum of data changes, but making it more difficult to see how a specific series changes over time. When viewing the chart types, stacked charts show a dark marker on top of or to the right of a light marker. The stacks are of differing heights.

- **100% stacked**—In a 100% stacked chart, the markers are plotted on top of each other. All stacks are scaled to have a height of 100%, allowing you to see which data points make the largest percentage of each stack. When viewing the chart types, stacked charts show a dark marker on top of or to the right of a light marker. The stacks are of the same heights.

 CAUTION   With the variety of charts available and the settings to make them eye catching, you might be tempted to choose a chart type based on its visual appeal—but keep in mind that not all chart designs will properly convey a true interpretation of the data. For example, look at the chart in Figure 11.2. A 3D pyramid is a fun way of looking at data, especially during a long presentation. But compare the three sections—do they really tell the truth of the data? The value of the base of the pyramid is less than half of the top value. But that is difficult to tell from just the image. Imagine if the data values weren't turned on? And compare the middle section with the top. They look about the same, with perhaps the middle slightly larger, but the data values tell a different story.

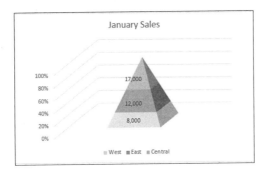

FIGURE 11.2

A bad chart design can distort the truth about the data.

Adding a Chart to a Sheet

There are three ways to add a chart to a sheet. With two of the methods—Quick Analysis tool and Recommended Charts—you pick from a group of charts Excel has selected for you. You can still customize the chart after it's placed on the sheet—Excel just offers a place to start. The third method allows you to choose from all available charts.

Once you've added a chart to a sheet, you can select it by clicking anywhere in the chart area. No matter which method you choose, you'll have to add a chart title after the chart is inserted. See the section "Editing and Formatting a Chart Title" for instructions on how to do this. You'll also be able to change the color and apply a chart style (see the section "Applying Chart Styles and Colors").

Using the Quick Analysis Tool

The Quick Analysis tool is a quick way to insert a chart on a sheet. When you select data on the sheet, the Quick Analysis tool appears in the lower-right corner of the selection, as shown in Figure 11.3. When you click on the icon and select Charts, Excel suggests different chart types based on its analysis of the selected data. Although the data in Figures 11.3 and 11.4 is the same, the selections differ and Excel's chart type recommendations differ, too.

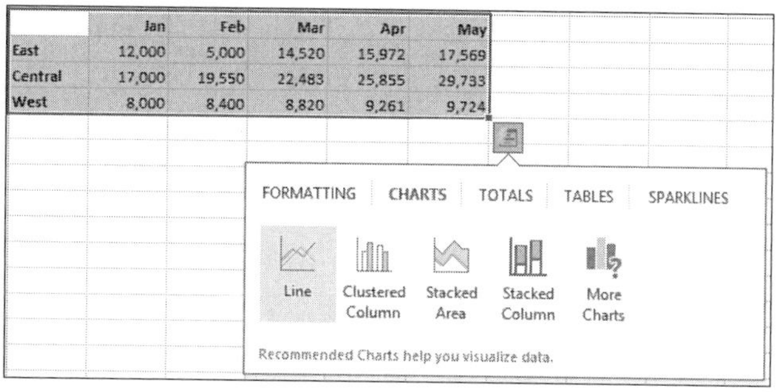

	Jan	Feb	Mar	Apr	May
East	12,000	5,000	14,520	15,972	17,569
Central	17,000	19,550	22,483	25,855	29,733
West	8,000	8,400	8,820	9,261	9,724

FORMATTING | CHARTS | TOTALS | TABLES | SPARKLINES

Line | Clustered Column | Stacked Area | Stacked Column | More Charts

Recommended Charts help you visualize data.

FIGURE 11.3

Use the Quick Analysis tool to bring up a list of suggested chart types.

	A	B	C	D	E	F	G
		Jan	Feb	Mar	Apr	May	
East		12,000	5,000	14,520	15,972	17,569	
Central		17,000	19,550	22,483	25,855	29,733	
West		8,000	8,400	8,820	9,261	9,724	

FORMATTING | CHARTS | TOTALS | TABLES | SPARKLINES

Clustered Column | Stacked Column | Stacked Area | Clustered Bar | Stacked Bar | More Charts

Recommended Charts help you visualize data.

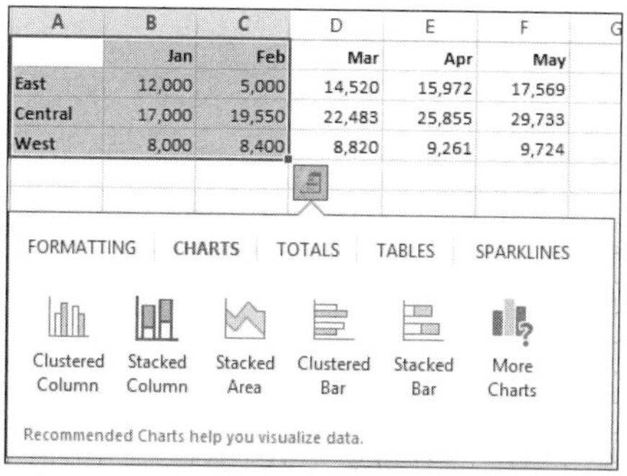

FIGURE 11.4

The list of suggested chart types will change depending on the selected data.

As you move your cursor over the suggestions, a preview image appears, so you can see what your data would look like in the selected chart type. When you've decided which chart you want, click on the icon and Excel inserts the chart on the sheet. If you don't see a chart type you like, selecting More Charts opens up a list of the Recommended Charts. See the following section "Viewing Recommended Charts."

Viewing Recommended Charts

You don't have to select your data range before viewing Excel's recommended charts, but it does ensure that Excel properly interprets the range. You must have at least one cell in the source data selected, then go to Insert, Charts,

Recommended Charts and the Insert Chart dialog box shown in Figure 11.5 opens.

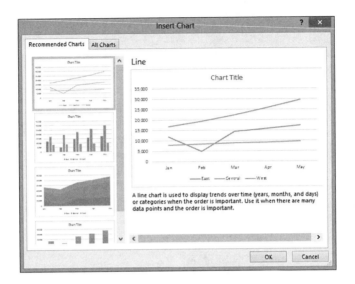

FIGURE 11.5

Excel recommends charts based on its interpretation of your data.

On the left side of the dialog box are Excel's recommended charts. Click on a chart and a larger version appears on the right side of the dialog box. When you see one you like, select it and then click OK. It is added to the active sheet. If you don't see a chart type you like, select the All Charts tab to see all the charts available in Excel. See the following section "Viewing All Available Charts" for more information.

Viewing All Available Charts

For access to all available charts—not just the ones Excel thinks you might find useful—select at least one cell in your source data and then select one of the chart type drop-downs in the Charts group of the Insert tab or click on the See All Charts dialog launcher in the lower-right corner of the Charts group.

If you open a drop-down from the Charts group, you can move your cursor over the individual charts and a preview appears on the sheet. If you see the chart you want, click on its icon and the chart is added to the sheet.

If you don't see the chart you want, select the More [chart type] Charts text at the bottom of the drop-down to open the Insert Chart dialog box to the chart group you were looking at previously. If you click the ribbon shortcut instead, it opens the Insert Chart dialog box to the Recommended Charts tab. Click the All Charts tab to view all charts.

The left side of the Insert Chart, All Charts dialog box, shown in Figure 11.6, lists all the chart groups available. When you select a group, the available types are shown along the upper-right side of the dialog box. If you select a type, a preview appears below the types. Depending on the source data setup, you might get two or more previews, reflecting possible data series configurations. If Excel cannot interpret the source data, you don't get a preview image. For example, an Open-High-Low-Close Stock chart requires a very specific setup of opening price, high price, low price, closing price.

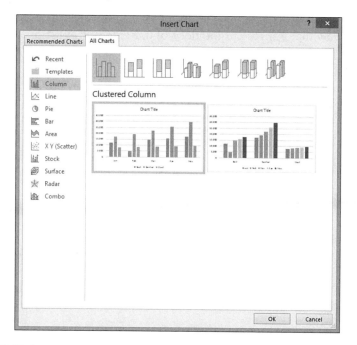

FIGURE 11.6

Choose from all the charts Excel has to offer through the All Charts option.

When you place your cursor over a preview, a larger version appears. Once you find the chart you want, select it, and then click OK; it is added to the sheet.

Adding, Removing, and Formatting Chart Elements

When you select a chart, three icons appear on the right side of it. The first, which looks like a plus sign, is for Chart Elements, the items reviewed in the section "Elements of a Chart."

 NOTE You can also access a list of elements by going to Chart Tools, Design, Chart Layouts, and opening the Add Chart Elements drop-down. This list doesn't offer the ability to turn elements on/off by just selecting the element. Instead, you must open the element's submenu and make a selection.

Select an element to have it appear in the chart. Deselect it to hide it. For additional options concerning the element, such as its location in the chart, click on the arrow that appears to the right of the element. A list of options appears, as shown in Figure 11.7. Selecting More Options opens a task pane on the right side of Excel. Depending on the selected element, the options shown change, but it is from this task pane that you can make more changes to the element's formatting, such as the color, 3D design, and alignment.

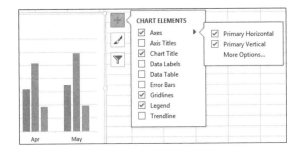

FIGURE 11.7

The Chart Elements list allows you to turn an element on or off and adjust its settings.

Editing and Formatting a Chart Title

Unless you have a single data series with a row header, when you insert a chart, Excel places a "Chart Title" placeholder at the top of the chart. To change the text, click in the text box and replace the generic "Chart Title." You can also apply formatting to the title. If you select the entire text box, the formatting will apply to the entire title. Else, you can select a single character or word and format just that.

 CAUTION   The selection frame around the text box changes depending on the mode the selection is in. When the frame is selected and the frame is solid, any formatting will apply to the entire frame and its contents. If the frame is dashed, then the selection is inside the frame.

 TIP   To move the text box to a custom location, place your cursor along the box edge until it turns into a four-headed arrow. At this point, hold down the mouse button and drag the box to a new location.

Excel doesn't have the built-in ability, but with a little work, you can create a dynamic chart title linked to a cell. To do this, select the title text box, ensuring the selection frame is solid, not dashed. Next, place your cursor in the formula bar, type an equal sign (=), and then click on the cell containing the title text. Press Enter and the title updates to reflect the cell's text. As the text in the cell changes, the chart title also updates.

If you decide to make the title static again, right-click on the title and select Edit Text. You can also toggle the chart title on and off to reset the title.

Changing the Display Units in an Axis

Excel bases the units shown in an axis off the data. Excel displays units in millions or billions if that is what your data contains, taking up quite a bit of room. You can change the display units, reducing the amount of space used and making the axis easier to read. To do this, right-click on the axis and select Format Axis. From the task pane, select Axis Options, the last icon that looks like a chart. Near the bottom of the Axis Options section is a section for Display Units, as shown in Figure 11.8. Open the drop-down and select how you want the units abbreviated. If you don't want abbreviation text appearing by the axis, deselect Show Display Units Label on Chart. Instead, you can customize the chart title, as shown in Figure 11.8.

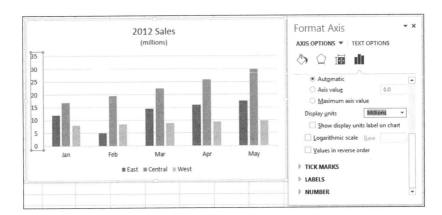

FIGURE 11.8

Change the display units of a numerical axis to reduce the amount of space used.

Applying Chart Styles and Colors

Once you've inserted a chart, you may want to move the chart title, move the legend, add a background, change the color of the series, or apply any number of changes to make the chart more attention getting. You can apply each change yourself, or you can see what chart styles Excel has available.

When you select a chart, three icons appear along the right side of it. Clicking the second icon with the paintbrush opens up a Style dialog box, in which you can scroll and view various styles, as shown in Figure 11.9. As you place your cursor over each one, your chart updates and provides a preview of the style. When you find a style you like, click it and your chart will update.

 NOTE You can also access this list of styles by selecting your chart and going to Chart Tools, Design, Chart Styles.

If you click the Color tab of the Styles dialog box (or go to Chart Tools, Design, Change Colors), various color combinations are shown. If you place your cursor over a color sample, the data series in the chart updates. When you find a color scheme you like, click it and your chart updates.

 TIP If you click once on a single series in the chart so that only the series is selected, then go to Chart Tools, Format, Shape Styles, Shape Fill, you can change the color of the selected series. If you click twice (two single clicks, not a double-click) on a specific data point in a series so that only it, not the entire series, is selected, you can apply a color to just that data point.

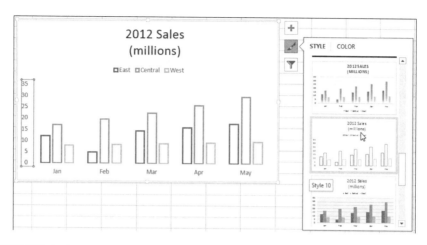

FIGURE 11.9

Apply one of Excel's existing chart styles to create an eye-catching chart.

Applying Chart Layouts

Chart layouts are predefined layouts offering combinations of the chart elements: legend, chart title, axis title, data labels, and data table. From Chart Tools, Design, Chart Layouts, Quick Layout, up to 12 layouts are available, depending on the type of chart selected. If you place your cursor over a layout sample, the chart updates and provides a preview. When you find a layout you like, click it and your chart updates. If none of the predefined combinations is what you want, you can manually modify each element.

Moving or Resizing a Chart

The default location for a chart is the same sheet as the data. If you create your chart using the Quick Analysis tool or the Recommended Charts options, you have no control on where the chart is initially placed. But a chart can be moved to another location on the same sheet, to a new sheet, or to its own chart sheet.

To move a chart elsewhere on the same sheet, click anywhere in the chart area and drag the chart to the new location. Be careful not to click in the plot area or you'll move the actual chart itself within the frame.

To relocate the chart to another sheet, first make sure the new sheet exists. Then, select the chart and go to Chart Tools, Design, Location, Move Chart. From the Move Chart dialog box that opens, select the new sheet from the Object In drop-down.

A chart sheet is a special type of sheet in Excel used to display only charts. It doesn't have cells like the other sheets and you can't add any information to it, other than the chart components. To relocate the chart to its own chart sheet, select the chart and go to Chart Tools, Design, Location, Move Chart. From the Move Chart dialog box that opens, select the New Sheet option. Charts on a chart sheet cannot be resized, except by zooming in and out on the sheet.

To resize a selected chart, place the cursor at any of the four corners or midway along any of the edges of the frame. When the cursor changes to a double-headed arrow, click and drag the chart to the desired size.

Switching Rows and Columns

If, after inserting a chart, you want to switch the row/column setup being used for the data series, select the chart and then click the Switch Row/Column button found on the Chart Tools, Design tab in the Data group. Excel switches the range used for the series and the range used for the category labels.

Changing an Existing Chart's Type

You don't have to re-create a chart from scratch if you want to change the chart type. Just select the chart; go to Insert, Charts; and select a new chart type from the drop-downs. Any formatting that can transfer over will be included in the new chart type. You can also go to Chart Tools, Design, Type, Change Chart Type. See the section "Viewing All Available Charts" for instructions on using the dialog box.

Creating a Chart with Multiple Chart Types

Some of the chart types can be used together in a single chart, as shown in Figure 11.10, where region series are column charts and the monthly average a line chart. You can do this by selecting Combo as the chart type. If you need to change an existing chart into a combo chart, see the preceding section, "Changing an Existing Chart's Type."

TIP Excel does not show a combo chart as a recommendation when you select from the Quick Analysis tool or Recommended Charts. You must insert the chart using the instructions in the section "Viewing All Available Charts."

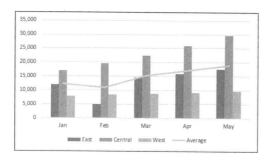

FIGURE 11.10

Use a combo chart to add a line to show how each region compares with the average.

Select Combo from the Insert Chart or Change Chart Type dialog box and Excel provides a few predesigned combo charts to choose from. If none of the options is what you want, click the last icon, Custom Combination, which looks like a pencil over a column chart. At the bottom of the dialog box, shown in Figure 11.11, each series has its own line, which shows the series name, chart type, and whether the series should be shown on a secondary axis. As you select different chart types, the preview window updates. Once you have the chart types you want, click OK.

FIGURE 11.11

You can mix a variety of chart types using the Combo chart type.

NOTE A secondary axis is an axis that appears on the right side of the chart. It is often used for charting data of a different scale. For example, if you're charting dollars and percentages, you could have the dollar data attached to the left axis and the percentages attached to the right axis.

Updating Chart Data

Unless the source data is a Table, the chart won't automatically update as new data is added to the data set. To manually update the data source of a chart, do one of the following:

- Go to Chart Tools, Design, Data, Select Data, or right-click the chart and choose Select Data. Update the Chart data range in the Select Data Source dialog box, shown in Figure 11.12.

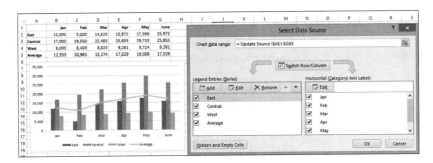

FIGURE 11.12
The original data range was A1:F5. After adding the June data, the source data range is updated to include the new data in the chart.

- When the chart is selected, the data source is highlighted with a colored border. The borders can be manually modified, changing the source range, by clicking and dragging to include the new rows. Make sure you place your cursor in the corner of the range and get a two-headed arrow, not a four-headed arrow. If using this method, be careful to not move the range when trying to expand it.

In addition to the two previous methods, the existing series on a chart can be updated by copying the new data and pasting it into the chart. To do this, follow these steps:

1. Ensure that the new data has a header similar to the existing data. It is especially important that a heading entered as a Date is still a Date and not Text.

2. Select the new data, including the header.

3. Right-click over the selection and choose Copy.

4. Select the chart.

5. Go to Home, Clipboard, Paste. The chart updates with the new data.

Creating Stock Charts

There are four types of stock charts that you can create using historical stock data. Each type has specific requirements for included columns and their order. If the order of the data is not met, the chart will not be created. The charts and their required columns and order are as follows:

- **High-Low-Close**—Requires four columns of data: Date, High, Low, Close

- **Open-High-Low-Close**—Requires five columns of data: Date, Open, High, Low, Close

- **Volume-High-Low-Close**—Requires five columns of data: Date, Volume, High, Low, Close

- **Volume-Open-High-Low-Close**—Requires six columns of data: Date, Volume, Open, High, Low, Close

After the data is in the correct column order, the chart can be selected from the Other Charts drop-down. See "Viewing All Available Charts" for inserting a stock chart.

 TIP Excel doesn't read the column labels to determine if you have set up your data correctly. It can only count the number of columns in the data source. So make sure the data source includes only the columns for the desired stock chart, not including a Date or Stock Name column.

Creating Bubble Charts

You may want to use a bubble chart because they are unusual, but there is also a practical reason for using one. With a bubble chart, you can display a relationship among three variables. The x,y coordinate represents two variables, and the size of the bubble is the third.

In Figure 11.13, Age and Miles are charted along the x- and y-axes, respectively. The Price becomes the size of the bubble at the intersection of the x,y coordinate. See "Viewing All Available Charts" for inserting a bubble chart.

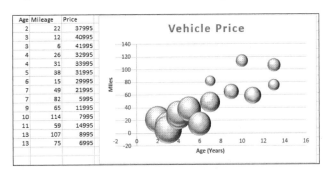

FIGURE 11.13

The size of the bubble at the intersection of the x- and y-axes represents the relative price of the vehicle.

Pie Chart Issue: Small Slices

When creating a pie chart, you may end up with slices that are very difficult to see. Two possible ways of dealing with this are to rotate the pie or create a bar of pie chart.

Rotating the Pie

Rotating the pie works best if the chart is 3D. By rotating the chart so the smaller slices are toward the front, they are easier to see, as shown in Figure 11.14. To rotate the pie, follow these steps:

1. Select the chart by clicking along the chart's frame.

2. Go to Chart Tools, Format, Current Selection, and select the series from the Chart Elements drop-down.

3. Select Format Selection.

4. From the Series Options category (the far-right icon that looks like a column chart), move the Angle of First Slice slider to the right. The chart updates when you let go of the mouse button, so you can see how far you need to move the slider.

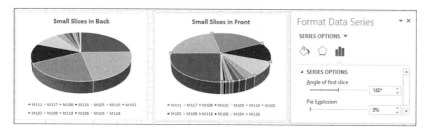

FIGURE 11.14

Rotate the pie chart to place the smaller pie slices toward the front, making them easier to see.

Creating a Bar of Pie Chart

Bar of Pie is one of the options listed under Pie (see "Viewing All Available Charts"). It's used to explode out the smaller pie slices into a stacked bar chart, as shown in Figure 11.15, making the smaller slices more visible. Excel will create a new slice called Other, which is a grouping of the slices now in the bar. But the default explosion might not be adequate to your needs—you might want to include more smaller pieces in the bar chart. You can include more pieces by going into the Format Data Series task pane and changing the number of values included in the bar.

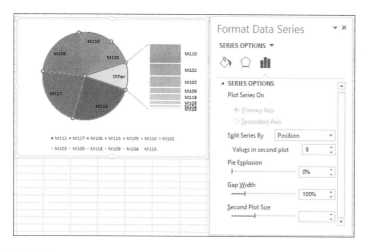

FIGURE 11.15

Use a bar of pie chart to group smaller slices into a stacked bar chart, making the smaller slices more visible.

To change an existing pie chart to a bar of pie chart and modify the number of slices used in the stacked bar in the chart, follow these steps:

1. Select the pie chart.

2. Go to Chart Tools, Design, Type, Change Chart Type.

3. In the Change Chart Type dialog box, select Bar of Pie from the Pie options.

4. Click OK. The chart changes to a bar of pie chart. If you're happy with the default selection for the number of slices moved to the stacked bar, you're done. Otherwise, continue to step 5 to change the number of slices used in the bar.

5. With the chart still selected, go to Chart Tools, Format, Current Selection, and select the series from the Chart Elements drop-down.

6. Click Format Selection. The Format Data Series task pane opens.

7. From the Series Options category, change the number of Values in the Second Plot field. As the value is changed using the spin buttons, the chart updates.

8. When satisfied with the chart, click Close.

 TIP Adjust the size of the bar chart by changing the Second Plot Size value in the Format Data Series task pane.

Adding Sparklines to Data

A sparkline is a chart inside of a single cell based on a single row or column of data. It can be placed right next to the data it's charting or on another sheet. Because the sparkline is in the background of the cell, you can still enter text in that cell.

There are three types of sparklines available: Line, Column, and Win/Loss. Different colors can be applied to them, and various settings in the Show group of the Sparkline Tools, Design tab affect how the sparkline will be designed.

To add a sparkline to your data, select either the cell where you want the sparkline to go or the data set (not including the headers) and go to Insert, Sparklines. Fill in the fields of the Create Sparklines dialog box and the sparklines are added to the selected location.

TIP   As long as Excel can tell you have the same number of sparkline cells and corresponding ranges, you can create adjacent sparklines based on adjacent data sets. Just select the multiple sparkline cells or data sets at the same time. If you create sparklines together using this method, they will be grouped, and changes to the settings will affect them all.

Adding Points to a Sparkline

After you've created a sparkline, you can choose to show the High Point, Low Point, Negative Points, First Point, Last Point, and Markers (line charts only), as shown in the first three examples in Figure 11.16. To add points to a sparkline, select the sparkline and go to Sparkline Tools, Design, Show, and select the desired points. Each point can be assigned its own color by going to the Marker Color drop-down in the Style group of the tab. For example, to create the first set of sparklines in Figure 11.16, follow these steps:

1. Select F3:F5, the cells where the sparklines will be placed.

2. Go to Insert, Sparklines and select Column.

3. Place your cursor in the Data Range field, and then select range B3:E5 on the sheet.

4. Verify the Location Range is correct, and then click OK.

5. From the Show group on the Sparkline Tools, Design tab, select High Point. Excel colors the high point in each sparkline a different color.

6. To change the color of the high point, go to the Marker Color drop-down in the Style group. From the drop-down, select High Point, and then select a new color for the marker.

Spacing Markers in a Sparkline

The fourth set of charts in Figure 11.16 uses the Date Axis Type option to space the columns out in respect to the date of the data set. Note the space in the sparkline between the first and second columns. This is parallel to the date difference between the first two columns of data. The setting is available in the sparklines Axis drop-down in the Group group.

▲	A	B	C	D	E	F	G	H
1	Column Chart with High Point Indicators (Dark Columns)							
2		Q1	Q2	Q3	Q4			
3	East	9,853	7,141	2,339	634	■ ■ _		
4	Central	6,826	6,599	7,594	1,839	■ ■ ■		
5	West	6,411	260	755	2,074 ■	_		
6								
7	Line Chart with Markers							
8		Jan-12	Feb-12	Mar-12	Apr-12	May-12	Jun-12	
9	East	2,689	1,332	3,233	1,369	2,970	21	⋁⋀⋁
10	Central	1,028	1,931	1,894	2,089	1,279	1,388	⟋‾
11	West	121	3,181	3,415	4,887	3,545	1,313	⟋‾
12								
13	Win/Loss Chart with Negative Points Highlighted							
14		Jan	Feb	Mar	Apr	May	Jun	
15	East	84	67	-26	43	3	-97	■■₋■■₋
16	Central	96	-70	-14	-26	-4	88	■₋₋₋₋■
17	West	42	-45	15	-28	-50	90	■₋■₋₋■
18								
19	Column Chart with Date Axis							
20		1/1/2012	1/4/2012	1/5/2012	1/6/2012	1/7/2012	1/8/2012	
21	East	9,853	7,141	2,339	634	2,689	2,970	▌ ▐₋₋₋
22	Central	6,826	6,599	7,594	1,839	1,028	1,279	▌ ▐▌₋₋
23	West	6,411	260	755	2,074	121	3,545	▌ ₋₋₋■

FIGURE 11.16

Use Sparklines to add in-cell charts to your data.

CAUTION   The date range must include real dates. For example, Jan, Feb, Mar, and the like won't work because these are not actual dates, but if the actual dates are 1/1/12, 2/1/12, 3/1/12 and they are simply formatted to just show the month, they will work to space out the data in the sparkline.

To space out sparklines based on the dates in the data set, as shown in Figure 11.16 where there are two days (1/2/12 and 1/3/12) missing between the first and second dates, follow these steps:

1. Select a cell in the sparkline group.

2. Go to Sparkline Tools, Design, Group, Axis, and select Date Axis Type from the drop-down.

3. The Sparkline Date Range dialog box opens. Select the date range, B20:G20 in Figure 11.16, to apply to the sparklines.

4. Click OK. The sparklines update to accommodate the spacing in the selected date range.

Deleting Sparklines

You cannot simply highlight a sparkline and delete it. Instead, to delete a sparkline, go to Sparkline Tools, Design, Group, Clear, and choose either Clear Selected Sparklines to clear just the selected sparkline or Clear Selected Sparkline Groups, to clear a set of sparklines grouped together.

Creating a Chart Using a User-Created Template

If you have a chart design you want to apply to multiple charts, you can save the design as a template. All the settings for colors, fonts, effects, and chart elements are saved and can be applied to other charts. Because the template is saved as an external file, you can share it with other users.

To create the template, build and customize a chart. Then right-click on the chart and select Save as Template. Give the template a name and click Save. The template is now available in the Templates option of the Insert Chart dialog box and can be applied just like the Excel-defined charts.

CAUTION You must use the default location for saving charts so the chart will appear in the Insert Chart dialog box.

TIP If you receive a chart template, save it to the following folder:
\\Appdata\Roaming\Microsoft\Templates\Charts
Any templates saved to this location appear in the Insert Chart dialog box.

THE ABSOLUTE MINIMUM

A well-designed chart can be very informative at a glance. By using different chart types together with a secondary axis, you can relate even more information to users a lot quicker than with a table of numbers. Sparklines, too, can quickly relay a story of the data to users.

IN THIS CHAPTER

- Create a PivotTable.
- Sort and filter a PivotTable.
- Group dates in a PivotTable.
- Insert slicers to help users filter a PivotTable.

12

PIVOTTABLES AND SLICERS

PivotTables can summarize one million rows with five clicks of the mouse button. For example, if you have sales data broken up by company and product, you can quickly summarize the sales by company then product or, with a few clicks, reverse the report and summarize by product then company. Or, you're in charge of all the local kids soccer leagues and you want to create a report showing the number of boys versus girls, grouped by age. A PivotTable can do all this and more.

They're so powerful with so many options that this chapter cannot cover it all. This chapter provides you with the tools to create straightforward, but useful, PivotTables. For even more details, refer to *PivotTable Data Crunching: Microsoft Excel 2013* (ISBN 978-0-7897-4875-1) by Bill Jelen and Michael Alexander.

CAUTION There is an advanced version of PivotTables called PowerPivot that this book does not review. PowerPivot is a powerful data analysis tool for working with very large amounts of data. For information on PowerPivot, refer to *PivotTable Data Crunching: Microsoft Excel 2013* (ISBN 978-0-7897-4875-1) by Bill Jelen and Michael Alexander.

Preparing Data for Use in a PivotTable

To take full advantage of a PivotTable's capabilities, your data should adhere to a few basic formatting guidelines:

- There should be no blank rows or columns.

- If a column contains numeric data, don't allow blank cells in the column. Use zeros instead of blanks.

- Each row should be a complete record.

- There shouldn't be any Total rows.

- There should be a unique header above every column.

- Headers should be in only one row; otherwise Excel will get confused, unable to find the header row on its own.

Figure 12.1 shows a data set properly formatted for working with PivotTables. Figure 12.2 shows a data set not suitable for PivotTables. Instead, the dates should all be in one column. And although a person might understand that all the data shown is relevant to the Central region, Excel does not.

Region	Product	Date	Customer	Quantity	Revenue	COGS	Profit
Central	Laser Printe	1/2/2011	Alluring Shoe Company	500	11240	5110	6130
Central	Laser Printe	1/3/2011	Alluring Shoe Company	400	9204	4088	5116
East	Laser Printe	1/9/2011	Alluring Shoe Company	900	21465	9198	12267
West	Laser Printe	1/11/2011	Alluring Shoe Company	400	9144	4088	5056
Central	Multi-Funct	1/26/2011	Alluring Shoe Company	500	10445	4235	6210
Central	Basic ColorJ	2/5/2011	Alluring Shoe Company	200	4280	1968	2312
Central	Basic ColorJ	2/19/2011	Alluring Shoe Company	800	18504	7872	10632
East	Laser Printe	2/23/2011	Alluring Shoe Company	1000	20940	10220	10720
East	Laser Printe	3/2/2011	Alluring Shoe Company	400	8620	4088	4532

FIGURE 12.1

This data is great for PivotTables.

Region	Customer	Product	1/1/2011	1/2/2011	1/3/2011	1/4/2011	1/6/2011
Central	Alluring Shoe Company	Laser Printers		6130	5116		
		Basic ColorJet Printers	5290		3723		
		Multi-Function Printers					
	Appealing Calculator Corporat	Laser Printers					
		Basic ColorJet Printers					
		Multi-Function Printers	9882		3472	4293	
	Best Vegetable Company	Basic ColorJet Printers					
	Bright Eggbeater Corporation	Basic ColorJet Printers					
		Multi-Function Printers					
	Bright Hairpin Company	Laser Printers		12690			
		Basic ColorJet Printers					5890

FIGURE 12.2

This data set is not suitable for a PivotTable.

PivotTable Limitations

As incredibly powerful as PivotTables are, they do have a few limitations:

- You cannot add a calculated item to a grouped field.

- If a field is grouped by days, grouping by months, quarters, or years will undo the group by days.

- Changing the source data does not automatically update the PivotTable. You must click the Refresh button.

- Blank cells confuse Excel. A single blank cell in a numeric column will make Excel think the column contains text values, changing the default behavior for that column.

- You cannot insert rows or columns in a PivotTable.

PivotTable Compatibility

PivotTable compatibility between Excel 2013 and the legacy versions is a bit tricky:

- If you open an .xlsx file with a converter in a legacy version, the PivotTables will not work.

- If you create PivotTables in an .xlsx file (file type used by Excel 2007 and newer) and then save the file as an .xls file (file type used by legacy Excel), the PivotTables will not work. The Compatibility Checker dialog box will open when you save the file, warning of the incompatibilities, such as Show Values As.

- To get a PivotTable created in 2013 to work in legacy Excel, save the file as an .xls file before creating the PivotTable. Close and reopen the file, and then create the PivotTable. Any options not compatible with older versions of Excel, such as slicers (which you can read more about later in this chapter), will not be available. Strangely enough, you can apply Show Values As and save the file. Excel will not warn of compatibility issues and the PivotTable will open fine in legacy versions.

PivotTable Field List

There are two parts to a PivotTable report—the PivotTable itself and the PivotTable Field List, which appears only when a cell in the PivotTable is selected. The PivotTable Field List consists of a list of the column headers in the data set (the fields) and the four areas of a PivotTable.

Figure 12.3 shows a basic PivotTable, using all four areas of a PivotTable to summarize product profit by year and quarter on a regional basis. The four areas are as follows:

- **Filters**—Limits the report to a specific criteria; in this case, we are looking at only the Central region's revenue. Instead of creating a separate report for each region, use the Report filter to view the desired region.

- **Columns**—The headers going across the top of the PivotTable—in this case, the breakdown by year and quarter.

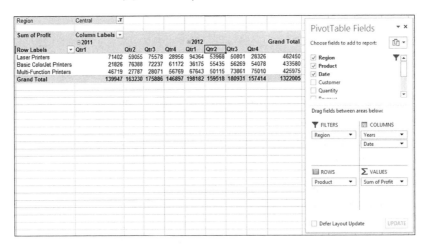

FIGURE 12.3

A basic PivotTable using all fields to summarize 2011 and 2012 quarterly product sales for the Central region.

- **Rows**—The headers going down the left side of the PivotTable—in this case, the Products. If there is more than one field, the fields will appear in a hierarchical view, with the second field under the first field.

- **Values**—The data being summarized—in this case, Profit. The data can be summed, counted, and many other calculation types.

Not all four areas must be used. Each area can have more than one field.

Creating a PivotTable

There are three ways to create a PivotTable. With two of the methods—Quick Analysis tool and Recommended PivotTables—you pick from a group of PivotTables Excel has selected for you. You can still customize the report after it's placed on the sheet—Excel just offers a place to start. The third method allows you to design a report from scratch.

Using the Quick Analysis Tool

The Quick Analysis tool is a quick way to create a PivotTable. When you select data on the sheet, the Quick Analysis tool appears in the lower-right corner of the selection. When you click on the icon and select Tables, Excel suggests different PivotTables based on its analysis of the selected data. Placing your cursor over a PivotTa… icon opens a preview window, as shown in Figure 12.4. If you click the icon, Excel creates the PivotTable on a new sheet. If none of the previews show what you want, select the More icon to open the Recommended PivotTables dialog box.

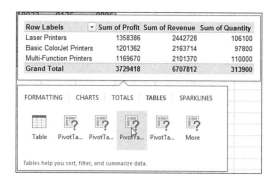

FIGURE 12.4

Use the Quick Analysis tool to bring up a list of suggested PivotTables.

TIP You don't have to select the entire data set. As long as your data is set up properly, Excel will be able to extrapolate the table from the selection of two cells.

Viewing Recommended PivotTables

As long as your data is set up properly, you don't have to select the entire table before viewing Excel's recommendations. You must have at least one cell in the source data selected, and then go to Insert, Tables, Recommended PivotTables and the Recommended PivotTables dialog box shown in Figure 12.5 opens.

FIGURE 12.5

Excel recommends PivotTables based on its interpretation of your data.

On the left side of the dialog box are Excel's recommended PivotTables. Click on a PivotTable and a larger version appears on the right side of the dialog box. When you see one you like, select it and then click OK. The PivotTable is created on a new sheet.

If you don't see a PivotTable you like, click the Blank PivotTable button to create your own PivotTable. See the following section, "Creating a PivotTable from Scratch," for more information.

Creating a PivotTable from Scratch

Creating a PivotTable is simple if the data set is suitable for PivotTables. Once you've told Excel what the data source is, it can be quickly created by selecting the desired fields in the field list. Based on the data in a field, Excel places the selected field in the area it thinks it should go. Text fields are placed in the Rows area. Numeric fields are placed in the Values area and summed.

When you select fields in the field list and add them to an area that already contains fields, the new fields are placed below the existing fields. The up/down layout in the area corresponds to a left/right layout of the fields in the PivotTable, except for the Filters area, which also goes up/down.

The order of the fields and the area in which they're located can be changed by clicking the field and dragging it to a new location. You can also drag fields from the field list to an area, instead of selecting them and letting Excel choose their locations.

The PivotTable in Figure 12.6 summarizes product quantity and profit by customer. It also allows users to filter by region.

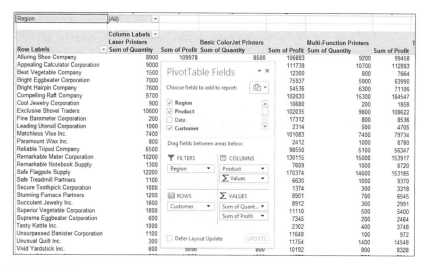

FIGURE 12.6

You aren't limited to PivotTable reports Excel thinks would be useful. Design your own or customize one from Excel's suggestions.

To create this report, follow these steps:

1. Make sure the data set is set up properly, as explained in the section "Preparing Data for Use in a PivotTable."

2. Select a cell in the data set.

3. Go to Insert, Tables, and click the PivotTable button (not the drop-down arrow).

4. The Create PivotTable dialog box, shown in Figure 12.7, opens and Excel selects the data set. The address is shown in the Table/Range field. If the selection is correct, continue to step 5. If the selection is not correct, return to step 1.

FIGURE 12.7

Use the Create PivotTable dialog box to identify the source data and where the PivotTable should be created.

 CAUTION You could correct Excel's selection, but if Excel didn't select the data set properly, then there is likely something wrong with its layout, which could affect the PivotTable created.

5. Select the location where the PivotTable is to be placed. The default location is always a new sheet. If using an existing sheet, ensure there is enough room on the sheet for the PivotTable's rows and columns.

6. Click OK. The PivotTable template and field list appear on a new sheet (or on an existing sheet, if that is what you selected), as shown in Figure 12.8.

7. Select the fields that should be the row labels, Customer. If there needs to be more than one field for the row labels, select them in the order they need to appear in, left to right, on the report.

8. Select the fields the report should summarize, Quantity and Profit. Notice that when you select two or more fields to summarize, Excel adds a Values field to the Columns area.

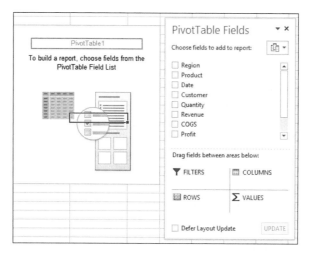

FIGURE 12.8

Once the PivotTable template and field list appear, you can start designing the report.

9. Add a column label, Product, by clicking and dragging the field from the list to the Columns area.

10. Click and drag the Region field from the list to the Filters area.

Removing a Field

To remove a field from a PivotTable, deselect it from the field list or click it in the area and select Remove Field. You can also click and drag the field from the area to the sheet until an X appears by the cursor. When the X appears, release the mouse button.

Renaming a Field

You can rename a field as it appears in the PivotTable by typing a new name directly in the cell. The name must be unique and cannot be the same as the field's original name before it was placed in the PivotTable.

CAUTION   Do not double-click on a PivotTable cell to edit it as this command is often reserved for the drill downs. For more information on drill downs, see the section "Viewing the Records Used to Calculate a Value."

Changing the Calculation Type of a Field Value

When Excel identifies a field as numeric, it automatically sums the data. If it cannot identify the field as numeric, it will count the data. No matter which calculation type Excel appoints to a value field, it can be changed by selecting the field in the PivotTable; going to PivotTable Tools, Analyze, Active Field, Field Settings; and selecting an option from the Summarize Values By list in the Value Field Settings dialog box. You can also open the Value Field Settings dialog box by right-clicking on a value in the PivotTable and selecting Value Field Settings.

Changing How a PivotTable Appears on a Sheet

There are three ways the PivotTable report will appear, as shown in Figure 12.9. The view can be changed by going to PivotTable Tools, Design, Report Layout, and selecting the desired layouts from the drop-down:

- **Compact**—This is the default configuration for .xlsx, .xlsm, and .xlsb files. All the fields in the row labels area share the same column. The Total, such as the West Total, appears in the same row as the field.
- **Outline**—The fields in the row labels area each have their own column. The Total, such as the West Total, appears in the same row as the field.
- **Tabular**—This is the default configuration for an .xls file. The fields in the row labels area each have their own column. The Total, such as the West Total, appears in its own row beneath its group.

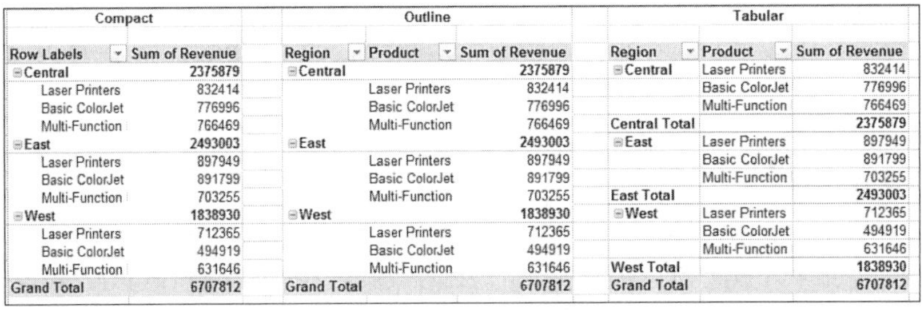

Compact

Row Labels	Sum of Revenue
Central	2375879
Laser Printers	832414
Basic ColorJet	776996
Multi-Function	766469
East	2493003
Laser Printers	897949
Basic ColorJet	891799
Multi-Function	703255
West	1838930
Laser Printers	712365
Basic ColorJet	494919
Multi-Function	631646
Grand Total	6707812

Outline

Region	Product	Sum of Revenue
Central		2375879
	Laser Printers	832414
	Basic ColorJet	776996
	Multi-Function	766469
East		2493003
	Laser Printers	897949
	Basic ColorJet	891799
	Multi-Function	703255
West		1838930
	Laser Printers	712365
	Basic ColorJet	494919
	Multi-Function	631646
Grand Total		6707812

Tabular

Region	Product	Sum of Revenue
Central	Laser Printers	832414
	Basic ColorJet	776996
	Multi-Function	766469
Central Total		2375879
East	Laser Printers	897949
	Basic ColorJet	891799
	Multi-Function	703255
East Total		2493003
West	Laser Printers	712365
	Basic ColorJet	494919
	Multi-Function	631646
West Total		1838930
Grand Total		6707812

FIGURE 12.9

Excel offers three ways of viewing and working with a PivotTable report.

If you have either Outline or Tabular applied, you can choose to repeat the item labels by selecting Repeat All Item Labels from the Report Layout drop-down.

PivotTable Sorting

Excel automatically sorts text data alphabetically when building a PivotTable. Any row label, column label, or record can be dragged to a new location. To reset the table back to its default state, remove the affected field from the area, refresh the table, then put the field back.

Another option is to sort using one of the methods in the following sections. When a sort is applied in a PivotTable, it remembers the settings, so as you pivot the table, the sort sticks.

PivotTable Quick Sort

The quick sort buttons offer one-click access to sorting cell values. There are four entry points to the quick sort buttons:

- On the Home tab, select Editing, Sort & Filter, Sort A to Z or Sort Z to A.

- Go to Data, Sort & Filter; select either the AZ or ZA quick sort buttons to sort the active field.

- Right-click a cell in the PivotTable, select Sort, and choose from Sort A to Z or Sort Z to A.

- From a pivot label drop-down, select Sort A to Z or Sort Z to A.

 NOTE   The actual button text may change depending on the type of data in the cell. For example, if the column contains only values, the text will be Sort Smallest to Largest. If the column contains text, it will be Sort Z to A.

Unlike sorting outside PivotTables, it doesn't matter if you have more than one cell selected during the sort. Excel automatically sorts the entire PivotTable. If multiple columns are selected, Excel sorts by the leftmost column in the selection.

To quickly sort a field, select a cell in the field you want to sort by or a label to sort by labels. Apply the desired quick sort method outlined previously. The data re-sorts based on the selection. The Sort dialog box, discussed in the following section, is updated for the selected field.

 CAUTION   A downside of using the quick sort buttons on the Home and Data tabs is that if you continue to pivot the table, Excel forgets the sort settings. However, if you use the PivotTable sort options, Excel remembers the sort settings.

Sort Text Columns with Sort (Fieldname) Dialog Box

The Sort (Fieldname) dialog box provides advanced options for sorting text columns, such as sorting the selected column based on the total of another field. For example, you could sort customers by the sum of all profit. To bring up the dialog box shown in Figure 12.10, select a cell containing text and use one of the following methods:

- Select a cell in the desired field, go to the Home tab, and then select Editing, Sort & Filter, Custom Sort.

- Select a cell in the desired field, and then go to Data, Sort & Filter, Sort.

- Right-click a cell in the desired field in the PivotTable, select Sort, and select More Sort Options.

- From a pivot label drop-down, select More Sort Options. You can select the field to sort at the top of the drop-down.

FIGURE 12.10

Use the Sort (Fieldname) dialog box for advanced sorting options of text columns.

The Sort (Fieldname) dialog box provides the following additional sorting options, which the PivotTable will remember as the table layout is changed:

- **Manual**—This option is the default sort, which clears, but doesn't undo, any previous settings.

- **Ascending/Descending**—These options sort the selected column based on the original field or a value field selected from the drop-down.

If sorting a text column, a More Options button is available in the dialog box. Clicking the button reveals the following options:

- **AutoSort**—Select to have the sort updated when the PivotTable is updated.
- **First Key Sort Order**—Available when AutoSort is deselected, allowing the field to be sorted by a custom list.
- **Sort by Grand Total**—Available when either Ascending or Descending is selected with another field; this option sorts the data using the Grand Totals.
- **Sort by Values in Selected Column**—Available when either Ascending or Descending is selected with another field; this option sorts the data using the column of the selected cell.

Sort Rows or Columns by Value

When you right-click on a calculated value cell and select Sort, More Sort Options, the Sort By Value dialog box opens. With this dialog box, you can sort the report by the selected value's row or column.

To sort by column, select Top to Bottom from the Sort Direction options. This is similar to sorting using the quick sort buttons. To sort by the value's row, select Left to Right. This sorts all the value columns by the values in the selected row. For example, Figure 12.11 is sorted left to right, largest to smallest by row 6. This reorganizes the columns so that the Laser Printers are the leftmost column, because it contains the largest value in row 6. If you select a cell in row 7 and perform the same sort, Multi-Function Printers will move to become the leftmost column because the largest value in that row is in the Multi-Function Printers group.

4		Laser Printers		Multi-Function Printers		Basic ColorJet Printers	
5	Row Labels	Sum of Revenue	Sum of Profit	Sum of Revenue	Sum of Profit	Sum of Revenue	Sum of Profit
6	⊞2/25/2011	40047	22673	12145	6216		
7	⊞1/1/2011			10245	6010		
8	⊞1/2/2011	11240	6130				
9	⊞1/3/2011	9204	5116				
10	⊞1/4/2011			6860	3472		
11	⊞1/6/2011	13806	7674				

FIGURE 12.11

Sort columns left to right based on a specific record.

Expanding and Collapsing Fields

If the rows area contains multiple fields, row labels appear in groups that can be quickly expanded and collapsed by clicking the + and - icons. Additional methods, including the capability to expand or collapse all the groups in a field are the following:

- Select a cell in the field and go to Data, Outline, Show Detail or Hide Detail, which affects all the groups in the field.

- Select a cell in the field and go to PivotTable Tools, Analyze, Active Field, Expand Field or Collapse Field, which affects all the groups in the field.

- Right-click a cell in the field and from the Expand/Collapse submenu, choose one of the following:

  - **Expand or Collapse**—Affects the selected group.

  - **Expand Entire Field or Collapse Entire Field**—Affects all the groups in the field.

  - **Collapse to (Fieldname) or Expand to (Fieldname)**—One or more menu options, depending on the number of grouped fields available, affects the selected group.

If you try to expand a data item instead of a field, Excel opens a Show Detail dialog box allowing you to add a new field within the selected data item. If you try to expand a calculated value, Excel inserts a new sheet and shows the records that were used to calculate the value. This is known as *drilling down*. See the following section, "Viewing the Records Used to Calculate a Value," for more information.

Viewing the Records Used to Calculate a Value

Double-clicking a data item, or right-clicking and selecting Show Details, creates a new sheet with a table showing the records from which the data item was derived. This is known as *drilling down* and can be useful if you notice a value in the PivotTable that stands out and you need to investigate it in more detail.

The new table is not linked to the original data or the PivotTable. If you need to make corrections to the data, make them to the original source and refresh the PivotTable. You can then delete the sheet that was created for the drill down.

Grouping Dates

A common issue with PivotTables occurs when someone tries to group a date field and receives the error "Cannot group that selection." The reason may be that the dates are not real dates, but instead text that looks like dates. If that's the case, see the "Using Text to Columns to Convert Text to Numbers" section in Chapter 3, "Getting Data onto a Sheet," to convert the text dates to real dates (because real dates are numbers).

The Grouping dialog box allows dates to be grouped by number of days, months, quarters, and years. When dates are grouped into more than one type, such as month and year, virtual fields are added to the PivotTable field list, which can be used just like the regular fields.

To access the Grouping dialog box, do one of the following:

- Right-click a date and select Group.

- Select a date cell and go to PivotTable Tools, Analyze, Group, Group Selection or Group Field.

- Select a date and go to Data, Outline, Group.

When grouping dates, if Months is the only selection, multiple years will be combined into the month. To get the months grouped into their respective years, also select Years from the dialog box, like this:

1. Select a cell in the PivotTable with a date value.

2. Go to PivotTable Tools, Analyze, Group, Group Field. If you receive the error "Cannot group that selection," see the "Using Text to Columns to Convert Text to Numbers" section in Chapter 3 to convert the text dates to real dates. Otherwise, continue to step 3.

3. The date range found by Excel appears in the Group dialog box, as shown in Figure 12.12. Make changes if needed.

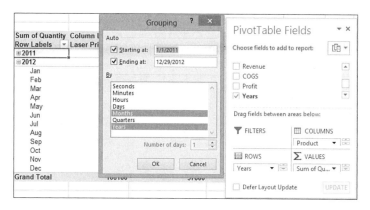

FIGURE 12.12

When dates are grouped, the new field, such as Years, is added to the field list.

4. Select Months and Years from the list box.

5. Click OK. The data is grouped into months and years, and a Years field is added to the field list.

To return the dates to normal, you have to ungroup the field. Unselecting the original or virtual field will not ungroup the dates. To ungroup the dates, do one of the following:

- Right-click a grouped date and select Ungroup.

- Select a date cell and go to PivotTable Tools, Analyze, Options, Group, Ungroup.

- Select a date and go to Data, Outline, Ungroup.

 TIP   At first glance, there doesn't appear to be a way of creating a weekly report as there is no Weeks option in the Grouping dialog box. But by using the Days option in the Group dialog box, seven days can be grouped together to create a week, 14 days for a biweekly report, and so on. Excel will group the selected number of days based on the range in the dialog box, so if the weeks need to represent a normal week, such as Sunday to Saturday, change the starting date to be a Sunday that will include the first date in the data set.

Filtering Data in a PivotTable

Filtering allows you to view only the data you want to see. Unlike Excel's AutoFilter (see Chapter 8, "Filtering and Consolidating Data"), filtering a PivotTable doesn't hide the rows. Instead, the rows are removed from the report. An icon that looks like a funnel replaces the drop-down arrow of the labels that have had a filter applied to them. This section reviews several filtering methods available for viewing only specific records. These methods can be accessed with one of the following steps:

- In the PivotTable Field List, highlight a field and click the drop-down arrow to open the filter listing.

- In the PivotTable, click the label drop-down.

- Right-click a label in the PivotTable and select Filter.

Filtering for Listed Items

The filter listing is probably the most obvious filter tool when you open the drop-down. If the PivotTable is formatted in Compact form (the default) and the selected area contains more than one field, a Select Field drop-down will appear at the top, allowing another field to be selected if the incorrect one is active, as shown in Figure 12.13. All items in the filter listing will be selected, because they are all visible the first time you open the drop-down, but you can select just the items that should appear in the data. Any item that no longer bears a check mark will be hidden.

FIGURE 12.13

A drop-down at the top of the filter window allows the correct field to be selected if the area has more than one field and the report is in Compact form.

TIP For instruction on how to search for items to include or exclude from the filter, see the section "Using the Search Function to Filter for or Exclude Items" in Chapter 8.

If you have a long list of items and only want to hide or show a few, it might be easier to select a few items directly on the sheet, then right-click, select Filter, and then select Keep Only Selected Items or Hide Selected Items.

Using Label, Value, and Date Special Filters

Special filters are available in the Filter drop-down and also by right-clicking a label and selecting Filter. If the selected field is a date field, Date Filters will appear. If the selected field is anything other than a date, Label Filters will appear, as shown in Figure 12.14. In both cases, Value Filters will be included. All the special filters, except for ones that take action immediately, open a Filter dialog box in which specifics for the filter are entered.

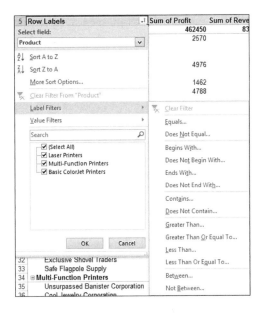

FIGURE 12.14

Numerous methods are available in the Label Filters option.

Selection of any of the Label Filters opens the Label Filter (Fieldname) dialog box in which text can be entered. Wildcards can also be used in the text fields. Use an asterisk (*) to replace multiple characters or a question mark (?) to replace a single character.

Value Filters include various options that will bring up the Value Filter (Fieldname) dialog box in which values can be entered. There is also a Top 10 option, described in more detail in the section "Top 10 Filtering."

Date Filters offer a wide selection of options, including additional options under All Dates in the Period. The Custom Filter (Fieldname) dialog box for dates includes calendars to aid in date entry. The options dealing with quarters refer to the traditional quarter of a year, January through March being the first quarter, April through June being the second quarter, and so on.

The report in Figure 12.15 contains data for two years, 2011 and 2012. To show only the fourth quarter profit for both years, first group the data by quarter, month, and year, and then apply the fourth quarter filter, like this:

1. Right-click over a date cell and select Group.

2. From the Grouping dialog box, select Months, Quarters, Years.

3. Click OK and the data will be grouped by year. Within each year, it will be grouped by quarter, and within each quarter, it will be grouped by month.

4. Open the Row Labels drop-down. Go to Date Filters, All Dates in the Period and select Quarter 4. The PivotTable updates, showing only the fourth quarter records for 2011 and 2012 by month.

Sum of Profit	Column Lab ▼		
Row Labels ▼	Laser Printers	Basic ColorJet Printers	Multi-Function Printers
⊟2011			
⊟Qtr4			
Oct	62063	45223	64706
Nov	57872	94286	16555
Dec	114469	43149	28730
⊟2012			
⊟Qtr4			
Oct	72676	50857	44398
Nov	36954	51411	40842
Dec	39409	42541	78311

FIGURE 12.15

Compare the fourth quarters of multiple years with a few clicks of the mouse.

Top 10 Filtering

The Top 10 option has a flexible dialog box allowing you to specify the top or bottom items, percentages, or sums to view. For example, you could choose to view the bottom 15% or the top 7 items. The Top 10 option is available under the Value Filters listing and also by right-clicking a specific label and selecting Filter, Top 10.

The original report shown in Figure 12.16 originally listed 27 companies. Using the Top 10 option, you can filter the list down to the top companies that have helped bring in $2,500,000 in revenue. To filter for those records, follow these steps:

1. Right-click over a customer name and select Filter, Top 10.

2. From the first drop-down, select Top.

3. In the second field, enter the value to sum for, **2,500,000**. The actual summed value may surpass this.

4. Select Sum from the third drop-down.

5. Select the value field to sum, Revenue.

6. Click OK. The PivotTable filters to the companies that meet the entered criteria.

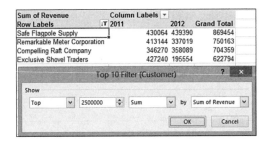

FIGURE 12.16

Use the Top 10 option to create a report of top customers who account for a specific amount of revenue.

Clearing Filters

To clear all filters applied to a PivotTable, go to PivotTable Tools, Analyze, Actions, Clear, Clear Filters.

You can use two ways to clear a filter from a specific field:

- Right-click the field, go to Filter, and select Clear Filter from (Fieldname).

- Open the label's Filter drop-down, select the field from the drop-down at the top (if more than one field in the area), and select Clear Filter from (Fieldname).

Creating a Calculated Field

A calculated field is a field you create by building a formula using existing fields and constants. For example, the report shown in Figure 12.17 includes fields for revenue and profit, but not for the price of the items sold. You could create a formula outside the report, but when the table is updated, the formula may be overwritten. Instead, create a calculated field to calculate the average price.

Go to PivotTable Tools, Analyze, Calculations, Fields, Items, & Sets, and select Calculated Field from the drop-down. The entry fields in the dialog box, shown in Figure 12.17, are the following:

- **Name**—The unique name you assign the new field.

- **Formula**—The formula for the field. It should consist of one or more selections from the Fields listing, operators, and constants.

- **Fields**—A list of all available fields.

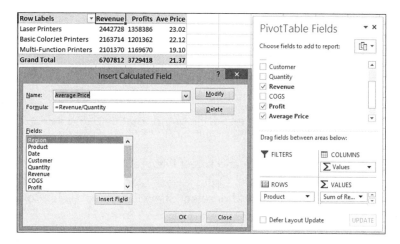

FIGURE 12.17

Create calculated fields to add calculations that will become part of the PivotTable.

Creating the formula isn't that different from building one in the formula bar, but instead of cell references, use the fields. Double-click or highlight and select Insert Field to insert a field in the formula. When the formula is complete, click Add to accept it. When you return to the PivotTable, the new field will appear in the field list and can be used in the same way as the existing fields.

To create the average price field discussed previously, follow these steps:

1. Go to PivotTable Tools, Options, Calculations, Fields, Items, & Sets and select Calculated Field.

2. In the Name field, enter the name of the field, `Average Price`, as it will appear in the field list.

3. Highlight the 0 in the Formula field.

4. Enter the formula in the Formula field. Double-click or highlight and click Insert Field to insert fields into the formula. Type any operators, constants, or parentheses as needed directly in the Formula field. In this example, the formula is Revenue/Quantity.

5. Click Add to accept the formula.

6. Click OK. The new field is added to the field list and can now be arranged and formatted as needed in the PivotTable.

Hiding Totals

By default, subtotals and grand totals are automatically added to the PivotTable as the fields are arranged. To hide grand totals, do one of the following:

- Right-click a specific grand total field and select Remove Fieldname.

- Right-click the header of a specific grand total field and select Remove Grand Total.

- Right-click the PivotTable and select PivotTable Options or go to PivotTable Tools, Analyze, PivotTable, Options. From the dialog box that opens, go to the Totals & Filters tab and deselect Show Grand Totals for Rows and Show Grand Totals for Columns.

- Go to PivotTable Tools, Design, Layout, and click the Grand Totals drop-down. From there, you can turn all grand totals on or off, or turn on only row grand totals or column grand totals.

To hide subtotals:

- Right-click a specific subtotal field and select Subtotal Fieldname.

- Select a cell in the specific field. Go to PivotTable Tools, Analyze, Active Field, Field Settings. From the Field Settings dialog box that opens, on the Subtotals & Filters tab, select None.

- Go to PivotTable Tools, Design, Layout, and click the Subtotals drop-down. From there, you can turn all subtotals off or choose where they appear in respect to their data.

Formatting Values

If you right-click a cell in a PivotTable, select Format Cells, and apply formatting to the cell, only the one cell will be formatted. To apply formatting to an entire field, the formatting must be applied through the PivotTable's Format Cells dialog box. The dialog box is similar to the normal Format Cells dialog box, except only the Number tab is available. To access this dialog box, do one of the following:

- Right-click a cell in the field and select Number Format.

- Right-click a cell in the field and select Value Field Settings. From the dialog box that opens, click the Number Format button.

- Select a cell in the field and go to PivotTable Tools, Analyze, Active Field, Field Settings. From the dialog box that opens, click the Number Format button.

 NOTE   Refer to the section "Applying Number Formats with Format Cells" in Chapter 4, "Formatting Sheets and Cells," for details on the various number formats.

Slicers

Slicers allow you to filter a PivotTable, but in a much more user-friendly way. Unlike the filter drop-downs, slicers are always visible and you can change their dimensions to better fit your sheet design, as shown in Figure 12.18. There are three filters—Region, Product, and Customer—in the figure.

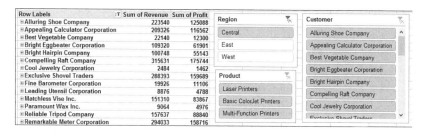

FIGURE 12.18

Slicers offer a more visually pleasing and user-friendly way of filtering PivotTables.

To insert a slicer, go to PivotTable Tools, Analyze, Filter, Insert Slicer. The Insert Slicers dialog box opens, listing all fields except calculation fields. The field for which a slicer is added does not need to be visible in the PivotTable. Slicers can be sized and placed as needed. Use the Slicer Tools tab, available when you select a slicer, to modify many settings, such as changing the look of the slicers and attaching the slicer to multiple PivotTables.

 NOTE   For an in-depth look at slicers, refer to *PivotTable Data Crunching: Microsoft Excel 2013* (ISBN 978-0-7897-4875-1) by Bill Jelen and Michael Alexander.

THE ABSOLUTE MINIMUM

PivotTables are incredibly useful, and this chapter just touches on what they can do. You can experiment with moving the fields to different areas in the field list and see how the data is summarized. Sort and filter to get even more information out of the table, such as the top 10 producers in the last year. And if you need to share the PivotTable with others, add slicers to make it easier for them to filter and view the data important to them.

IN THIS CHAPTER

- Create charts you can scroll through.
- Highlight a specific item in multiple reports with one click.
- Apply a single filter to multiple reports at the same time.
- Place your data on a map.

USING POWER VIEW TO CREATE REPORTS

Dashboard is a word you hear a lot when it comes to Excel reports. A dashboard is a sheet with multiple charts and tables that provide various ways of interpreting data. Depending on the number of charts and tables, it can take time to build and update. And it would take a bit of knowledge to make a dashboard you can filter or sort, or quickly focus on a particular item with a click. In Excel 2013, Microsoft has made creating dynamic dashboards a lot easier (and cooler!) with Power View. With Power View, you can create a sheet with multiple tables, charts, and maps. With a few clicks, you can filter, sort, or focus all the visualizations on one or more selected records. The downside, though, is that you cannot share the workbooks with pre-Excel 2013 users.

Power View Requirements

Power View is a COM add-in in the Professional Plus Office version of Excel available on PCs. The add-in must be enabled before you can use the tool. See the "COM Add-Ins and DLL Add-Ins" section in Chapter 1, "Understanding the Microsoft Excel Interface," to enable the Power View add-in.

Power View requires Microsoft Silverlight to be installed, and if it's not, it prompts you the first time you try to create a report, as shown in Figure 13.1. Click the Install Silverlight link in the message bar and follow the prompts to download and install the program. When the installation is complete, return to Excel and click the Reload button in the message bar to continue with the creation of your report.

FIGURE 13.1

You are prompted to install Silverlight if it's not already installed.

Creating Reports

Creating a Power View report is simple. Make sure the data table is properly set up with no blank rows or columns, and each column must have a unique heading. Select a cell in the data table and go to Insert, Reports, Power View. A new sheet is added with the Power View template, as shown in Figure 13.2.

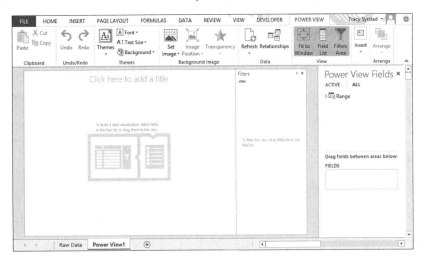

FIGURE 13.2

You start your Power View report with a blank template that you build visualizations on.

Once you have the template, open the group (Range in Figure 13.2) and choose the report fields by selecting them from the field list (select the check box, not the field name) or dragging them down to the Fields list box below the listing. Select the fields in the order you want them to appear from left to right in a table. As you select fields, a table is created in the report area, as shown in Figure 13.3. This table is just one of the data visualizations available. See the section "Changing Data Visualizations" for information on how to change the data visualization to another type, such as a bar chart.

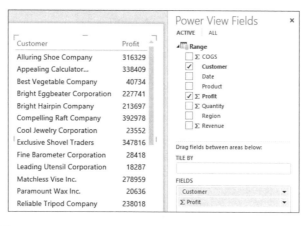

FIGURE 13.3

As you select fields, they're added to a table, the default visualization.

Changing the Values Field Calculation

When Excel identifies a field in the Values area as numeric, it automatically sums the data. If it cannot identify the field as numeric, it counts the data. No matter which calculation type Excel appoints to a value field, it can be changed by clicking the arrow to the right of the field and selecting the desired calculation type, as shown in Figure 13.4.

Moving and Resizing a Visualization

Once you've added a visualization, you can move it around the report and resize it. To select a visualization, click on it and sizing handles appear in all four corners and in the center of each side, as shown in Figure 13.5. To resize the visualization, place your cursor on a handle. When it turns into a double-headed arrow, click and drag to resize. To move the visualization, place your cursor along the frame of the visualization until you see a dotted frame line and the cursor turns into a hand, as shown in Figure 13.5. Click and drag the visualization to a new location on the template.

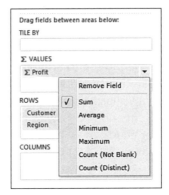

FIGURE 13.4

You can apply a variety of calculations, such as Sum and Average, to the data.

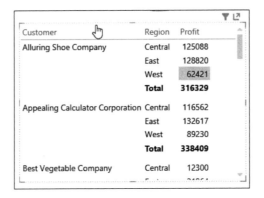

FIGURE 13.5

Proper placement of the cursor is required to be able to drag and move a visualization.

 NOTE   Unlike normal charts and tables, the visualizations have scrollbars as part of their frames. So, you don't have to size a visualization to show all the data. Size it to fit your report and you can scroll to specific data, or filter it, as discussed in the "Filtering" section.

Undoing Changes to a Report

To undo a change to a visualization, such as resizing, use the Undo button found on the Power View tab in the Undo/Redo group. The undo/redo buttons in the Quick Access toolbar are disabled while on a Power View sheet.

Inserting and Formatting a Report Title

To add a title to the report, click where it says "Click Here to Add a Title" and enter your title. When the cursor is in the title area, the Text tab appears to the right of the Power View tab. Highlight the title and use the options on the Text tab to change the font style or size and text alignment.

 NOTE   The formatting options on the Home tab are not available for formatting the title.

Changing Data Visualizations

The default data visualization is a table, but it can be changed to other types of tables, to charts, or even to maps. To change the visualization, select it, go to Design, Switch Visualization, and select the desired data visualization. Depending on the visualization selected, different options are available on the Design and Layout tabs.

 TIP   If you find a data visualization unavailable, try switching back to the default Table visualization. Some options, such as Tiles, are only available from one of the Table visualization options.

Inserting Table Data Visualizations

The Table drop-down has three options to choose from: Table, Matrix, and Card. Figure 13.6 shows those three options and also another option: Table with Tiles. Each option groups and summarizes data in a different way, allowing you to choose the layout that works best for your data. For example, the Matrix option grouped the regions together by company, allowing the user to see, at a glance, how a company is doing across the regions.

Table is the default report type. The selected fields are displayed from left to right in a table format. Matrix is similar to a pivot table, where you have row, column, and value fields, as shown in Figure 13.7. You can change the layout of the matrix by selecting and dragging the fields between the areas in the task pane. Card creates mini reports, summarizing the selected data.

 NOTE   See the section "Adding Tiles to a Visualization" to learn how the visualization Table with Tiles in Figure 13.6 was created.

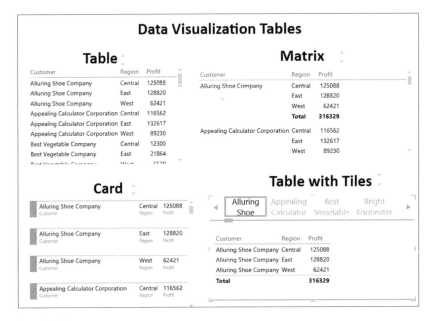

FIGURE 13.6

You can choose from several table visualizations to best represent your data.

FIGURE 13.7

Creating a matrix visualization is similar to setting up a pivot table—they both have row and column fields.

Inserting Chart Data Visualizations

Although the charts available in Power View don't offer as many formatting and layout options as normal charts, they do have functionality other charts do not have. Power View charts can be scrolled through, filtered, and viewed as multiple mini charts (see Figure 13.8).

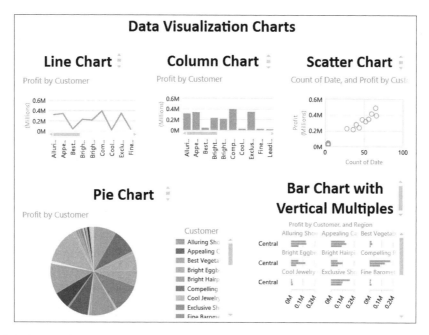

FIGURE 13.8

You can choose from several chart visualizations to display your data in the best way.

There are five chart types available. Bar and Column charts each have their own buttons with the following options: Stacked, 100% Stacked, and Clustered. Line, Scatter, and Pie are found in the Other Chart drop-down and do not have additional options.

You can change the layout of the charts by selecting and dragging the fields between the areas in the task pane. In addition to standard chart areas, like Values and Axis, there are areas for Vertical Multiples and Horizontal Multiples. These areas are used to make mini charts like the bar chart with vertical multiples in Figure 13.8. That chart was created by placing the Customer field in the Vertical Multiples area in the task pane.

 NOTE See the section "Adding Tiles to a Visualization" for information about the Tile By area in the task pane.

Inserting Map Data Visualizations

Power View uses Bing Maps to plot your data to a map. If you have a table with location information, such as the city and state or longitude and latitude, and the value you want plotted, a bubble is placed on a map, its size based on value relative to the other data being mapped. For example, the map in Figure 13.9 shows company profit in Rapid City, South Dakota; Pierre, South Dakota; and Sioux Falls, South Dakota. You can tell from the size of the bubble that Rapid City had the lowest profit margin of the three cities.

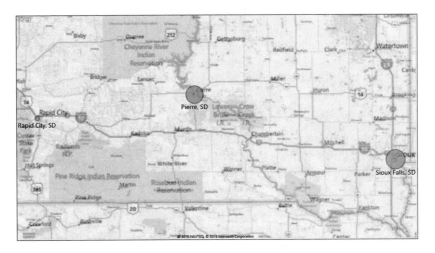

FIGURE 13.9

Use a map to compare values between cities. The larger the bubble, the larger the value.

When you select the Map visualization, you have at least two areas you must fill in—the Size and either Locations or Longitude or Latitude. Size is the field that controls the size of the bubbles. Locations or Longitude or Latitude control where on the map the bubble is placed.

 NOTE   The first time you place a field in the Locations area, you may get the prompt shown in Figure 13.10. Select Enable Content to allow the data to be sent to Bing.

⚠ PRIVACY WARNING To be displayed on the map, some of your data needs to be geocoded by sending it to Bing. | Enable Content |

FIGURE 13.10

Allow Excel to send location information to Bing so it can map your data.

For different-colored bubbles, place the field used to define the differences in the Color area. If each bubble is equivalent to only one value, then the bubble will only have one color. For example, the three locations in the sample map are equivalent to West, Central, and East regions in the data. If the Region field is placed in the Color field, then each bubble will be a different color. But if the Customer field is placed in the Color field, each bubble will be like a pie, each slice being a different color to represent a different company being summarized in the profit.

Adding Tiles to a Visualization

Tiles add a dynamic navigation strip to the top of a visualization, filtering the visualization to show only values selected from the strip, as shown in the Table with Tiles visualization in Figure 13.6. The Design, Tiles, Tiles option is only available in the ribbon when you have a table visualization selected, but you can add a tile to any visualization by dragging a field down to the Tile By area in the task pane.

 TIP If the Tile Type drop-down isn't enabled after adding a tile to a visualization, make a selection from the tile. The drop-down should become active.

To remove tiles from a visualization, select the field in the Tile By area and drag it up to the field listing or click the arrow to the right and select Remove Field.

Combining Multiple Visualizations

You aren't limited to a single visualization or only certain fields in a report. You can mix visualizations and fields, as shown in Figure 13.11 where we have a profit by customer chart, a region and profit by customer matrix, and a profit by product card.

To create extra visualizations, after creating your first, click elsewhere on the template so the first visualization is no longer selected. Then, create your new one. Power View places it where it finds an empty space.

When you have multiple visualizations on a report, they are all linked, even if they use different fields, because they come from the same data set. You can apply a filter that affects them all at the same time (see the section "Filtering" for more information).

To delete a visualization, select it and press Delete on the keyboard or right-click on the visualization and select Cut.

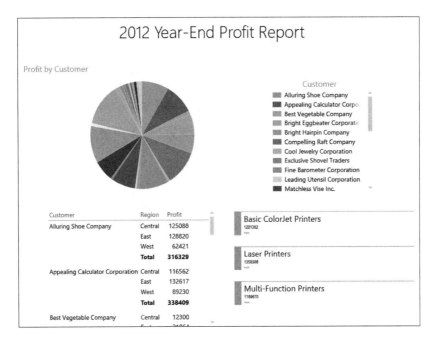

FIGURE 13.11

You can create multiple visualizations that can update together.

Changing Colors

To change the colors in a chart, you have to apply a theme to the report, which affects all of its visualizations and any other Power View sheets in the workbook. You cannot select a single visualization on a multivisualization report or a single series on a chart and change just its colors.

Themes are found in the Themes group of the Power View tab. Click on the Themes drop-down and it opens to show a variety of themes available. Each theme consists of a color and font palette. You do not get a preview when you place your cursor over an option. Instead, you must select an option and update your report to see how it looks.

If you decide you like a color but not the font type, you can select a new font from the Font drop-down. Again, this affects all the visualizations in the active report. You can also change the Text Size.

NOTE For more information about themes, see the section "Using Themes to Ensure Uniformity in Design" in Chapter 4, "Formatting Sheets and Cells."

Sorting

Most visualizations can be sorted by value or category in ascending or descending order. For example, you can show the largest profit makers at the top of a table by sorting the profit value in descending order.

To sort a table visualization, click on the column header and an arrow appears on the far right of the column, showing the sort order. Only one column at a time can be sorted in a table.

Matrix visualizations can be sorted by one or more nonvalue columns. Click on the column header and an arrow appears on the far-right side of the column. If you sort by a value header, then any previous sort selections are lost.

Chart sort options appear in the upper-left corner of a chart when you place your cursor over it. Pie, bar, and column charts can be sorted by selecting the sort field from the category drop-down, as shown in Figure 13.12. Click Asc or Desc to change the sort order.

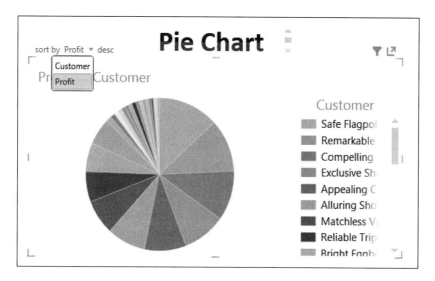

FIGURE 13.12

Charts that can be sorted have the sorting options in the upper-left corner.

NOTE Cards, line charts, scatter charts, and visualizations with tiles cannot be sorted. The exception for line charts and scatter charts is if they have been designed as multiples. In that case, the sort options are available.

Filtering

You can filter the data used by the visualizations to show one or more categories. If you have multiple visualizations in a report, you can apply a filter that affects them all, or filter a single visualization.

If the Filters area isn't visible, go to Power View, View, Filters Area and the area appears to the right of the report. Depending on your selection in the template area, you see a View option and possibly another, such as Chart. Selecting the View option allows you to click and drag fields from the field listing to the Filters area for filtering. Applying a filter in this way filters all the visualizations on that template, as shown in Figure 13.13 where all the visualizations only show data pertaining to Alluring Shoe Company.

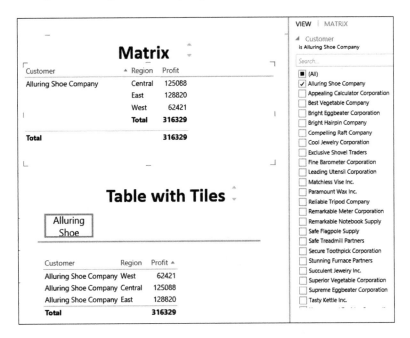

FIGURE 13.13

Setting up a filter in the View option filters all the visualizations on the report.

If you select a specific visualization, such as a matrix table, then a second filter option, Matrix, appears. Select that option to see and filter the fields used for that visualization. This filters only the selected visualization, as shown in Figure 13.14.

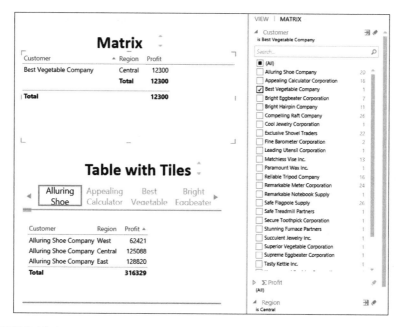

FIGURE 13.14

You can filter a specific visualization by selecting it then choosing its option in the Filters area.

NOTE You can only filter visualizations with tiles using the View option. Such visualizations do not allow specific visualization filtering.

To select the items to include in the filter, click the field in the Filters area. This opens and shows all the items in the field. If you want to filter by only one item, you can select the item name. But if you want to filter by multiple items, you *must* select the check box.

You can also type text in the search field and press Enter to return matching values from the filter list. The search is additive. That is, if you select the check box of the results and perform another search and selection, the first item remains selected.

> **TIP** You can directly access the filter specific to a visualization by clicking the funnel you see in the upper-right corner when you place the cursor over the visualization.

To clear a filter, click the eraser-like icon to the right of the field name. To delete a filter from View mode, click the X icon to the right of the field name.

Advanced Filter Mode

If you have a long list of items to scroll, it might be easier to filter by a range or logic value. When filtering all the visualizations (in the View option), you have the Advanced Filter Mode. To access this option, click the icon with an arrow, shown in Figure 13.15. If you're filtering a text field, you toggle between two options: List Filter Mode (the original mode) and Advanced Filter Mode. If you're filtering a value field, you toggle between three options: List Filter Mode, Advanced Filter Mode, and Range Filter Mode.

Advanced Filter Mode allows you to select a logic option, such as Contains or Does Not Contain, and then enter the value you want to compare the data with. For example, in Figure 13.15, the list was filtered for all customer names that contain the word *Shoe* or *Raft*. Press Enter or click Apply Filter to update the visualizations with the results.

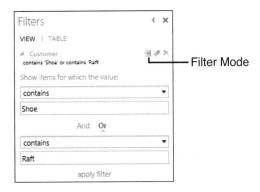

FIGURE 13.15

Select the Filter Mode icon to toggle through the different filter modes, including the Advanced Filter Mode, which allows you to use logic items to filter your data.

Range Filter Mode gives you a slider bar where you can move the ends to define a value range. Figure 13.16 shows the data filtered for revenue records greater than or equal to 10,504.

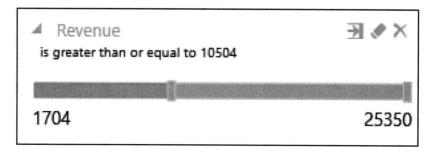

FIGURE 13.16

Use the slider bar to narrow down a range to filter a value field by.

Highlighting

If you have a chart on a report, you can use that chart like a filter to highlight a specific item in all visualizations in the report. To do this, click on the series in the chart, such as a pie slice, that represents the item you want to filter by. This updates all the tables to show only records for the selected item and all series in the charts dim, except for the selected series. To highlight multiple series, hold down the Ctrl key as you select them.

To return the visualization to normal, select any selected item again.

Using Slicers

Just like the slicers in pivot tables, slicers in Power View allow you to filter a report, but in a more user-friendly way. To create a slicer, create a table visualization with the field you want to filter by, then go to Design, Slicer, Slicer. You can then select items from the slicer to filter the other visualizations on the report. To select multiple items, hold down the Ctrl key as you make your selections. To quickly clear all selections, click the eraser-like icon in the upper-right corner of the slicer.

Sharing Power View Reports

Currently, Power View reports created in Excel 2013 can only be shared with other Excel 2013 users. If you send it to someone using an earlier version of Excel, a generic picture with Power View across the top will be in place of the reports.

THE ABSOLUTE MINIMUM

Power View allows you to easily create dynamic dashboards. Not only can you scroll through the tables and charts, but you can also quickly filter one or all items. With a single click, you can focus on a specific item, filtering all the visualizations to that item. Or, place the data on a map, allowing you to see how one location compares with another.

IN THIS CHAPTER

- Insert SmartArt.
- Design a WordArt logo.
- Add special effects to imported pictures.

14

INSERTING SMARTART, WORDART, AND PICTURES

You can add a little pizzazz to your workbooks by using graphic text and images. This chapter introduces you to SmartArt, which combines graphics and text to depict ideas, WordArt to twist colorful text, and the Picture tools to manipulate imported images.

Working with SmartArt

SmartArt is a collection of similar shapes, arranged to imply a process, a relationship, or a hierarchy. You can add text to SmartArt shapes, and for some shapes, include a small picture or logo. For example, you could use SmartArt to create an organization's hierarchy chart with pictures of the employees. Excel 2013 has more than 130 available diagrams, grouped into nine categories of SmartArt:

- **List**—Designs for nonsequential lists of information.
- **Process**—Designs for sequential lists of steps.
- **Cycle**—Designs for steps that repeat.
- **Hierarchy**—Designs for organization charts, decision trees, and other hierarchical relationships.
- **Relationship**—Designs for showing the relationships between items.
- **Matrix**—Designs to show four quadrants of a list.
- **Pyramid**—Designs to show overlapping, proportional, containment, or interconnected relationships.
- **Picture**—Designs for use with pictures in either sequential or nonsequential layouts. The picture tools can be used to adjust the imported images.
- **Office.com**—Various designs that you can download from Microsoft. The available designs will change with time. Note that these designs will also appear in their specific categories.

 CAUTION   SmartArt diagrams are removed when you open a workbook in the Excel Web App. In legacy versions of Excel, SmartArt will be turned into Pictures.

Inserting a SmartArt Diagram

To insert a SmartArt diagram, go to Insert, Illustrations, SmartArt, and select the desired layout. Excel places the diagram in the middle of the screen with the Text pane to the left, as shown in Figure 14.1. When you're done entering text, click any cell on the sheet and the Text pane disappears.

 CAUTION   Do not click the x in the upper-right corner of the Text pane to close it or the next time you place SmartArt, the Text pane will not automatically appear. If this happens, you can manually open the Text pane by going to SmartArt Tools, Design, Create Graphic, and selecting Text Pane.

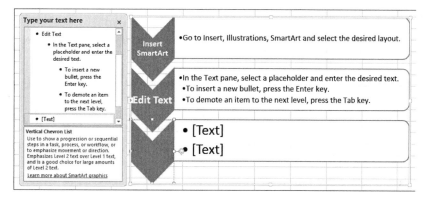

FIGURE 14.1

Use the Text pane to insert and organize the text in the SmartArt diagram.

You should keep a few things in mind concerning the Text pane:

- Click a bulleted placeholder to enter the text.

- Navigate between bulleted items by using the mouse or arrow keys.

- The Tab key will not work to move between the placeholders. Instead, use the Tab key to demote an item to the next level. Use Shift+Tab to promote an item.

- Press Enter to add a new item beneath the currently selected item.

- Deleting a bullet will promote the ones beneath it if they are of a lower level.

To insert a SmartArt layout and enter text, follow these steps:

1. Go to Insert, Illustrations, SmartArt, and select the desired layout.

2. In the Text pane, select a placeholder and enter the desired text.

3. Use the mouse to select the next placeholder or use the down-arrow key to move to the next placeholder for entering text.

   - To insert a new bullet, press the Enter key.

   - To demote an item to the next level, press the Tab key.

   - To add a new graphic, select the last bullet, press the Enter key to insert a new bullet, and then click Promote, found under SmartArt Tools, Design, Create Graphic, as many times as necessary to make the selected bullet a level 1 item.

4. Repeat step 3 as many times as necessary.

5. When you are done entering information, click any cell on the sheet.

Inserting Images into SmartArt

Some SmartArt layouts include image placeholders, as shown in Figure 14.2. To insert an image, click the image placeholder and the Insert Pictures dialog box opens. Browse to and select the desired image. When an image in SmartArt is selected, the Picture Tools tab becomes visible in the ribbon and you can use any of the picture tools on the image.

FIGURE 14.2

Use images in SmartArt diagrams to create a business organization chart.

 NOTE This section covers the specifics of working with images in SmartArt. If this is the first time you've inserted SmartArt, refer to the previous section "Inserting a SmartArt Diagram" for instructions on entering text, adding new SmartArt graphics, and promoting or demoting the bulleted items.

Keep the following in mind when working with SmartArt images:

- To change the image, select it and go to Picture Tools, Format, Adjust, Change Picture.

- You cannot delete the accompanying text placeholder, but if you do not need it, enter a space in the field.

 NOTE The picture tools are reviewed in the section "Inserting Pictures."

To insert a SmartArt layout that includes images, follow these steps:

1. Go to Insert, Illustrations, SmartArt, and select a layout from the Picture category. Layouts from other categories include image placeholders, but they can more easily be found in the Picture category.

2. Click OK to place the layout on the sheet.

3. Click an image placeholder and the Insert Picture dialog box opens. Browse to the desired image and click Insert.

4. Use the options on the Picture Tools, Format tab to make any required changes to the image.

5. If you do not want any text in the image's accompanying text placeholder, enter a space in the text's placeholder.

6. Repeat steps 2 through 4 as many times as required.

Selecting SmartArt Diagrams

Selecting a SmartArt component must be done carefully. If you have the incorrect frame selected, you will move that shape instead of the entire SmartArt frame. You can tell if a shape is selected because the frame around it becomes visible. Only the frame around the entire SmartArt diagram is visible when you've selected the entire diagram. Also, nothing will be selected in the Text pane when the entire diagram is selected.

If a shape is selected, move your cursor over the frame until it turns into a four-headed arrow, then click on the frame and the entire diagram will be selected. When the frame is selected, you can move it to a new location, resize it, or delete it. Keep the following in mind when manipulating the SmartArt's frame:

*   When moving or resizing the diagram, the Text pane momentarily disappears.

*   To move the diagram, place the cursor on the frame until it turns into a four-headed arrow; then click and drag the diagram to a new location.

*   To resize the diagram, place the cursor in any corner or place it in the center of any edge until it turns into a double-headed arrow. You can then click and drag the diagram to a new size.

Adding and Deleting Shapes

Use Add Shape to add a new shape to the SmartArt diagram. The new shape will be added above the selected shape or at the bottom if the entire diagram is selected.

To delete a shape, select it so you see the frame around it and press the Delete key.

To add a new shape in the middle of the diagram, follow these steps:

1. Select the shape where you want the new shape.

2. Go to SmartArt Tools, Design, Create Graphic, and select Add Shape.

3. The shape selected in step 1 will be moved down and the new shape inserted in its location.

4. If the new shape is not in the correct location, select level 1 of the shape (the topmost bulleted item) and go to SmartArt Tools, Design, Create Graphic, and choose Move Up or Move Down.

Reordering Placeholders

To move a text or image placeholders to a new location, use Move Up and Move Down found under SmartArt Tools, Design, Create Graphic. Move Up and Move Down refer to the order of the items as shown in the Text pane, not their actual position in the diagram. To move an item to a new shape, it must be cut from its current location and pasted to the new location. Keep in mind the following when moving placeholders in the SmartArt:

- Any customized formatting of a placeholder will move with the placeholder.

- Each level can be moved individually, with any sublevels moving with their parent level.

- A level can be moved only within its group; it cannot be moved beyond its group. So if an item is level 2, it cannot be moved past its level 1 parent.

To change the order of text placeholders, follow these steps:

1. In the Text pane, place your cursor in the text of the level to be moved. Any children of the selected level will move with the parent. So if you're moving an entire shape, select level 1. If a level 2 item includes level 3 items, place your cursor at level 2 and the level 3 items will also move.

2. Go to SmartArt Tools, Design, Create Graphic, and choose Move Up to move the selected item up the Text pane or Move Down to move the item down the Text pane.

3. If an item needs to be moved to an entirely different shape, highlight the text in the Text pane.

4. Press Ctrl+X to cut the text out of the Text pane.

5. Place your cursor in the new location for the text.

6. Press Ctrl+V to paste the text to the new location.

Formatting the Placeholder Text

The text formatting options found in the Font group of the Home tab can be applied to any selected item in SmartArt. If you select a shape, the formatting will be applied to all text entries in the shape. If you select a single word, the formatting will apply to just that word.

The exception to this formatting is font size. Selecting a single item in a shape, such as just one word in a sentence, will have unexpected results, as shown in Figure 14.3. But you can change the font size of all the text in a selected shape.

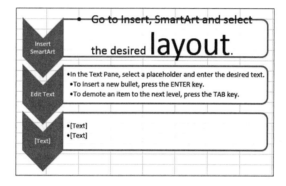

FIGURE 14.3

Changing the font size of "layout" to 54 changed the rest of the sentence's font size from 11 to 18.

Changing the Selected Layout

You can change the layout of the current diagram to a new layout by going to the Layouts group of the SmartArt Tools, Design tab. The drop-down will show the available layouts of the current diagram's category. As you place your cursor over a layout, your current layout temporarily changes, giving you a preview. You can access all the categories and their layouts by selecting the More Layouts option at the bottom of the drop-down. This opens the Choose a SmartArt Graphic dialog box with all available categories and layouts. Existing levels and text will transfer over to the new layout.

Changing an Individual Shape

You can change the shape of an individual shape in a diagram by selecting the shape and going to SmartArt Tools, Format, Shapes, Change Shape, and selecting a new shape in the drop-down. Every component in the diagram can be replaced, as shown in Figure 14.4.

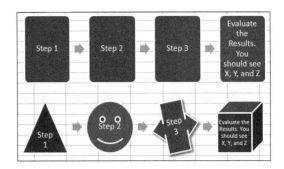

FIGURE 14.4

You can replace every shape in a diagram to create your own custom SmartArt.

Linking a Cell to a SmartArt Shape

You can't actually link a SmartArt shape to a cell, but you can create the layout in SmartArt, convert it to shapes, and then replace the text with formulas linking the component to a cell. This allows the text in the layout to update automatically when the cell's text updates.

 NOTE Your selected SmartArt can only have one placeholder per shape. If you need to show multiple placeholders, then you will have to design the linked cell with multiple lines.

There are two reasons why it's important to make sure the SmartArt is designed perfectly before converting it. First, after you convert it to shapes, it's no longer SmartArt and you will not have access to the SmartArt tools to make changes. The second reason is that it is much easier to select the correct frames when they have text in them already.

To link SmartArt to a cell, follow these steps:

1. Set up the data on the sheet, including the cells with dynamic text that you will link the shapes to.

2. Completely design the SmartArt, including the placement of sample text.

3. Select the diagram.

4. Go to SmartArt Tools, Design, Reset, Convert to Shapes. This converts the SmartArt to individual shapes.

5. Go to Drawing Tools, Format, Arrange, Selection Pane. The Selection pane opens on the right side of the window.

6. Many components in SmartArt consist of layers of shapes, which are all now visible in the Selection pane. Select one of the components called Freeform. The corresponding shape will be selected on the sheet. If this is not the desired shape, select another in the Selection pane until the shape you want is highlighted. Freeform is usually the shape used to hold text.

7. After the desired shape is selected, place your cursor in the formula bar, type an equal sign, and then type the cell address of the cell you want to link the shape to, as shown in Figure 14.5. Press Enter to save the change.

8. Repeat steps 6 and 7 until all components are linked.

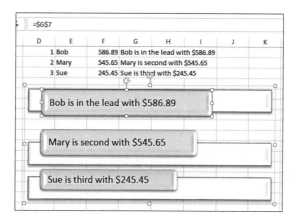

FIGURE 14.5

Insert the formula in the formula bar to link the shape to a cell.

 CAUTION Converted SmartArt diagrams will be removed when you open a workbook in the Excel Web App.

Inserting WordArt

WordArt allows you to design text beyond the capabilities of the normal font settings on the Home tab, as shown in Figure 14.6. For example, you can use it to create a logo for the header of a report. After inserting the WordArt, go to the

Drawing Tools, Format tab to access the various tools for modifying the color and shape.

FIGURE 14.6

Use WordArt to bend and twist text.

To insert WordArt and customize it, follow these steps:

1. Go to Insert, Text, WordArt, and select a text style from the drop-down. The WordArt will be added to the active sheet.

2. Excel adds generic text in the preset WordArt. Select the default text and type your own text.

3. To change the font style, select the text and choose a new font style from the Font group of the Home tab. As you move your cursor over the different font styles, your WordArt updates to reflect the style.

4. To add effects to the WordArt, such as the curve in Figure 14.6, go to Drawing Tools, Format, WordArt Styles, Text Effects. An option from Transform was used in the figure.

 CAUTION WordArt is removed when you open a workbook in the Excel Web App. In legacy versions of Excel, WordArt may not appear as designed.

Inserting Pictures

A picture is worth a thousand words. If you're creating order sheets for new uniforms for various soccer teams, inserting a picture of the team's uniform can differentiate the sheets at a glance.

To insert a picture, follow these steps:

1. Select the cell where you want the upper-left corner of the picture to be.

2. Go to Insert, Illustrations, Pictures to choose a picture from your local or network drive, or Online Pictures to search online or insert one from your SkyDrive.

3. Select the image to import and click Insert.

When an image on the sheet is selected, the Picture Tools, Format tab appears with tools for modifying your image, such as picture correction, cropping, and special effects.

If you right-click on the image and select Format Picture, the Format Picture task pane opens on the right side of the window. While some of the options found here can also be found on the Format tab, such as most of the Picture Effects, some options are only in the task pane, such as the Picture Position settings under the Picture, Crop option.

Resizing and Cropping Pictures

When you import a picture, it comes in it's true size. That is, if the image is 8x10, then it will be 8x10 on the sheet. When you select the image, small squares appear in the corners and along the edge of the picture. These squares are called *handles* and are used to change the size of the picture.

To resize the selected image, click and drag one of the handles along the edge or in the corners of the picture. For more specific sizing, enter the size in the Shape Height or Shape Width fields of the Size group on the Picture Tools, Format tab.

If you want only a part of the imported picture, you can *crop* it, removing what you don't need. You can manually crop an image or crop it to a specific shape, as shown in Figure 14.7. To crop the selected image, go to Picture Tools, Format, Size, and select an option from the Crop drop-down. If you later decide you've made a mistake, go to Picture Tools, Format, Adjust, Reset Picture, Reset Picture & Size, and the image will return to its original state.

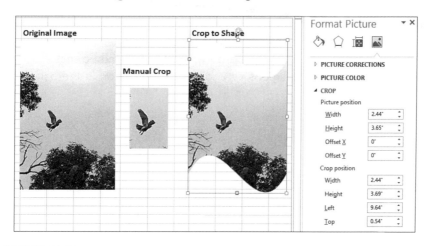

FIGURE 14.7

Use the cropping tools to crop an image to a particular size or place the image in a shape.

The Crop option is for a manual crop. On the image, black cropping handles appear in the corners and along each edge. Click and drag the handles to outline where you want the image cropped. The part of the picture you are cropping away will appear grayed out.

Choose Crop to Shape to crop the image to one of the shapes available in the drop-down. The image will be recut to the selected shape. To nudge the image within the shape, right-click the image and select Format Picture. In the task pane, select the Picture icon. Select the Crop category and under the Picture Position options, change the values in the Offset X and Offset Y fields. Adjusting the Offset X value moves the image left or right in the shape; adjusting the Offset Y value moves the image up or down in the shape.

 CAUTION Cropped images are removed when you open a workbook in the Excel Web App.

Applying Corrections, Color, and Artistic Effects

You can correct the brightness and contrast, change a color image to a black-and-white image, or apply artistic effects to the selected image through the options in the Adjust group of the Picture Tools, Format tab. As you move your cursor over an option in a drop-down, the image automatically adjusts, providing a preview of the option. Click the option to accept the change to the selected picture.

Corrections

The Corrections drop-down consists of options to sharpen and soften the image and to adjust brightness and contrast. If none of the predefined options are what you want, you can manually make the adjustments by selecting Picture Corrections Options at the bottom of the drop-down. This opens the Format Picture task pane to the Picture Corrections category. Changes made in the pane apply automatically to the image. To undo a change, click the Undo button in the Quick Access Toolbar.

Color

The Color drop-down includes options for adjusting color saturation, color tone, or recoloring the image. The More Variations option at the bottom of the drop-down is part of the Recolor group. The Set Transparent Color allows you to select a pixel in the image, and all pixels of the same color will become transparent, showing whatever is behind the image. For more control of saturation, tone, and recolor options, select Picture Color Options, which opens the Format Picture task pane to the Picture category. Changes made in the pane apply automatically to the image. To undo a change, click the Undo button in the Quick Access Toolbar.

Artistic Effects

Artistic effects include Glow Edges, Film Grain, Light Screen, and many other effects that will change the way an image looks, as shown in Figure 14.8. After you select an effect, you can fine-tune it through the Effects, Artistic Effects category of the Format Picture task pane. The fine-tuning options differ depending on the effect chosen. Changes made in the task pane apply automatically to the image. To undo a change, click the Undo button in the Quick Access Toolbar.

FIGURE 14.8

The Pencil Grayscale effect was used to change a photograph into an image that looks like a sketch.

Arranging Pictures

The Arrange group of the Picture Tools, Format tab consists of several options for arranging imported images:

- **Bring Forward**—Brings the selected image forward, placing it on top of other images it is stacked with. Includes Bring to Front, which places the selected image as the topmost image.

- **Send Backward**—Sends the selected image backward, placing it below other images it is stacked with. Includes Send to Back, which places the selected image behind all other images.

- **Selection Pane**—Opens a task pane that lists all the shapes on the active sheet. You can use this pane to select a specific shape.

- **Align**—Includes various alignment options, as shown in Figure 14.9, to quickly line up the selected images.

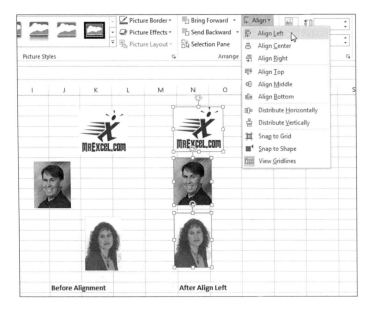

FIGURE 14.9

Align Left lines up the selected images based on the left edge of the topmost image.

- **Group**—Includes the options to group and ungroup the selected images. Grouping images allows you to move them together without losing their alignment or order. If selective images were grouped together at one point and then ungrouped, Regroup will re-create the group without your having to reselect all the images.

- **Rotate**—Rotates or flips the selected image.

To align selective images, follow these steps:

1. Place the images approximately how you want them. For example, if you want to align the images left, place them in a vertical layout. If you want to line them up by their centers, place them in a horizontal layout. Each command's icon provides an example of how the images should be laid out.

2. Select the images by holding down the Ctrl key and clicking each image in turn.

3. Go to Picture Tools, Format, Arrange, and select the desired alignment from the Align drop-down.

Reducing a Picture's File Size

Importing a picture into a workbook can dramatically increase the file size. Picture Tools, Format, Adjust, Compress Pictures offers multiple options for compressing images based on how you will be using the workbook, as shown in Figure 14.10. You can further reduce the file size by selecting the Delete Cropped Areas of Pictures option, but this means that you will be unable to return the image to its original state.

FIGURE 14.10

The Compress Pictures dialog box offers multiple options for how much the image resolution should be reduced based on how you will be distributing the workbook.

THE ABSOLUTE MINIMUM

Excel is a very versatile program, not limited to just colorful tables and charts. You can use it to create graphic instructions with SmartArt and pictures. Or use WordArt to add a bit of flair to a logo.

IN THIS CHAPTER

- Get the most out of the macro recorder.
- Run a macro from a button on a sheet.
- Change a complex embedded IF statement into a simpler custom function.

AN INTRODUCTION TO USING MACROS AND UDFS

Excel has a great tool called the Macro Recorder. It records your mouse and keyboard actions in Excel, allowing you to play them back at a later time. It does this by turning your actions into programming code, using a language called Visual Basic for Applications, or VBA. You can also use VBA to write User-Defined Functions (UDFs), functions that you can use on sheets, similar to how you use the SUM function.

VBA macros enable you to automate any process in Excel. For example, every day you import data that you apply formatting to, place formulas, and move columns. It can be time consuming to repeat these steps. A macro can reduce the work to the push of a button.

You don't need to be a programmer to record macros or create UDFs. Just follow the rules in this chapter and you'll successfully record simple macros that can deal with data sets of any size. This chapter also introduces you to user-defined functions, which are useful when a built-in function doesn't exist for your needs.

TIP Even if you don't record your own macros or write your own UDFs, understanding where code goes and how to navigate the editor is a useful skill. You may find sample code or UDFs online that you want to incorporate into your workbooks and this chapter helps you understand where it goes and how it works.

NOTE To really get beyond the macro recorder and write your own code, check out *VBA and Macros for Microsoft Excel 2013* by Bill Jelen and Tracy Syrstad from Que Publishing (ISBN 0789731290).

Enabling VBA Security

Security settings can be set for all workbooks or for specific, trusted locations. Workbooks stored in a folder that are marked as a trusted location automatically have their macros enabled.

Macro settings are found under File, Options, Trust Center, Trust Center Settings, Macro Settings. The four macro settings options are as follows:

- **Disable All Macros Without Notification**—Prevents all macros from running. With this setting, only macros in the Trusted Locations folders can run.

- **Disable All Macros with Notification**— Displays a message in the Message Area that macros have been disabled. This is the recommended setting as it allows you to choose to enable content by clicking that option, as shown in Figure 15.1.

- **Disable All Macros Except Digitally Signed Macros**—Requires you to obtain a digital signing tool from VeriSign or another provider. This setting is appropriate if you are going to be selling add-ins to others, but a bit of a hassle if you just want to write macros for your own use.

- **Enable All Macros (Not Recommended: Potentially Dangerous Code Can Run)**—Allows all macros to run without warning. Although this option requires the least amount of hassle, it opens your computer to attacks from malicious viruses. Microsoft suggests that you do not use this setting.

The recommended macro setting is Disable All Macros with Notification. With this setting, if you open a workbook that contains macros, you'll see a security warning in the area just above the formula bar, as shown in Figure 15.1. Assuming you were expecting macros in this workbook, click Enable Content.

FIGURE 15.1

The Disable All Macros with Notification setting gives you control over whether to allow macros to run.

If you do not want to enable macros for the current workbook, dismiss the security warning by clicking the X at the far right of the message bar.

If you forget to enable the macros and attempt to run a macro, a message informs you that you cannot run the macro because all macros have been disabled. You must close the workbook and reopen it to access the message bar again and enable the macros.

After you enable macros for a workbook stored on a local hard drive and then save the workbook, Excel remembers that you previously enabled macros in this workbook. The next time you open this workbook, macros will be automatically enabled.

Developer Tab

By default, the Developer tab is hidden in Excel. The Developer tab contains useful tools such as buttons for recording macros and adding controls to sheets. To access it, do the following:

1. Go to File, Options, Customize Ribbon.

2. In the rightmost list box, select the Developer tab, which is near the bottom.

3. Click OK to return to Excel. Excel displays the Developer tab shown in Figure 15.2.

FIGURE 15.2

You'll need the Developer tab to access tools specific to working with macros.

The buttons in the Code group on the Developer tab are used for recording and playing back macros:

- **Visual Basic**—Opens the Visual Basic Editor (VB Editor or VBE).

- **Macros**—Displays the Macro dialog box, where you can choose to run or edit a macro from the list of macros.

- **Record Macro**—Begins the process of recording a macro.

- **Use Relative Reference**—Toggles between using relative or absolute recording. With relative recording, Excel records that you move down three cells. With absolute recording, Excel records that you selected cell A4 (if you started in A1).

- **Macro Security**—Opens the Trust Center, where you can choose to allow or disallow macros to run on this computer.

 TIP   If you don't want to make the Developer tab visible, you can access options to View Macros, Record Macros, and Use Relative References from the Macros drop-down on the View tab, Macros group. But you won't have quick access to other useful buttons, such as the Visual Basic button that opens the editor.

Introduction to the Visual Basic Editor

Click the Visual Basic button in the Code group of the Developer tab. This will open the VB Editor, shown in Figure 15.3, which is the interface used for writing and editing macros. On the left side is the Project Explorer, which lists all the workbooks and add-ins and their components. On the right side is the Code pane, where you view and edit the macros you create.

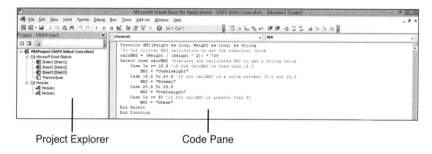

Project Explorer   Code Pane

FIGURE 15.3

The Project Explorer on the left side of the screen is the primary method of navigating through the components of the workbook in the editor.

Project Explorer

The Project Explorer lists any open workbooks and add-ins that are loaded, as shown in Figure 15.3. If you click the + icon next to VBAProject, it becomes a - icon and opens up to show a folder with Microsoft Excel objects. There can also be folders for Forms, Class Modules, and (standard) Modules. Each folder includes one or more such components. If the Project Explorer is not visible, select View, Project Explorer from the menu.

A *module* is a component in the Project Explorer where you enter code. A *userform*, or form, is a pop-up window, for example a window that asks you to type in more information. Forms also include code.

Right-clicking a component, such as Module1, and selecting View Code or just double-clicking the desired component brings up any code in the module in the Code pane. The exception is userforms, where double-clicking displays the userform in Design view.

Inserting Modules

A project consists of sheet modules for each sheet in the workbook and a single ThisWorkbook module. Code specific to a sheet, such as controls or sheet events, is placed on the corresponding sheet. Workbook events—code that runs automatically when something happens, for example when the workbook is opened—is placed in the ThisWorkbook module. The code you record and the UDFs you create will be placed in standard modules.

To insert a standard module, follow these steps:

1. Right-click the project you need to insert the module into.

2. From the context menu, select Insert, Module.

3. The module is placed in the Modules folder.

You can insert a module from the menu by selecting the project and going to Insert, Module.

Understanding How the Macro Recorder Works

This section is about the difference between recording a macro that will run successfully on a new data set and one that will make you cry in frustration when it fails on a new data set. You'll rarely be able to record all of your macros and have them work on different data sets, but with the tips in the following subsections, you'll greatly improve your chances.

The macro recorder is very literal, especially with the default settings. For example, if you have cell A1 selected and then begin the macro recorder and use the mouse to select your entire data set in range A1:B10, this is what will be recorded:

```
Range("A1:B10").Select
```

If the next time you run the macro, the data set is A1:B20, your macro won't run on rows 11–20 because the macro only covers rows 1–10. There are two things you need to change to make the recorded macro work properly. First, don't use the mouse when selecting ranges. Second, don't use the default settings of the macro recorder.

Navigating While Recording

To get the most out of the macro recorder, you should use keyboard shortcuts to navigate the sheet, not the mouse. The reason is that some of the keyboard shortcuts translate to commands instead of specific cell selections. For example, if you record pressing Ctrl+down-arrow to jump to the last row in a column, you will get

```
Selection.End(xlDown).Select
```

If your data set changes in size the next time you run the macro, the preceding line of code will be much more useful than if you'd recorded the macro by using the mouse. That's because the line doesn't mention a specific cell. Instead what it says is that, from the currently selected cell, select the last row of data before an empty cell, which is what the keyboard shortcut did.

Relative References in Macro Recording

The second rule to successful macro recording is to know when to turn relative referencing on and off. By default, it is off, which has its uses, but you'll often want it on. You can turn relative referencing on and off as needed while recording a macro.

 NOTE   For more information on relative referencing, refer to the "Relative Versus Absolute Formulas" section in Chapter 5, "Using Formulas."

When relative referencing is off, the macro records specific cell addresses. Imagine you have a list of addresses similar to Figure 15.4. Each address is exactly three rows, and a blank row separates each address. To transpose an address to a single row, you would follow these steps:

	A
1	HARRY SANTIAGO
2	248 MILL LANE
3	RIVERSIDE, VA 74720
4	
5	WHITNEY HARRIS
6	1292 PINE HIGHWAY
7	ST JOSEPH, ME 93197
8	
9	VELMA TALLEY
10	1845 HILL AVENUE
11	GREENWOOD, VI 24124
12	

FIGURE 15.4

Transposing this long list of addresses to multiple columns and rows would make it easier to use them in a mail merge.

 NOTE   Don't worry about actually recording this macro. The results are shown in figures so you can compare the results.

1. Start in cell A1.

2. Press the down-arrow key.

3. Press Ctrl+X to cut the address.

4. Press the up-arrow key and then the right-arrow key (to move to cell A2, remember to use the keyboard to navigate).

5. Press Ctrl+V to paste the address next to the name.

6. Press the left-arrow key once and the down-arrow key twice to move to the cell containing the city, state, and ZIP Code.

7. Press Ctrl+X to cut the city.

8. Press the up-arrow key twice and the right-arrow key twice to move to the right of the street cell.

9. Press Ctrl+V to paste the city.

10. Press the left-arrow key twice and the down-arrow key once to move to the new blank row just beneath the name.

11. Hold down the Shift key while pressing the down-arrow key twice to select the three blank cells.

12. Press Ctrl+- to bring up the Delete dialog box.

13. Press R to select the Entire Row option and then press Enter to accept the command.

If you record these steps with relative referencing off, you will get code that is cell specific, A2, B1, A3, etc., as shown in the text box in Figure 15.5. The results of running this code repeatedly on the data from Figure 15.4 are shown in Figure 15.5. A couple of repetitions of the code overwrite the first address line, ruining the record.

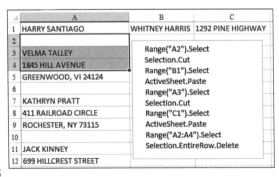

FIGURE 15.5

Recording the macro with relative referencing off recorded the specific cell address for processing the first address, making the code useless for subsequent addresses.

If this example was your first recorded macro, you might despair, as many before you have, at the uselessness of the recorder. But there is a way to make it work, and that's to turn on the Use Relative References option found in the Code group on the Developer tab. Performing the same steps with relative referencing on returns the results shown in Figure 15.6. As the active (or selected) cell moves down the column, the correct fields are cut and pasted to the proper row and column.

 NOTE Looking at the code in Figure 15.6, you may notice that there are cell addresses, A1 and A1:A3. But this is deceptive. It's actually an A1 reference based off of the active cell.

	A	B	C	D	E
1	HARRY SANTIAGO	248 MILL LANE	RIVERSIDE, VA 74720		
2	WHITNEY HARRIS	1292 PINE HIGHWAY	ST JOSEPH, ME 93197		
3	VELMA TALLEY	1845 HILL AVENUE	GREENWOOD, VI 24124		
4	KATHRYN PRATT	411 RAILROAD CIRCLE	ROCHESTER, NY 73115		
5	JACK KINNEY	ActiveCell.Offset(1, 0).Range("A1").Select			
6	699 HILLCREST STREET	Selection.Cut			
7	BLOOMINGDALE, PA 56701	ActiveCell.Offset(-1, 1).Range("A1").Select			
8		ActiveSheet.Paste			
9	BENJAMIN WILKERSON	ActiveCell.Offset(2, -1).Range("A1").Select			
10	478 THIRD HIGHWAY	Selection.Cut			
11	MIDDLETON, OK 49122	ActiveCell.Offset(-2, 2).Range("A1").Select			
12		ActiveSheet.Paste			
13	BEATRICE WILSON	ActiveCell.Offset(1, -2).Range("A1:A3").Select			
14	1409 THIRTEENTH ROAD	Selection.EntireRow.Delete			

FIGURE 15.6

Turn on the relative reference option while recording to record your movements instead of the specific cell addresses.

Basically, if you always want the exact same cells modified, such as a header in A1:C1 that you always bold, don't use relative referencing while recording. But if you need the flexibility of changing cell addresses, such as repeating a series of steps based on where the active cell starts, then turn on relative referencing.

Avoiding the AutoSum Button

If you use the AutoSum button while recording a macro, Excel will record the actual formula entered in the cell in R1C1 notation. It doesn't record that you wanted it to select the range above or to the left of the formula. It's just not that flexible. So, instead of using the AutoSum button, manually type in the formula mixing relative and absolute referencing.

 NOTE For more information on relative referencing, refer to the "Relative Versus Absolute Formulas" section in Chapter 5.

For example, if you want to sum G2:G13, the AutoSum function will create the formula =SUM(G2:G13), or in R1C1 notation, =SUM(R[-12]C:R[-1]C). When viewed in R1C1 notation, you see how fixed the formula is. Although it will work in any column that it's placed in, it specifically includes the cells 12 cells above (row 2) and directly above (row 13) the formula cell. The problem is if you add more rows, then the first cell is no longer 12 rows above—it's more. The solution is to type in the formula manually, fixing the row for the first argument, as shown in Figure 15.7.

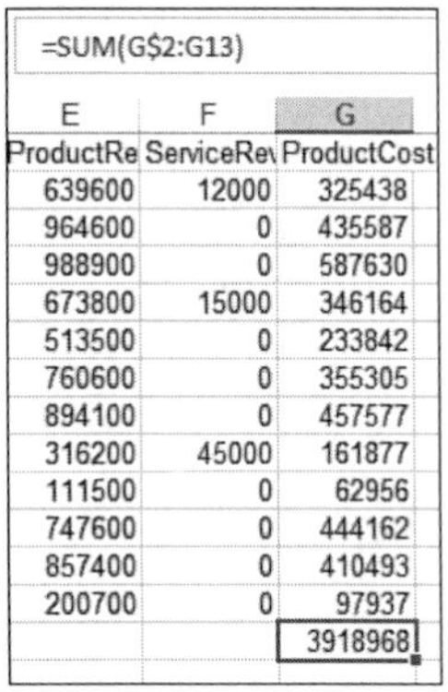

=SUM(G$2:G13)		
E	F	G
ProductRe	ServiceRe	ProductCost
639600	12000	325438
964600	0	435587
988900	0	587630
673800	15000	346164
513500	0	233842
760600	0	355305
894100	0	457577
316200	45000	161877
111500	0	62956
747600	0	444162
857400	0	410493
200700	0	97937
		3918968

FIGURE 15.7

Instead of using the AutoSum button, type in SUM formulas manually, making sure to fix the row of the first argument.

Recording a Macro

To begin recording a macro, select Record Macro from the Code group of the Developer tab. Before recording begins, Excel displays the Record Macro dialog box shown in Figure 15.8. The dialog box gives you a chance to customize details about the macro, for example, replacing Excel's generic macro name, like Macro1, with a more useful one, like FixAddressRecords.

To begin recording a macro and fill in the Record Macro dialog box, follow these steps:

1. Go to Developer, Code, Record Macro. The Record Macro dialog box opens. You can also quickly access the dialog box by clicking the Record Macro button in the status bar.

2. In the Macro Name field, type a name for the macro, making sure not to include any spaces or start with a number or symbol. Use a meaningful name for the macro, such as **FixAddressRecords.**

FIGURE 15.8

Provide details for the macro you're about to record.

3. The Shortcut Key field is optional. If you type J in this field, and then press Ctrl+J on the sheet, this macro runs. Note that most of the lowercase shortcuts from Ctrl+a through Ctrl+z already have a use in Excel. Rather than being limited to the unassigned Ctrl+J, you can hold down the Shift key and type Shift+A through Shift+Z in the shortcut box. This assigns the macro to Ctrl+Shift+A.

4. From the Store Macro In drop-down, choose where you want to save the macro: Personal Macro Workbook, New Workbook, This Workbook. It is recommended that you store macros related to a particular workbook in This Workbook.

The Personal Macro Workbook (Personal.xlsb) is not a visible workbook; it's created if you choose to save the recording in the Personal Macro Workbook. This workbook is used to save a macro in a workbook that will open automatically when you start Excel, thereby allowing you to use the macro. After Excel is started, the workbook is hidden.

5. Enter a description of the macro in the optional Description field. This description is added as a comment to the beginning of your macro.

6. Click OK and record your macro. When you are finished recording the macro, click the Stop Recording icon in the Developer tab or in the status bar.

Running a Macro

If you assign a shortcut key to your macro, you can play the macro by pressing the key combination. Macros can also be assigned to the ribbon, the Quick Access

Toolbar, forms controls, drawing objects, or you can run them from the Macros button in the Code group on the Developer tab.

Running a Macro from the Ribbon

You can add an icon to a new group on the ribbon to run a macro. This is appropriate for macros stored in the Personal Macro Workbook. Follow these steps to add a macro button to the ribbon:

1. Go to File, Options, Customize Ribbon.

2. In the list box on the right side of the dialog box, choose the tab name where you want to add the macro button.

3. Click the New Group button below the list box on the right side of the dialog box. Excel adds a new entry called New Group (Custom) to the end of the groups in that ribbon tab.

4. To move the group to the left in the ribbon tab, click the up-arrow icon on the right side of the dialog box several times.

5. To rename the group, click the Rename button. Type a new name, such as **Report Macros**, and click OK.

6. Open the upper-left drop-down and choose Macros from the list. Excel displays a list of available macros in the list box below the drop-down.

7. Choose a macro from the list box.

8. Click the Add button in the center of the dialog box. Excel moves the macro to the selected group in the list box on the right side of the dialog box. Excel uses a generic VBA icon for all macros, which you can change in step 9.

9. To rename or change the icon used for the macro, follow these steps:

    a. Select the macro in the list box on the right side of the dialog box.

    b. Click the Rename button.

    c. Excel displays a list of possible icons. Choose an icon or type a new name for the macro in the Display Name field, such as **Fix Addresses**, as shown in Figure 15.9.

    d. Click OK to return to the Excel Options dialog box.

10. Click OK to close the dialog box. The new button appears on the selected ribbon tab.

FIGURE 15.9

Create a custom group on the ribbon to add buttons for your macros.

Running a Macro from the Quick Access Toolbar

You can add a button to the Quick Access Toolbar to run your macro. If your macro is stored in the Personal Macro Workbook, you can have the button permanently displayed in the Quick Access Toolbar. If the macro is stored in the current workbook, you can specify that the icon should appear only when the workbook is open.

Follow these steps to add a macro button to the Quick Access Toolbar:

1. Go to File, Options, Quick Access Toolbar.

2. If the macro should be available only when the current workbook is open, open the upper-right drop-down and change For All Documents (Default) to For *filename.xlsm*. Any icons associated with the current workbook are displayed at the end of the Quick Access Toolbar.

3. Select Macros from the list in the upper-left drop-down, Choose Commands From. Excel displays a list of available macros in the list box below the drop-down.

4. Choose a macro from the list and click the Add button in the center of the dialog box to move the macro to the list box on the right side of the dialog box. Excel uses a generic VBA icon for all macros, which you can change by following steps 5 and 6.

5. To rename and change the icon used for the macro, follow these steps:

   a. Select the macro in the list box on the right side of the dialog box.

   b. Click the Modify button.

c. Excel displays a list of possible icons. Choose an icon or type a new name for the macro in the Display Name field, such as `Fix Addresses`, as shown in Figure 15.10. The name will appear as the ToolTip when you place your cursor over the button.

FIGURE 15.10

Add a button to the Quick Access Toolbar to run the macros saved to a specific workbook.

6. Click OK to close the Modify Button dialog box.

7. Click OK to close the dialog box. The new button appears on the Quick Access Toolbar.

Running a Macro from a Form Control, Text Box, or Shape

You can create a macro specific to a workbook, store the macro in the workbook, and attach it to a form control or any object on the sheet to run it. Macros can be assigned to any sheet object, such as an inserted picture, a shape, SmartArt graphics, or a text box. To assign a macro to any object, right-click the object and select Assign Macro.

Follow these steps to attach a macro to a button on a sheet:

1. In the Controls group of the Developer tab, click the Insert button to open its drop-down list. Excel offers 9 form controls (though 12 are shown, three are not usable) and 12 ActiveX controls.

2. Click the Button (Form Control) icon in the upper-left corner in the drop-down.

3. Move your cursor over the sheet; the cursor changes to a plus sign.

4. To draw a button, click and hold the mouse button while drawing a box shape. Release the button when finished and the Assign Macro dialog box opens.

5. Choose the macro from the Assign Macro dialog box and click OK. The button is created with generic text such as Button 1. To customize the text, refer to steps 6 and 7.

6. To give the button a new caption, follow these steps:

a. Right-click over the button and select Edit Text. The cursor within the button becomes visible.

b. Replace the current caption with your own text.

c. When finished, click anywhere outside the button.

7. For further text formatting options, right-click over the button and select Format Control. Click OK when done to return to Excel.

8. Click the button to run the macro.

User-Defined Functions

Excel provides many built-in formulas, but sometimes you need a custom formula not offered in the software, such as a commission rate calculator. You can create functions in VBA that can be used just like Excel's built-in functions, such as SUM, VLOOKUP, and MATCH, to name a few. After the user-defined function (UDF) is created, a user needs to know only the function name and its arguments.

When you create a UDF, keep the following in mind:

- UDFs can only be entered into standard modules. Sheet and ThisWorkbook modules are a special type of module; if you enter the function there, Excel won't recognize that you are creating a UDF.

- A variable is a word used to hold the place of a value, similar to an argument. Variables cannot have any spaces or unusual characters, such as the backslash (\) or hyphen (-). Make sure any variables you create are unique. For example, if your function is called BMI, you cannot have a variable with the same name.

- A variable type describes the variable as string, integer, long, and so on. This tells the program how to treat the variable—for example, integer and long—though both numbers have different limitations. The type also tells the program how much memory to put aside to hold the value.

- A simple UDF formula is not that different from a formula you write down on a sheet of paper. For example, if asked how to calculate the final cost of a store item, you would explain that it's the sale price *(1 + tax rate). Similarly, in a FinalCost UDF, you might enter FinalCost = SalePrice* (1+ TaxRate), where SalePrice and TaxRate would be arguments for the function, FinalCost.

- A UDF can only calculate or look up and return information. It cannot insert or delete rows or color cells. The UDF has the same limitations as built-in functions.

Structure of a UDF

Like a normal function, a UDF consists of the function name followed by arguments in parentheses. To help you understand this, the following example will build a custom function to add two values in the current workbook. It is a function called ADD that will total two numbers in different cells. The function has two arguments, Number1 and Number2. The syntax of the function is as follows:

```
ADD(Number1,Number2)
```

Number1 is the first number to add; Number2 is the second number to add. After the UDF has been created, it can be used on a sheet.

To create a UDF in the VBE, follow these steps:

1. Open the VBE by going to Developer, Code, Visual Basic.

2. Find the current workbook in the Project Explorer window.

3. Right-click over the current workbook and select Insert, Module. A new module is added to the Modules folder.

4. Double-click the new module to open it in the Code pane.

5. Type the following function into the module's Code pane, as shown in Figure 15.11:

```
Function ADD(Number1 As Long, Number2 As Long) As Long
ADD = Number1 + Number2
End Function
```

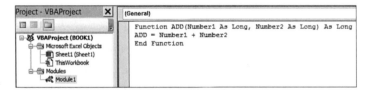

FIGURE 15.11

A UDF's code must be entered in a standard module.

Let's break this down:

- Function name: ADD.

- Arguments are placed in parentheses after the name of the function. This example has two arguments: Number1 and Number2.

- `As Long` defines the variable type as a whole number between –2,147,483,648 and 2,147,483,647. Other variable types include the following:

  - `As Integer` if you were using a whole number between –32,768 and 32,767

  - `As Double` if you were using decimal values

  - `As String` if you were using text

- `ADD =Number1 + Number2`: The result of the calculation is returned to the function, ADD.

Not all the variable types in the function have to be the same. You could have a string argument that returns an integer—for example, FunctionName(argument1 as String) as Long.

 NOTE When computers were slower and every bit of memory mattered, the difference between Integer and Long was crucial. But with today's computers, in most cases memory doesn't matter and Long is becoming preferred over Integer because it doesn't limit the user as much.

How to Use a UDF

After the function is created in the VBE, follow these steps to use it on a sheet:

1. Type any numbers into cells A1 and A2.

2. Select cell A3.

3. Press Shift+F3 to open the Insert Function dialog box (or from the Formulas tab, choose Insert Function).

4. Select the User Defined category.

5. Select the ADD function and click OK. The Function Arguments dialog box opens.

6. Place your cursor in the first argument box and select cell A1.

7. Place your cursor in the second argument box and select cell A2.

8. Click OK. The function returns the calculated value, as shown in Figure 15.12.

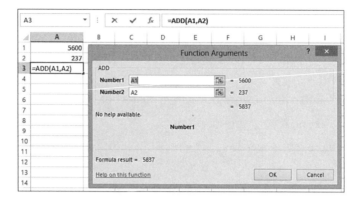

FIGURE 15.12

Using your UDF on a sheet is not different from using one of Excel's built-in functions.

Sharing UDFs

Where you store a UDF affects how you can share it:

- **Personal.xlsb**—If the UDF is just for your use and won't be used in a workbook opened on another computer, you can store the UDF in the Personal Workbook.

- **Workbook**—If the UDF needs to be distributed to many people, you can store it in the workbook in which it is being used.

- **Template**—If several workbooks need to be created using the UDF, and the workbooks are distributed to many people, you can store it in a template.

- **Add-in**—If the workbook is to be shared among a select group of people, you can distribute it via an add-in. For more information on add-ins, refer to the VBA book mentioned at the beginning of this chapter.

Using Select Case to Replace Nested IF

A really useful application of a UDF is with a Select Case statement. A Select Case statement is similar to a nested IF statement, but much easier to read. Also, because the 64 nested IF statements allowed in 2013 are not compatible in legacy versions of Excel, using a UDF with Select Case statements ensures compatibility.

 NOTE For more information on nested IF statements, refer to "Nested IF Statements" in Chapter 6, "Using Functions."

The statement begins with Select Case and then the variable you want to evaluate. Next, follow the Case statements, which are the possible values of the variable, each including the action you want to take when the variable meets the Case value. You can also include a Case Else, as a catchall for any variable that doesn't fall within the predefined cases. The statement ends with End Select.

Within the Case statements, you have the option of using comparison operators with the word Is, such as Case Is <5 if the variable is less than 5. You also have To, used to signify a range, such as Case 1 To 5.

Example: Calculate Commission

Imagine you have the following formula on a sheet. For the different type and dollar of hardware, there's a different commission percentage to use in the commission calculation. It's rather difficult to read and also to modify.

```
=IF(C2="Printer",IF(D2<100,ROUND(D2*0.05,2),ROUND(D2*0.1,2)),IF(C2=
➡"Scanner",IF(D2<125,ROUND(D2*0.05,2),ROUND(D2*0.15,2)),IF(C2=
➡"Service Plan",IF(D2<2,ROUND(D2*0.1,2),ROUND(D2*0.2,2)),ROUND(D2*0.01,2))))
```

The continuation character (➡) indicates that code is continued from the previous line.

Instead, take the same logic, make it a Select Case statement, and see the commission percentage breakdown for each hardware item. You can easily make changes, including adding a new Case statement. In addition, because in the original formula the commission calculation for each hardware type is the same (price*commission percentage), that formula doesn't need to be repeated in each Case statement. Use the Select Case statements to set the commission percentage and have a single formula at the end to do the calculation. You can also provide more flexibility in case users enter a different hardware description, for example "Printers" instead of just "Printer."

NOTE   In the following code, there is text following an apostrophe ('). For example: 'If Hardware is Printer or Printers, do the following.

Any text following an apostrophe is called a comment and is not treated as code. Use comments to leave yourself notes about what the line of code is for. Comments do not have to be after the corresponding line of code. They can be anywhere within the Sub or Function, except directly inline before code—because then you are also turning the code into a comment.

```
Function Commission(Hardware As String, HDRevenue As Long) As Double
Select Case Hardware 'Hardware is the variable to be evaluated
    Case "Printer", "Printers" 'If Hardware is Printer or Printers, do the following
        If HDRevenue < 100 Then 'If Hardware is less than 100
            ComPer = 0.05 'then ComPer is 5%
        Else 'else, ComPer is 10%
            ComPer = 0.1
        End If
    Case "Scanner", "Scanners"
        If HDRevenue < 125 Then
            ComPer = 0.05
        Else
            ComPer = 0.15
        End If
    Case "Service Plan", "Service Plans"
        If HDRevenue < 2 Then
            ComPer = 0.1
        Else
            ComPer = 0.2
        End If
    Case Else
            ComPer = 0.01
End Select
'Once a value is assigned to ComPer, do the calculation and return it to
'the function
        Commission = Round(HDRevenue * ComPer, 2)
End Function
```

Example: Calculate BMI

This example takes the user input, calculates the BMI (body mass index), then compares that calculated value with various ranges to return a BMI descriptive, as shown in Figure 15.13. When creating a UDF, think of the formula in the same way you would write it down because this is very similar to how you will enter it in the UDF. The formula for calculating BMI is as follows:

```
BMI=(weight in pounds/height in inches(squared)) *703
```

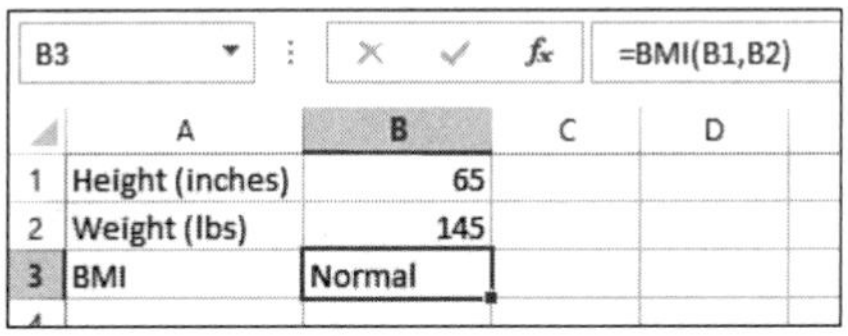

FIGURE 15.13

A UDF can perform calculations based on user input and return a string.

The table for returning the BMI descriptive is as follows:

Below 18.5 = underweight

18.5–24.9 = normal

25–29.9 = overweight

30 & above = obese

The code for calculating the BMI then returning the descriptive is the following:

```
Function BMI(Height As Long, Weight As Long) As String
'Do the initial BMI calculation to get the numerical value
calcBMI = (Weight / (Height ^ 2)) * 703
Select Case calcBMI 'evaluate the calculated BMI to get a string value
    Case Is <=18.5 'if the calcBMI is less than 18.5
        BMI = "Underweight"
    Case 18.5 To 24.9 'if the calcBMI is a value between 18.5 and 24.9
        BMI = "Normal"
    Case 24.9 To 29.9
        BMI = "Overweight"
    Case Is >= 30 'if the calcBMI is greater than 30
        BMI = "Obese"
End Select
End Function
```

THE ABSOLUTE MINIMUM

A macro can take a tedious, time-consuming process and reduce it to a button press. Understanding how to get the most out of the macro recorder can help you create that time-saving program. You can also create special types of macros called UDFs, which are custom functions you apply just like Excel's built-in functions.

IN THIS CHAPTER

- Share a workbook online.
- Create an online form to help users fill in a sheet and print the results.
- Create a survey that can be filled out anonymously by others.

INTRODUCING THE EXCEL WEB APP

The Excel Web App is a browser-based version of Excel that allows users to enter new data and formulas in an Excel workbook while online. Those users do not need to have Excel installed on their computers to use the app. Mobile workers might use the Excel Web App to access their data while they are out of the office. You also might expect college students to use the Excel Web App to collaborate on group projects using this free version of Excel.

This chapter helps you get started working on and sharing your Excel files online.

Requirements

You don't need much to get started with the Excel Web App:

- A current browser (minimum: Internet Explorer 7, Mozilla Firefox 3, or Safari 3)

- A Microsoft account, such as Hotmail, Microsoft SkyDrive, Xbox LIVE, Windows Phone, or other Microsoft services

- An Internet connection

With these three items, you can view your Excel workbooks anywhere in the world where you can access SkyDrive at skydrive.live.com.

Acquiring a Microsoft Account

With a Microsoft account, you can access the SkyDrive online storage where you can store, view, edit, and share your Excel workbooks. You don't need a Microsoft account if you are accessing a public file on someone else's SkyDrive. But if you want to upload your own files or access a SkyDrive requiring login, you will need a Microsoft account.

A Microsoft account enables you to log in to a variety of websites, such as Windows Live, Hotmail, and Xbox LIVE, using one account. If you already log in to a Microsoft-owned site, it is possible you already have a Microsoft account. You can create the account using an existing email address or obtain a new email address through the live.com or hotmail.com domains. Follow these steps to create a Microsoft account:

1. Use your browser to navigate to https://signup.live.com. If you don't see a web page similar to the one shown in Figure 16.1, it's possible you are already signed in to a Microsoft account. In that case, you may see a page with your login name in the upper-right corner. If that's the case, you don't need to create a Microsoft account because you already have one.

2. If you have an existing email address you want to use, type it into the Microsoft Account Name field, press the Tab key, and skip to step 6. Otherwise, click the Or Get a New E-Mail Address link to create a new email address and continue to step 3.

3. In the Microsoft Account Domain List drop-down, select the domain you want to have the address for (live.com or hotmail.com).

4. In the Microsoft Account Name field, type the username you want.

FIGURE 16.1

Create a Microsoft account to take full advantage of SkyDrive.

5. If Microsoft Account informs you that the ID isn't available, repeat steps 3 and 4; otherwise, if the ID is available, continue to step 6.

6. Type your password into the Create a Password field.

7. Type the same password again into the Reenter Password field.

8. Choose an option to reset your password in case you forget it:

- Enter a phone number that can receive a code in a text message.

- If you created a new Microsoft account, enter an alternate email address at which you can receive password reset information. The email address must be different from your Microsoft account.

- Select the Or Choose a Security Question link if you want to verify your identity online. Select a predefined question from the Question list and enter the correct response in the Secret Answer field. The response must be at least five characters.

9. Fill in the rest of the requested information: name, location, gender, and birth year.

10. In the last field, type the characters you see in the image.

11. Click I Accept. Microsoft Account will create your new ID.

Uploading and Downloading Workbooks

You no longer have to remember to move those important files to a USB flash drive and have that flash drive with you. From almost anywhere in the world, you can handle your boss's desperate call to fix the department budget numbers for his 11:00 a.m. presentation to corporate. All you need is a computer with access to the Internet. After you've logged in to your Microsoft account, you can upload your own workbooks or create new ones for viewing, editing, and sharing.

 CAUTION   Only unprotected workbooks can be opened online.

Accessing the SkyDrive

You can sign in to your Microsoft account from any site that supports the accounts, such as MSN.com or Bing.com, but to quickly get to your SkyDrive, go to skydrive.live.com. After you're signed in, you're brought to your SkyDrive, shown in Figure 16.2.

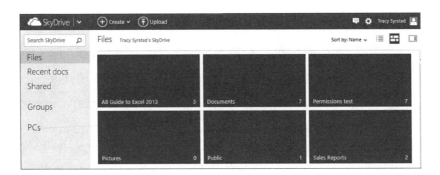

FIGURE 16.2

Log in to your SkyDrive to interact with it, such as uploading files and creating folders.

Uploading to SkyDrive

You can upload a workbook viewable by just you, selected individuals, or everyone. After it is uploaded, you can view, edit, and share the workbook. Follow these steps to upload your workbook while you're logged in to your SkyDrive:

1. Select the folder, such as Documents, to which you want to add your workbook.

2. Select Upload, found at the top of the web page.

3. Browse to the location of the file you want to upload and select it.

4. Click Open.

5. The file will be uploaded to your SkyDrive. When the upload is complete, the page will update to show an icon for the file.

Saving to SkyDrive from Excel

Save a file from Excel directly to your SkyDrive by choosing File, Save or Save As, SkyDrive. Excel attempts to log you in automatically, but if it can't, click the Sign In button and sign in with the account you created in the section "Acquiring a Microsoft Account."

Deleting a File from SkyDrive

To delete a file from your SkyDrive, right-click on the file and select Delete. A message box, shown in Figure 16.3, temporarily appears in the lower-right corner of the page, giving you the chance to undo the deletion.

FIGURE 16.3

You'll have about 15 seconds to undo an accidental deletion before it becomes permanent.

To delete multiple files, select the check box that appears when you place your cursor over the file. When all the desired files are selected, go to Manage, Delete. The files will be deleted but you will be given the option to undo the deletion.

Opening a Workbook

When you click on a folder, you'll open it and see all the workbooks in the folder, as shown in Figure 16.4. Place your cursor over a workbook without clicking on it and a check box appears in the upper-right corner of the workbook. Click the check box to select the workbook. An Open drop-down is added to the menu at the top of the web page.

FIGURE 16.4

Selecting a workbook adds options to the menu at the top of the web page.

TIP When another workbook is already selected, check boxes automatically appear on all other workbooks. You can then select another workbook by clicking anywhere on the workbook icon. Some menu options, such as Open, are not available when multiple workbooks are selected.

Open in Excel Web App

Selecting Open in Excel Web App opens the workbook in the Excel Web App in your browser.

When open in View Only mode, the workbook is read-only. Unlike Read-Only mode on the desktop version of Excel, where you can make changes and save them using the Save As command to save to a new file, you cannot make any changes while in View Only mode. There is no ribbon, either, as shown in Figure 16.5.

FIGURE 16.5

In View Only mode, the workbook has limited menu options.

When open in Edit mode, changes are automatically saved as they are made, unless the workbook has specific ranges configured for data entry. For more information, see the section "Configuring Browser View Options." A simplified ribbon is available with the features available in the Excel Web App, as shown in Figure 16.6.

FIGURE 16.6

A workbook in Edit mode has a simplified ribbon to access available features.

 TIP   You can also open the workbook in the Web App by clicking on its icon.

 CAUTION   Opening an Excel legacy file in the Web App converts it to an *.xlsx file.

Open in Excel

Selecting Open in Excel pops up a warning about viruses. If you trust the file, click Yes and it will open in Excel. If you do not trust the file, click No and the file won't be opened.

If you choose to open the file in Excel, the file remains on the SkyDrive, but you will view it in Excel. If you save changes, the changes will be saved to the online file. To save the file locally, see the section "Saving a File to Your Local Drive."

Creating a New Workbook Online

You aren't limited to workbooks created previously in Excel on your desktop PC. You can create a new workbook online and download it when you return to the office.

To create a new workbook on your SkyDrive, follow these steps:

1. Click the folder you want the workbook in.

2. Select Excel Workbook from the Create drop-down at the top of the web page, as shown in Figure 16.7.

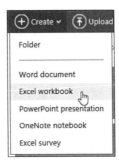

FIGURE 16.7

Create a workbook online.

3. Enter the name of the workbook and click Create. The file extension (.xlsx) is automatically appended for you.

4. The workbook is opened in the Web App where you can do your work.

Saving a File to Your Local Drive

Eventually, you will want to work on a workbook saved locally. This can be done in several ways:

*   With the workbook selected, click Download from the menu. You can also right-click on a workbook and select Download. Your browser will take over the download functionality.

*   With the workbook open in the Web App, select the File tab to reveal the following options:

    *   **Open in Excel**—Open the workbook locally in Excel. You can then do a Save As for your first save. Select a location on your computer to save the file.

    *   **Save As, Download**—Download the workbook to your computer.

*   With the workbook open in Excel, but not downloaded, do a Save As for your first save. Select a location on your computer to save the file.

Sharing a Folder or Workbook

SkyDrive doesn't just provide you with the convenience of being able to work with your workbooks wherever you are. It also helps you share your workbooks and the folders you create with other people.

Creating a New Folder

When you create an account, SkyDrive provides two folders for storing your documents: Documents, a protected folder only you can access, and Public, a folder available to anyone. You can share the Documents folder, but it is not recommended as other apps may save sensitive data to it. Instead, create a new folder to hold files you want to share by selecting Create, Folder from the menu, entering the name of the folder in the provided field, and pressing Enter.

Setting Folder Permissions

When you create a new folder on your SkyDrive, it is not shared. If you create the folder within another folder, it inherits the sharing properties of its parent folder. By setting the share properties of a folder, you can choose who has access to it and whether the person can only view existing files, add new files, or delete files.

To view the properties of a folder, right-click the folder's icon and select Properties. A task pane opens on the right side of the web page, as shown in Figure 16.8. Under Sharing, you can see the current sharing properties of the folder. The Sales Report folder can be viewed by users on Facebook with a link posted to your Timeline. Another link was created that allows logged-in users who click it to edit the folder.

FIGURE 16.8

You can share a folder in multiple ways, including with online services such as Facebook.

To configure the sharing properties of the selected folder, click the Share link, and the form in Figure 16.9 appears. Choose how you want to share the folder. The options for sharing are as follows:

Send email	Send a link to "Sales Reports" in email
Post to ⧉	To
Get a link		
	Include a personal message (optional)
	☑ Recipients can edit ☐ Require everyone who accesses this to sign in
Help me choose how to share	Share Cancel

FIGURE 16.9

Once you click the Share link, you can choose how you want to dispense access to the folder.

- **Send Email**—Send an email containing a link to your new folder and a link to view each file in the folder. Fill in the To field with the email addresses and include an additional message. Select the Recipients Can Edit check box if the recipients are allowed to edit the contents of the folder. Select the Require Everyone Who Accesses This To Sign In check box if the recipients must log in to their Microsoft accounts before accessing the folder.

- **Post to an Online Service**—If you have your Facebook, Twitter, or LinkedIn account linked to your Microsoft account, you can post a link to the folder at that service's site. Recipients will be required to log in to open files. Select Recipients Can Edit if the recipients are allowed to edit the contents of the folder. Select Add Services to add or manage the available services. Under Add Services, Manage My Services will take you to a web page to connect the services to your Microsoft account. Once you've posted to a service, you can configure whether recipients are limited to viewing or can also edit the contents of the folder.

 NOTE After setting up a service the first time, you must return to the share interface to post to the service.

- **Get a Link**—Create a link you can share, but also limit what users can do to the contents of the folder. Except for Public folders, users will be required to log in to open files. To retrieve a previously created link, return to the Get a Link option. The available links are as follows:

- **View Only**—Users can open the files in the folder but cannot make changes unless ranges have been configured for data entry. See "Configuring Browser View Options" for more information. Users will be able to download a copy of the file.

- **View and Edit**—Users can view and edit the files in the folder.

- **Public**—Anyone can access the files, even if they don't have a link.

To delete a share option, click the X to the right of the option. The option will no longer work, even if the users click the previously provided link.

 CAUTION   A user who creates a file in a folder becomes co-owner of the folder. This means if you delete the shared link previously sent to users, the co-owner will have access to any new workbooks added to the folder until the co-owner permission is also deleted from the Sharing list.

Setting File Permissions

Setting file permissions is the same as setting the folder permissions, except you right-click on a file and set its sharing permissions. For details on the sharing options, see the previous section "Setting Folder Permissions."

Simultaneous Editing

If you're allowing others to edit your workbook, eventually you will be editing the workbook at the same time as another person. When you are the sole person editing the workbook online, the text in the lower-right corner of your browser window reads 1 Person Editing. If other people are online editing at the same time, the text will update to reflect the number of people. Some limitations to working with a file in the Web App are as follows:

- A desktop user cannot edit the file at the same time as a user is editing it online. The desktop user will be limited to a read-only copy, saving a local copy, or waiting for notification when the file is available.

- If a workbook is open on the desktop, an online user is limited to viewing the file. The online user is not provided with options.

- If a workbook has been configured with specific ranges for data entry, each user who opens the file gets a copy. See the section "Configuring Browser View Options" for more information.

To see who else is in the workbook with you, click the arrow and a window opens up, showing everyone in the workbook, including you, as shown in Figure 16.10.

FIGURE 16.10

You can see who else is editing a workbook with you.

Because changes to workbooks are automatically saved, you can see what the other person is doing almost right away. There is no hierarchy of permissions or way to verify changes, so another user can change your changes as quickly as you can make them.

Interacting with a Sheet Online

Navigating in the Excel Web App isn't that different from navigating in the desktop version. For example, using keyboard shortcuts and using the mouse are still available. The two exceptions are as follows:

- You can't click and drag to move cells, rows, or columns.

- Right-click options are limited to cut, copy, and paste and manipulating hyperlinks.

Many of Excel's tools are still available, some with fewer options, such as charts. Other tools can be set up in Excel and used in the Web App, but not created in the Web App, such as conditional formatting and pivot tables. Some are not available at all, such as WordArt. The tools that are available to various degrees work very much as they do in the desktop version.

 CAUTION   Protected sheets and workbooks do not open in the Web App.

I've set up a public folder, AB Guide to Excel 2013, in my SkyDrive account, which you can access at http://sdrv.ms/YN1ajh. In it, you'll find workbooks with different Excel functionality, which you can test online or download and review locally.

Configuring Browser View Options

You can control which sheets are visible in the Web App. You can also configure specific ranges on the sheet for data entry, whether the user has View or Edit privileges. For example, you can create an online calculator. Or you can create an online entry form the user can save locally or print out. All of this is done through the Browser View Options available through the Save As dialog box in Excel.

When you go to File, Save As and select a folder on your SkyDrive, the Save As dialog box has a button for Browser View Options. Select the button and the Browser View Options dialog box opens. From the Show tab, you can choose to share the entire workbook, selected sheets in the workbook, or selected charts or pivot tables, as shown in Figure 16.11.

FIGURE 16.11

Let users only see specific items in a workbook, such as a PivotTable.

Go to the Parameters tab and you can specify named ranges, which the user can edit. Figure 16.12 shows a sheet in the Web App with a task pane in which the user enters data. When the user clicks Apply, the data is entered onto the sheet.

FIGURE 16.12

Use data entry parameters to limit the users to entering only the required data.

When you add parameters to a sheet, a few of the Web App rules change:

- Recipients with view-only links can enter information in the parameters.

- Recipients with view and edit links can only enter information in the parameters. The rest of the workbook is protected.

- Workbooks with data entry parameters are not shared. Each user opens a unique copy.

- Entries are not automatically saved. The user can save a copy by going to File, Save As, Save a Copy or File, Save As, Download.

- Parameters only affect the online sheet. Once downloaded, the data entry limitations are removed.

 TIP   Use short names that will make sense to users as they fill in the form. See the section "Using Names to Simplify References" in Chapter 5, "Using Formulas," for instruction on creating names.

Follow these steps to allow a user to enter temporary data in specific cells:

1. Select the cell you want the user to edit during the session.

2. Type the name of the cell in the Name box. Press Enter.

3. Repeat steps 1 and 2 for each cell you want editable.

4. Choose File, Save As and select a folder on your SkyDrive. The Save As dialog box opens.

5. Click the Browser View Options button.

6. Select the Parameters tab.

7. Click the Add button and the Add Parameters dialog box opens, listing all defined names in the workbook, as shown in Figure 16.13. Select the named ranges you want users to edit.

8. Click OK twice to return to the Save As dialog box.

9. Enter the name of the workbook in the File Name field and click Save.

To view the workbook as a user would, open the workbook online and go to View, Document View, Reading View. The names you defined will appear in a task pane to the right. To return to the creator's view, go to Edit Workbook, Edit in Excel Web App.

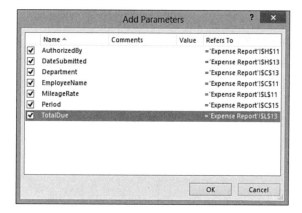

FIGURE 16.13

Use named ranges to define which cells users can edit.

Setting Up a Survey

You can create an online survey from within the Web App and provide a link to others to fill it out. The anonymous results will appear in an online workbook. To create the survey, create a new workbook and go to Insert, Tables, Survey, New Survey.

Figure 16.14 is a small sample survey I created. You can access it at http://sdrv. ms/RAwy2x. You can view the results in the workbook Survey found in the shared folder mentioned in the previous section "Interacting with a Sheet Online." To create the survey, follow these steps:

1. Create a new workbook in the Web App.

2. Go to Insert, Tables, Survey, New Survey. A data entry form opens.

3. Fill in the title, `Getting to Know You`, and the description, `A survey to learn more about Excel users`.

4. Click in the Enter Your First Question Here field and a form to fill in the question details appears.

5. In the Question field, type `What year were you born?`

6. In the Question Subtitle field, type `Age Category`.

7. The Response Type field is a drop-down, as shown in Figure 16.15. Select Number.

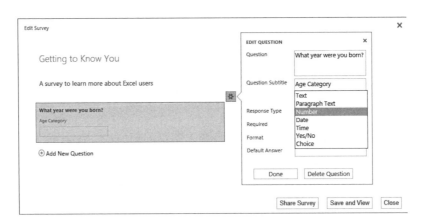

FIGURE 16.14

Create a survey web page that users can fill out anonymously. The results will feed into your workbook.

FIGURE 16.15

Each question can have a different response type.

8. Select the Required box.

9. Because Number is selected as the response type, an additional field, Format, appears. This allows you to format the number as Fixed Decimal, Percent, or Currency. Because we're asking for the year, leave it blank.

10. Leave Default Answer blank.

11. Click Done.

12. Click Add New Question.

13. In the Question field, type `Choose one`.

14. In the Question Subtitle field, type `Gender`.

15. Select Choice from the Response Type drop-down.

16. Select the Required box.

17. Because Choice is selected as the response type, an additional field, Choices, appears. This allows you to enter the choices the user can select from. Type `Female`, press Enter, then type `Male`.

18. Leave Default Answer blank.

19. Click Done.

20. Click Save and View. The survey is saved and you're brought to a view of the survey as the users will see it. If you're happy with everything, click Share Survey and a link will be generated. Copy the link and share it so users can fill out your survey. As users fill in and submit their responses, the workbook is updated with the results, as shown in Figure 16.16. You can then filter or create reports as needed.

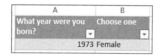

FIGURE 16.16

Survey results automatically update to the survey workbook.

To edit an existing survey, open its workbook and go to Insert, Survey, Edit Survey. When you click on a question, the Edit Question form appears and you can make changes.

THE ABSOLUTE MINIMUM

Using SkyDrive and the Excel Web App, you can share your workbooks with users around the world. Create a data entry form in which users enter data that flows to your workbook and the users can then print out. You can also set up a survey users can fill in anonymously while you collect the results.

Index

Q

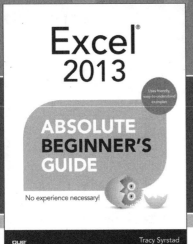

Excel 2013 ABSOLUTE BEGINNER'S GUIDE

No experience necessary!

Tracy Syrstad

Safari Books Online

FREE Online Edition

Your purchase of **Excel® 2013 Absolute Beginner's Guide** includes access to a free online edition for 45 days through the **Safari Books Online** subscription service. Nearly every Que book is available online through **Safari Books Online**, along with thousands of books and videos from publishers such as Addison-Wesley Professional, Cisco Press, Exam Cram, IBM Press, O'Reilly Media, Prentice Hall, Sams, and VMware Press.

Safari Books Online is a digital library providing searchable, on-demand access to thousands of technology, digital media, and professional development books and videos from leading publishers. With one monthly or yearly subscription price, you get unlimited access to learning tools and information on topics including mobile app and software development, tips and tricks on using your favorite gadgets, networking, project management, graphic design, and much more.

Activate your FREE Online Edition at informit.com/safarifree

STEP 1:   Enter the coupon code: QASZKCB.

STEP 2:   New Safari users, complete the brief registration form.
Safari subscribers, just log in.

If you have difficulty registering on Safari or accessing the online edition,
please e-mail customer-service@safaribooksonline.com